D0345244

LOVE THAT DOG
TRAINING PROGRAM

THE

LOVE THAT DOG
TRAINING PROGRAM

BY DAWN SYLVIA-STASIEWICZ
and LARRY KAY

WORKMAN PUBLISHING • NEW YORK

Copyright © 2010 by Dawn Sylvia-Stasiewicz

All rights reserved.
No portion of this book may be reproduced—mechanically,
electronically, or by any other means, including photocopying—
without written permission of the publisher. Published simultaneously
in Canada by Thomas Allen & Son Limited.

Library of Congress Cataloging-in-Publication Data is available.

ISBN 978-0-7611-6075-5

Cover design by David Matt
Design by Lisa Hollander
Original interior photography by Evan Sklar
Additional photography credits on page 289.

Workman books are available at special discounts when
purchased in bulk for premiums and sales promotions as well as
for fund-raising or educational use. Special editions or book
excerpts can also be created to specification. For details, contact
the Special Sales Director at the address below or send an e-mail to
specialmarkets@workman.com.

Workman Publishing Company, Inc.
225 Varick Street
New York, NY 10014-4381
www.workman.com

Printed in the United States of America
First printing September 2010
10 9 8 7 6 5 4 3 2 1

For my children,
Courtlandt, Blaise, and Paige.
My love and respect for you
is at the essence of all that I am
and all that I have done.
The greatest gift I have been given
is being your mother.

— DAWN SYLVIA-STASIEWICZ

For my parents,
Rima and Saul Kay, and my dog, Higgins.
The lovingkindness that is at the core
of this book's lessons
I learned from you.

— LARRY KAY

Contents

Introduction: The Call

I WAS IN THE KITCHEN with Maude, my African Grey parrot, when the phone rang. It was Vicki Kennedy, Senator Ted Kennedy's wife, calling.

"Dawn," she said to me, "I have a dog that I'd like you to evaluate. It's another Portuguese Water Dog and he'll be flying into Dulles in a few days. Do you have the time for this?"

I was a little surprised to hear that Vicki had her eye on another dog. The Kennedys had three dogs already—all Porties, as this adorable black-and-white curly breed is called by those of us who love them. I'd helped the Kennedys choose their dogs from Art and Martha Stern, breeders in Texas I worked with, and had trained all three at my country home in Hume, Virginia. Senator Kennedy and Vicki had recently taken home their third Portie, a puppy named Captain Courageous, or Cappy for short. It didn't seem likely that they'd already be looking to add another member to their family.

Senator Edward M. Kennedy and his wife, Vicki, as they return from sailing off the coast of Hyannisport, Massachusetts, with the Senator walking Splash and Mrs. Kennedy holding Sunny.

"He's not for us," Vicki said. "We're not sure yet where the puppy will go—we just want to see if you think he'd be good for a family with children." I agreed to evaluate the dog, but as we were about to hang up, Vicki stopped me.

"Oh, and Dawn," she said. "Keep this between us for a few days, okay?"

I drove from my home in the country to the Dulles Hilton a few days later, where I was scheduled to meet one of Senator Kennedy's assistants and a dog named Charlie. I still knew very little about Charlie except that he was about five-months-old and was a litter mate of Cappy's. He had been with a family who had returned him to Art and Martha because the family's older Portie and he didn't get along. Martha was looking for a family to "rehome" him with.

> "He's amazing. I think he's perfectly suited for a family and to be around children. I love him so much, I'm considering keeping him myself if the people you have in mind don't want him!"

After picking Charlie up, I drove him to my ex-husband's dental office, where I had an appointment scheduled to fix a chipped tooth. I carried Charlie's crate into a private room in the back of the office and closed the door. He'd been so quiet in the car—I couldn't wait to let him out. As soon as I opened the crate door, Charlie poked his head out. Most dogs need time to re-adjust to a flight and traveling in a crate, and tend to emerge very hesitant and unsure of their surroundings. Not Charlie. He was as happy as a clam and calm as a cucumber. I attached the leash I had brought for him and took him out to go potty. Back inside, I walked him around the office. He happily stopped to be petted by the staff members. I was worried that the noises of the machines would frighten him, but while I had my tooth fixed, Charlie lay quietly beside me on the floor, enjoying the new chew toy I'd bought for him.

I fell in love with Charlie immediately. I often have a number of guest dogs boarding with me, and, as a dog trainer and dog person, I come to love all of them. But I fell hard for Charlie. He was a handsome puppy of excellent breeding and a quick learner. He got along with the other dogs in my training classes (about twelve at a time), with my own dogs, with the neighbor's dogs, and even with my two parrots. Maude, who herself has a particular fondness for dogs, seemed to intrigue him most. He'd sniff around her cage, and Maude loved it. She'd climb down from her perch and put her beak through the wire door near his nose. "Gimme a kiss, arrh . . . That's nice!" she'd squawk, then throw him some kibble. Charlie would catch the treat and roll on the floor, hoping for more.

A few weeks later, Vicki called to check on Charlie.

"He's amazing," I told her. "I think he's perfectly suited for a family and to be around children. I love him so much, I'm considering keeping him myself if the people you have in mind don't want him!"

That's when she broke the news: The family considering Charlie wasn't just any family. It was the First Family.

While some people might have collapsed with fear, I wasn't worried at all. I looked at this job like any other job: I simply needed to prepare Charlie—or Bo, as he would eventually be known—for the home he was going to.

I BECAME A PROFESSIONAL DOG trainer out of a profound, abiding love of dogs. Throughout my childhood and teen years, I'd had a great fondness for my own family's pets and for dogs in general, and I always dreamed of one day having a houseful of children and animals. In 1982, I married a man I loved deeply, who was thirteen years my senior. He was a dentist with a growing practice near D.C. We agreed that I would stay home, raise our children, and help manage his dental practice, which we moved to the first floor of our home.

Four years after we married, we had a beautiful daughter we named Courtlandt. Fourteen months after that, we had Blaise, our son. And then, wouldn't you know it, nine months later I was pregnant again, this time with our second daughter, Paige. Having three very young children so close in age was crazy at times. Between the years 1986 and 1993 I was either pregnant or nursing (and always changing diapers). Despite the crazy scheduling, I was in heaven and had achieved what I always wanted: a house full of kids and pets. We had as many as five dogs at one time, including Boston Terriers, a Pomeranian, a Portuguese Water Dog, Border Collies, a Flat-Coated Retriever, an Irish Water Spaniel, a Giant Schnauzer, and an Ibizan Hound. Plus:

two ferrets, several pet rats, a few rabbits, numerous hamsters, four Siamese cats, one snake, and two very talkative parrots— Jules, a Yellow-naped Amazon, and Maude, our African Grey. It was hard just keeping their names straight at times and I often look back and wonder how I managed. At one point, I was nursing Paige while Jazz, my Boston terrier, nursed her puppies. I was one of those women others called Superwoman. Every morning I would get up, feed the children, feed the dogs, feed the birds, feed the cats, get the strollers, collect the leashes (taking extra care not to put the dogs in the stroller and the leashes on the children), head out for a walk around our neighborhood or take the kids to school, return and settle the dogs in their crates, and go to work at my husband's dental office downstairs. I was in constant motion, morning to evening. It was a hectic, frantic, wonderful life. Though my focus was on my family, I was involved in dog shows and began a side business training and boarding dogs, mainly to earn money for dog-show entry fees and conferences.

Then, one morning in 1995, I found myself sitting at my kitchen table, stunned, as my husband told me that he didn't want to be married any longer. At the time, our children were five, six, and seven years old. Now, without the financial security I had come to depend on, I needed to make some real money, and fast. The thought of getting a job and leaving my children every morning was unfathomable. I turned to dog training full-time, in between my children's school and sports schedules.

I knew from working with my own dogs that the talent I had when it came to training was special, and I had already gained a small reputation as a trainer who could teach owners how to raise dogs to be joyful, obedient, and devoted members of the family—especially families with children. That gave me some confidence as I started to spread the word about my business, and I put the deposit down on a small studio for my classes. It was such a scary but exciting time for me. Superwoman was also a business owner! I named my training program Positive Puppy Care, and later changed it to the name I use now, Merit Puppy Training. I continued to build up a reputation, and my list of clients grew. I moved out of our Washington home and into a house in the country: a wonderful place to live, and a perfect spot to train and board dogs.

I think involving children in the training process is a terrific idea. It's an experience that teaches them so many things—not only about dogs but about themselves. I certainly involved my own children, and they loved it. I held classes while they were in school in the morning, and then I'd pick them up and bring them to the next round of classes. In the evenings, my ex-husband would take them for dinner while I held more classes. I continued to expand my business, preparing dogs to compete in the show ring and, at the other end of the spectrum, teaching pet owners how to get their puppies learning at a very early age. Before long, my training services began to catch the attention of some of D.C.'s more powerful families. To be honest, I rarely paid attention to any of that. My main concern when it came to working with a family was that they were committed to training their dog and to providing a safe, happy home for their pet. In fact, I worked with Vicki and Senator Kennedy for months before I realized who they were. It was only after I received a check from them, and noticed the Edward Moore Kennedy printed on the top, that I realized that the Vicki Kennedy I had been speaking to on the phone about potty training and feeding schedules was the wife of that Ted Kennedy.

So, yes, it had been a long road to the White House, but it was one I felt ready to take.

THE
BASICS

My Approach to Training

AS THE MOTHER of three children and an animal trainer for more than twenty years, I have come to understand that the lessons learned in motherhood are applicable to dog training. This book shares my dog training system, which is based on the positive reinforcement approach. Unlike the traditional training programs currently in vogue, such as the one Cesar Millan uses in the *Dog Whisperer* series, positive reinforcement training holds at its core that dogs learn good behavior by being rewarded for doing well, and that punishment doesn't have to come in the form of a reprimand or, worse, physical force. In positive reinforcement training, our job is to love and respect our dogs and to reward and punish them the way we would our children. In positive reinforcement, the bottom line is that a dog is a living, breathing creation of God that desires love and security. A dog also feels pain, just as we do, and it is our job to minimize that pain.

In my professional judgment, positive reinforcement is the best dog training system, whether you are in a family with many children or a single adult. Right now, far too many dogs are still being subjected to more traditional, punishing training techniques, including the use of choke collars and physical force. Those aversive punishment techniques focus on the "bad" things a dog does, leaving a dog to try to figure out, through trial and error, what he must do in order *not* to be punished. As you will read, I used to practice those traditional training methods—until I had my moment of epiphany: Positive reinforcement is better all around.

I know that positive reinforcement works. I also know that if you stay committed to the principles of this approach, you will, by the end of this book's five-week fundamentals course, have a happy, spirited dog. If your dog has already been trained using traditional punishment techniques, and you're hoping to retrain her with this system, I applaud you, and I assure you that it's possible. I've seen it work countless times. Positive reinforcement training has even saved so-called "death row dogs"—dogs some people thought impossible to rehabilitate—from euthanasia.

I will guide you through each step of my program the same way I guide my students. We will start with an orientation, which will help you prepare yourself, your home, and your family for bringing your dog home. Next is the five-week fundamentals course, which will help you master the basics, from potty training to sit, stay, and come here. You and your dog will then graduate to tricks training, which is designed to keep your dog engaged and curious, as well as adding some elements for fun. Finally, you will discover how to make sure your dog does well in the world at large, so that you're comfortable sharing your family's canine experience with visitors, in your neighborhood dog park, and on the road.

Why Train?

FIRST AND FOREMOST, YOU TRAIN your dog because you want to control his behavior. I also believe there's another, equally important reason: Training, especially positive reinforcement training, is one of the best ways to bond with a dog. A well-trained dog that is truly connected to his owner will feel happy and safe, and have more success in our human world. *Not* to train a dog is like not teaching a child to read: It's wrong. The sad fate of an untrained dog—an animal unable to cope with the world—is usually a highly restricted life.

How will training make him feel happy and safe? Your dog is learning from you all the time, whether you're taking the time to train him or not. Dogs don't understand right and wrong as we do, but they're always trying to figure out, through trial and error, what is safe and what is dangerous, and what feels good and what doesn't. Since your dog is looking to you for those answers, it is best to direct his learning from the first day he enters your life. If you guide your dog to do what you want and reward him when he does it, he is more likely to do it again. In fact, as you'll see, your dog will try to figure out what he did to get rewarded.

A dog that feels safe will usually be a safer dog. According to the Centers for Disease Control, 4.5 million Americans are bitten by dogs every year, more than 2 million of them children. Nearly 400,000 of those children require medical attention. The vast majority of people who are bitten by dogs are bitten by one they know—either their family's dog or a friend's. A well-trained dog is far less likely to bite than an untrained or poorly trained dog.

I also believe that dog training makes all of us better humans; it can certainly help us instill good values in our children. When you involve your children in training, as I hope you will, not only are you helping your dog to enjoy children, you are teaching your children about safety, responsibility, caring, and what it takes to be a best friend.

Finally, as I said above, training is one of the best ways to bond with our dogs. If you've been the owner of a pet with which you've felt exceptionally bonded, you know that this type of relationship brings countless rewards. I loved witnessing the extraordinarily close relationship Senator Kennedy had with his dogs, especially Splash. Their relationship was legendary on Capitol Hill. Whenever I boarded the three Kennedy dogs in my home (which I still do frequently), and I took them back to the family, the Senator would interrupt whatever he was doing or

> When you involve your children in training, you are teaching your children about safety, responsibility, caring, and what it takes to be a best friend.

whomever he was meeting with to greet the dogs and me. This lion of a man turned into a boy when he got down on the floor and played with his dogs. One evening, when the Senator came to my house to pick up Splash on his way home from the airport, the two of them were so noisy with glee that my daughter Paige rushed downstairs to see what all the commotion was. When I introduced her to Senator Kennedy, she was speechless that this man frolicking on the floor of her home was the same man she had seen so many times on television—so speechless that she quickly but politely excused herself and went back upstairs to finish her homework.

I had another client named Nat, whose yellow Labrador Retriever, Zack, often boarded with me. They were so closely bonded that Zack knew when Nat was coming to pick him up. Zack would start pacing and hanging around the foyer, sometimes even picking up his doggy backpack and carrying it to the door. Without fail, about five minutes later, the doorbell would ring and there would be Nat. I began to test Zack, seeing if I could throw him off track. I would put his backpack out early, as if I knew that it was time for him to leave, but Zack never bought it. I would ask Nat to vary his evening arrival time, but that didn't work, either. Zack always knew. I don't know how Zack was able to do this, but I do know that to have such a powerful human–dog relationship is an extraordinary life experience.

Why Commit to Positive Reinforcement Dog Training?

THE IDEA THAT DOGS can—and should—be trained through positive reinforcement, rather than aversive punishment, was first *formally* developed by Ian Dunbar, a veterinarian with a doctorate in animal behavior. As he says, punishment does not have to be nasty, scary, or painful. Therefore, if it doesn't have to be, then it shouldn't be. For dogs, withholding a reward is punishment enough and is, in fact, more effective than physical punishment.

Let me use a real-life story to illustrate how dogs are trained using positive reinforcement, compared to traditional, aversive techniques. I once had a client named Peter, who came to my class at the Boys and Girls Club in Georgetown, distraught that his Australian Shepherd, Wallaby, wouldn't stop jumping. No matter how much Peter reprimanded Wallaby, the dog just loved to jump. Because Peter had been taught to use aversive punishment techniques, he would try to stop Wallaby from jumping by kneeing him in the chest when he jumped. It wasn't working. Wallaby kept jumping. He didn't understand that jumping was bad—he is, after all, a dog, and some dogs naturally love to jump. To Wallaby, Peter's kneeing felt like random bullying.

Rather than have Peter punish Wallaby for doing something bad, I wanted to help him learn to reward Wallaby for doing something good. I worked with them, using a positive reinforcement protocol that I've found extremely effective in getting dogs to stop jumping. First, I had Peter greet Wallaby *only* when Wallaby was sitting. If Wallaby jumped, Peter ignored him. Peter just kept quiet, turned his back, and refused to pay Wallaby any attention. But when Wallaby sat, he found something amazing happened: He got a treat. And not just any treat, but his favorite treat, a stuffed Kong (a nearly indestructible rubber chew toy with a hollow center that can be stuffed with all kinds of treats). When Wallaby jumped, there was no treat (nor were there any more knees to his chest). In time, Wallaby figured out that there was a clear pattern here: If he jumped, he got no treat. But if he sat? Well, jackpot! It took about five weeks of class time, plus Peter's patient practicing of this technique at home, but by the end of the exercise, Wallaby no longer jumped.

A few weeks later, Peter returned to class, upset that Wallaby had started jumping again. I asked Peter if he was consistently using the Kong technique we had practiced. Peter hesitated. "Well . . . sometimes." Aha! As you'll see, inconsistent training is the most common cause of good behaviors' falling apart. I worked with Peter on another technique: I had him *encourage* Wallaby to jump. That's right: We rewarded Wallaby for doing this "bad behavior" that he was already really good at. I had Peter ask Wallaby to jump at random times when Wallaby was least expecting it, even in the middle of class when we were working on something else. Over and over, Wallaby was rewarded with lavish praise and treats, just for jumping when asked to. If he jumped when Peter didn't ask, he got no reward. Instead, Peter turned his back.

Then a funny thing happened. Wallaby began to anticipate when Peter was about to ask him to jump and would wait for

Peter's cue, knowing that he would be rewarded. Before long, Wallaby knew that he was rewarded for jumping only when Peter cued him by saying, "Wallaby, Kangaroo!" As Peter succeeded in controlling his dog's jumping, he also taught Wallaby impulse control and turned this previously bad behavior into a fun trick they both *enjoyed!*

Peter's story helps illustrate that a punishment doesn't always have to be a physical reprimand like kneeing your dog in the chest, which could easily have taught Wallaby not to approach Peter at all. A punishment can also be a withheld reward, as long as it reduces the immediately preceding behavior so that it's less likely to occur in the future. In other words: Peter did punish Wallaby. How? If Wallaby jumped when Peter didn't ask for a jump, Peter didn't give Wallaby praise or a treat, but instead turned away and ignored him. Not giving a reward becomes the punishment. We call this a negative punishment, meaning Wallaby's punishment is that he did *not* get any *reward* that he valued (Peter's attention or a treat). Negative punishment is similar to grounding an older child, giving a young child a time-out, or revoking the much desired television time in the evening. It is *taking away* a privilege.

A positive punishment would have been Peter's physically reprimanding Wallaby with, say, a knee to the chest when Wallaby tried to jump. With a child, positive punishment might be being yelled at or getting a spanking. If all a parent did was spank a child when he

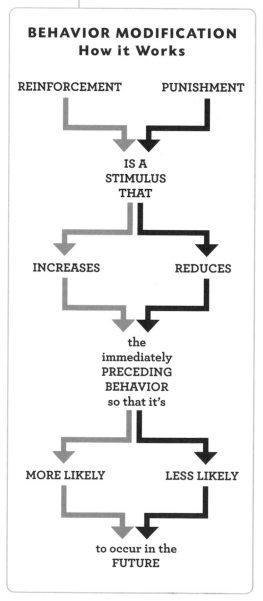

BEHAVIOR MODIFICATION
How it Works

REINFORCEMENT   PUNISHMENT

IS A
STIMULUS
THAT

INCREASES   REDUCES

the
immediately
PRECEDING
BEHAVIOR
so that it's

MORE LIKELY   LESS LIKELY

to occur in the
FUTURE

POSITIVE REINFORCEMENT VS. TRADITIONAL TRAINING

Both training systems attempt to modify the dog's behavior by using reinforcement to increase desired behavior and punishment to decrease unwanted behavior. The word *positive* means giving something (either a reward or a penalty), while *negative* means not giving that feedback (withholding the reward or penalty).

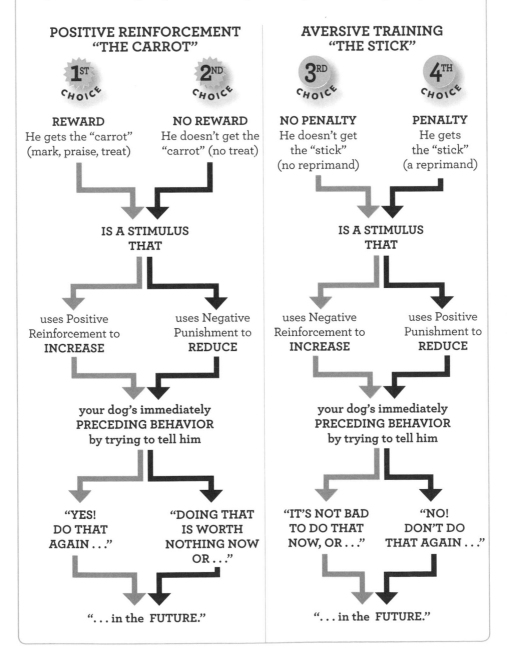

POSITIVE REINFORCEMENT "THE CARROT"

1ST CHOICE

REWARD
He gets the "carrot" (mark, praise, treat)

2ND CHOICE

NO REWARD
He doesn't get the "carrot" (no treat)

IS A STIMULUS THAT

uses Positive Reinforcement to **INCREASE**

uses Negative Punishment to **REDUCE**

your dog's immediately PRECEDING BEHAVIOR by trying to tell him

"YES! DO THAT AGAIN . . ."

"DOING THAT IS WORTH NOTHING NOW OR . . ."

". . . in the FUTURE."

AVERSIVE TRAINING "THE STICK"

3RD CHOICE

NO PENALTY
He doesn't get the "stick" (no reprimand)

4TH CHOICE

PENALTY
He gets the "stick" (a reprimand)

IS A STIMULUS THAT

uses Negative Reinforcement to **INCREASE**

uses Positive Punishment to **REDUCE**

your dog's immediately PRECEDING BEHAVIOR by trying to tell him

"IT'S NOT BAD TO DO THAT NOW, OR . . ."

"NO! DON'T DO THAT AGAIN . . ."

". . . in the FUTURE."

REHABILITATING PROBLEM DOGS

There are instances in which a dog is too fearful or damaged to be rehabilitated, but if a dog *can* be rehabilitated, positive reinforcement is the way to go.

Consider the most extreme case of animal abuse to garner public attention in recent history: Michael Vick's dogs. Who could have believed it? The quarterback for the Atlanta Falcons, convicted of running a dogfighting ring? Among the 47 dogs taken into custody, 22 were evaluated as beyond rehabilitation under the supervision of a guardian/special master appointed by the U.S. District Court for the Eastern District of Virginia. With the support of many experts, including some national humane organizations, these 22 "toughest case" pit bulls were slated for euthanasia. While those dogs were on death row, Best Friends Animal Society petitioned the court to be allowed to reevaluate them, and was then granted court permission to rehabilitate the dogs under continued supervision of the federal court's special master.

Best Friends practices only positive reinforcement methods at its Kanab, Utah, sanctuary. When the 22 Vicktory Dogs, as these pit bulls have become known, arrived at Best Friends' Dogtown Sanctuary, they were either frighteningly aggressive or completely shut down. Dogtown Manager John Garcia told us in interviews for this book that through positive reinforcement training, the Vicktory Dogs learned to trust people and came to believe that the world was a safe place, filled with benevolent people who would not harm them. Ann Allums was one of the trainers responsible for the Vicktory Dogs' rehabilitation. As she explains, had they used aversive training techniques, not only would these dogs have failed to be rehabilitated, they would likely have gotten worse, as typically happens to dogs with unchecked behavior problems. Today, some of the Vicktory Dogs have already earned their Canine Good Citizenship certificate (which we'll discuss in Appendix 1) and have been placed in private homes.

didn't behave, then the child's only reward would be *not* getting *spanked*—which is called negative reinforcement. (Child Protective Services would have other names for it.)

This concept of negative vs. positive isn't about bad vs. good. Negative means taking away; positive means giving. So, positive reinforcement means giving a reinforcement or reward. Negative punishment means not giving that reward. Positive reinforcement dog training is reward-oriented, which is why we use both positive reinforcement (giving rewards) and negative punishment (taking away rewards). Traditional dog training is punishment oriented. It emphasizes positive punishment (giving a physical correction such as a sharp rebuke or a yank on a choke chain) and negative reinforcement (taking away the punishment, such as not yanking the choke chain).

This distinction between negative and positive can be a little tricky to understand, so let's go back to Peter and Wallaby. Peter used the positive reinforcement model to change Wallaby's behavior by effectively saying to him, "I like your jumping; do that some more." The reward reinforced Wallaby's positive behavior. Peter punished Wallaby using negative punishment: no praise or treats if Wallaby jumped when Peter didn't ask him to, which was like saying, "You can jump all day, but I'm ignoring you. Doing that is worth nothing."

Let's assume that Peter continued to use the traditional, aversive training model. If Wallaby jumped on Peter, then Peter would be obligated to give the dog a positive punishment, a physical or verbal reprimand. This positive punishment would be designed to tell Wallaby, "Don't do that. Don't jump." When Wallaby didn't jump, Peter would do nothing, which would be a negative reward: Wallaby wouldn't get the punishment. In other words, Peter would be trying to tell Wallaby, "It's not bad to not jump." The negative reward would be an attempt to *reinforce* Wallaby's positive behavior (not jumping).

In my professional opinion, there's a flaw in that logic. Wallaby is never told specifically that he did the right thing— that *not* jumping is what Peter wants. Wallaby has to figure out what to do by process of elimination, but he is never told when he gets it right. Even a rat searching a maze finally gets a reward when he finds the cheese. But a dog that has been trained only through the traditional aversive punishment model has to figure it all out on his own. That would require abstract thinking, something that dogs' brains are not wired to do.

Moreover, when an animal is given "the stick" too many times, he either rebels or gives up and loses his spirit. Traditional trainers look forward to the moment in training when the dog gives up. They believe that the animal's weakened state of surrender is the moment when they can then build up desired behaviors. While that approach might be effective for extreme cases involving severe dog behavior problems under the care of a very skilled and experienced trainer like Cesar Millan, it is a dangerous weapon in the hands of the average dog owner, and even more dangerous in the hands of a child.

In fact, the American Veterinary Society of Animal Behavior (AVSAB) is very concerned about the idea of families using Cesar Millan's aversive punishment methods. In a recent position statement, the AVSAB gives nine reasons why aversive punishment can be ineffective and possibly dangerous, especially in the hands of an unskilled nonprofessional. They warn that it can trigger or even "cause aggressive behavior." They also caution that such training can suppress aggressive behaviors while making the dog more fearful, which makes that dog more likely to attack without warning.

Retraining a Traditionally Trained Dog

MY DOG EBONY AND I are proof that traditionally trained dogs and pet owners can be retrained to work in a more positive way, focusing on reinforcing good behaviors rather than on what the dog has done wrong. When I first started working with my dogs, I learned to train in the "old school" aversive style that I now preach against. At the time, it was difficult to find an alternative because, well, there wasn't any. That was the way things were done, and it never occurred to me to question it until Ebony taught me otherwise.

WHAT ABOUT BEING THE LEADER OF THE PACK?

Many traditional dog trainers who use aversive punishment techniques claim that we positive reinforcement folks don't understand dog pack psychology. They say that dogs desire a strong leader to dominate them and tell them what to do. Traditional trainers say that if the dog doesn't recognize you as the alpha dog, the leader of the pack, the dog will feel the need to become the leader and will end up being in charge of you.

It is true that dogs like to know who the leader is. But I believe that traditional dog trainers get themselves into trouble by concluding that the only kind of leadership that a dog respects is a bully boss who will yank him around by a choke chain; who will flip him on his back and sit on him, in what we trainers call the alpha roll position; who will pinch a dog's ear until he drops a training toy; who will give a dog only aversive correction.

Good leaders don't have to act like bullies to command respect—not in the human world or in the dog pack. Pet dogs don't need to be bullied to become your loyal follower. Pet dogs love to follow leaders who provide food, shelter, and safety: leaders they see as benevolent and fair. Good pack leaders provide social experiences and lots of fun.

Ebony was my first Portuguese Water Dog. I got her in the late 1980s with every intention of training her as a show dog. I soon found out, however, that she was dysplastic in one hip and carried the gene for progressive retinal atrophy. It would have been unethical to show her, earn a championship title, and then breed her. And so I didn't.

Instead, I took Ebony to the obedience ring, in which your dog is judged on how well she can obey cues and commands and follow your lead. To prepare her for the competitions, I trained with her on my own and with many other trainers, privately and in classes. Despite the hours we put in, Ebony didn't score well at the competitions. I kept trying, going to many competitions run by the American Kennel Club. Ebony progressed, but I could tell that something was off for her. She didn't like the choke chain and she lagged unhappily, with her tail tucked during practice and at obedience matches. She wasn't having any fun.

> Good leaders don't have to act like bullies to command respect—not in the human world or in the dog pack.

In 1991, I decided to stop tormenting poor Ebony; instead of entering competitions, we just went to watch. My kids were all very young, but I just loaded them, a diaper bag, the dogs, and their supplies into the car and off we'd go. When we got there, the kids would play, and I would watch the shows, taking notes. Afterward, I'd try to talk to the best trainers and pick their brains about how they got their dogs to perform so well. I was particularly taken by one superb trainer, Joan Woodard. Her dogs, a Golden Retriever and an Airedale Terrier, performed beautifully. What surprised me the most was that they were not wearing choke collars. I'd never seen that before. I tracked Joan down after one match.

"I saw you in the ring," I said to her. "Your dogs worked beautifully and you're not even using choke collars."

Joan smiled and pointed to Ebony's choke collar. "Too bad," she said. "But thank you for admiring my dogs' work." And then she walked away.

I understand now that she probably didn't want to waste time on another one of us choke folk, but I wouldn't give up. I kept after Joan, show after show, until I finally wore her down. She explained that there was a bit of a movement happening in dog training circles, and agreed to introduce me to a small,

"STOP THE VIOLENCE"

I am concerned about what happens to people when they harm an animal or—in the case of our children—see an animal get harmed, even if it's in the spirit of so-called training. If you'll allow me to get on my soapbox for a moment, I also believe that positive dog training strengthens our families and communities. This is one way in which we can stop the cycle of violence. Unfortunately, it's far too common that a youngster who first learns to commit violence against animals graduates to committing violence against people. The American Humane Association has launched a major initiative called The Link to study the connection between animal cruelty and human violence. The organization that issues the "No Animals Were Harmed" disclaimer for movies and TV shows, American Humane reports that violent criminals were significantly more likely than nonviolent offenders to have "committed childhood acts of cruelty toward pets" and that abuse against animals occurs in an overwhelming majority of households where there is documented child abuse and neglect.

If your child (or her friend) abuses or harms a pet, it's best to discuss it with her (or the friend's parent) immediately. If she has seen an animal being hurt, reassure her that you will do everything you can to help that animal. Praise her for being compassionate. Ask if she has ever hurt an animal; if she has, thank her for telling you, then together gently pet your dog (unless the dog is fearful). Remind your child that it is never okay to hurt an animal, and praise her once more for being a good kid who cares.

close-knit group of trainers who were doing things a different way.

The next week, I drove with Ebony to a class that Joan held in positive reinforcement techniques. I felt as if I were entering an underground fringe group, and in many ways, I was. This type of training was such a departure from what I had been accustomed to—to what I had been training others to do, as well—that I was amazed by how remarkably obedient, highly focused, and, most of all, happy the dogs in this room were. There were no choke collars, no physical corrections. Instead, there were treats and toys—lots of them. Even that was a difference. In traditional punishment-oriented training classes, treats are not allowed because, the thinking goes, they spoil dogs and make owners "soft."

The more I attended Joan's positive reinforcement classes, the more I got it. I began using this method with my own dogs, who took to it right away. Ebony, in particular, seemed like a completely different dog: She was spirited and joyful. *And she loved training.* She even loved her leash. Prior to this, she'd sulk and become dispirited when I put it on her, probably because she knew that before long, I'd be tugging at her neck and reprimanding her harshly. But after I began to train her with the methods of positive reinforcement, she would perk up when she saw me get the leash.

I never looked back.

Around that time, Dr. Ian Dunbar founded the Association of Pet Dog Trainers (APDT), a membership organization dedicated to promoting positive reinforcement training. I went to my first APDT conference in 1994, where I became even more inspired by many of the most dedicated dog trainers from around the country. I took along my (excuse the pun) dog-eared copy of Dr. Dunbar's 1979 landmark book, *Dog Behavior*, for him to autograph. Since that time, Dr. Dunbar has encouraged my work in positive reinforcement dog training, and we continue to exchange ideas, especially about dog training for families with children. I remain grateful to Dr. Dunbar and to Joan Woodard, my first positive reinforcement trainer, for helping me cross over.

I also remain eternally grateful to my dog Ebony, who passed away in 1995 at the young age of not yet seven years, having lasted only six months after being diagnosed with kidney failure. Ebony patiently showed me what a fast learner and happy dog she could be if I just rewarded her for all the good behaviors she offered me.

The Essentials: Patience and Practice

BEFORE YOU EMBARK ON this training program—from preparation, to the fundamentals course, and on to more advanced tricks training—I first want to applaud you for making the commitment to train your dog using positive reinforcement. And then I want to remind you that it won't always be easy. This program—and, indeed, any training program—will require a lot from your dog, and it will also require some things from you: mainly, consistent, patient practice. I want you to begin to keep in mind that *every* interaction with your dog is a training opportunity, starting, as I have said, with the moment he first walks into your home. I want you to know that the hard work happens between our classes, when I'll ask you to practice what you've learned, with constancy and consistency. I want you to do your homework assignments. I want you to understand that training includes making time for exercise, brushing, petting, and play.

This consistent, patient practice is what will make the difference between having a dog that is highly trained and spirited and one that is frustrated and unsure. Patient practice will teach your dog that his good behavior is appreciated and desired and will be rewarded. Patient practice will remind your dog, again and again, that he is a good dog who deserves the loving care that you give him. Patient practice will create an essential bond.

I believe that consistent, patient practice will also do wonders for you. The more you practice, the more confident you'll become. The same goes for children. I encourage you to involve your children in this program and the tasks and homework assignments. Successful dog training experiences can help teach children to take responsibility and to make and keep a commitment. If they become frustrated by the amount of time or consistent work that dog training requires, or with their dog's inability to master something quickly, we have an opportunity to show them that hard work pays off. So many times, I have seen children and families transformed through dog training. It is an opportunity to learn about ourselves, to become more understanding and accepting, and to laugh at our mistakes and challenges.

Believe me, if you commit to training your dog now and to following the lessons in this book, your work will pay off. Before long you will begin to reap the countless, wonderful, life-enriching rewards of having a well-behaved, well-socialized best friend.

Now, let's get started.

Preparing for Dog Training

I HOPE THAT YOU'RE reading this before you've brought your dog home, because the first question to consider in dog training is also the one I believe to be the most fundamental: Why are you getting a dog? If you've already found the new love of your life, you still ought to ask yourself that all-important question.

The "right" reason to get a dog is that you want a companion *and* are at a point in your life where you know that you have the time and lifestyle not only to care for your dog but to care for him well. You are fully aware of the commitment a dog requires, and are prepared and equipped to honor that commitment. You're emotionally ready to give part of yourself to raising this animal that

Now that you know you're ready for a dog, figure out which type would best suit your lifestyle—will he be large or small, hypoallergenic or hairy, purebred or mixed? The next step is preparation: Your house, yard, car, and even your family and other pets need to be prepped before the arrival of your new dog. You will also need to collect a number of supplies, and line up a responsible vet and groomer; I'll detail these processes in this chapter.

is completely dependent on you for his survival and well-being. Your finances are reasonably in order. Remember, desperately *wanting* a dog doesn't always mean that the time is right for *getting* a dog. If you're at an emotionally low moment in your life and are thinking of getting a dog to help you deal with depression or loneliness, I want you to really think about this decision before you take on the added responsibility. It's natural to want everyone to love your dog, but you should not get a dog in order to get approval or fulfillment from others.

If you are thinking of getting a dog for your child, while you yourself feel unsure about committing to a pet, I'd advise against doing it, because you must assume that you are going to be that dog's chief caretaker, despite your child's promises to the contrary. If you are thinking of getting your current dog a companion, be careful of falling into what dog trainers call second dog syndrome, in which you end up exerting less energy and spending less one-on-one time with the new dog than he needs, causing him to bond with your existing pet rather than with you. Second dog syndrome interferes with the bond you need to build with your new dog in order to train him successfully.

If, after giving these questions a lot of consideration, you determine that you are ready, congratulations are in order. The decision to bring a dog into your home and your family is, I believe, one of the most exciting, rewarding, and enriching decisions you can make.

Choosing the Right Dog for You

AS ANY FAMILY WITH A DOG will tell you, choosing the right pet for your family can be complicated. There are so many factors to consider. Would you prefer to rehome an older dog that is already trained? Are allergies an issue? If so, do you need to look for a breed that doesn't shed? Are you open to the joys (and mysteries!) of having a mixed-breed dog? What kind of dog will fit into your lifestyle, whether that means taking vigorous hikes every weekend or staying pretty close to home? Do you travel often? If so, would you find it easier to travel with a smaller dog that you can carry in the cabin of the airplane with you? What

YOUR SHELTER VISIT

Seeing dozens if not hundreds of adorable puppies and dogs at one time can make the head spin, so plan your shelter visits carefully. While you want to have an emotional connection to the pet you take home, you also want to make sure that you engage your rational brain in the process. Try to learn as much as you can about the history of the dog you are considering, and try to figure out if the dog is, or can easily become, well socialized with people and other dogs. For a rescued puppy, ask if she arrived with littermates, and find out what you can about those littermates. Was the dog found as a stray or given up by an owner? If she was given up, ask why. Occasionally (and unfortunately) dogs are given up simply because they have outgrown their cuteness (or because post-holiday doubts have set in). Ask if the dog has been potty and crate trained. What is the dog like with other dogs? Does she growl? Does she guard food or toys? Can you take a toy (or a shoe) from her mouth? How is she with children? Has she ever bitten someone? What is she like when she is touched and picked up?

There are no questions you can't ask. Remember this key fact: You are making a commitment to this dog for the duration of her life. Some reputable rescue organizations work with an animal behaviorist, a behavior specialist, or an experienced professional dog trainer to evaluate each dog that has been given up for rehoming or found abandoned; however, many shelters and rescue organizations are woefully underfunded. Their dedicated staff struggle to meet the demands of caring for the skyrocketing number of abandoned animals, and are unable to provide behavior evaluations for each one. In that case, if possible, enlist the help of an experienced, professional dog trainer to go with you to evaluate the dog once you have made your choice. Even if you need to pay for the trainer's time, it will be money well spent.

Different breeds have their charms—but all dogs are not good choices for all people.

about big dogs? Most big dogs require a lot of space and eat more than smaller dogs, so is space or the cost of food an issue for you right now?

Once you figure out what kind of dog is best for your family, you need to decide whether your preference is to adopt a dog from a shelter or rescue organization or to purchase one from a breeder.

If you are open to the idea of adopting your family's new best friend from an animal shelter, I'd like to thank you. According to the Humane Society of the United States, on average, between 15,000 and 20,000 dogs and cats are taken in at animal shelters every day across America. These adorable, lovable animals are just waiting for their new homes, and they are desperate to start a new chapter in their lives.

Working with a Breeder

IF YOU CHOOSE TO GO THE PUREBRED ROUTE, the first thing to understand is the big difference between good breeders and bad ones. Some unscrupulous people set up factory farms to breed puppies as a cash crop. Many pet stores that sell puppies have purchased them from these puppy mills, so it is best to deal directly with the breeder. Educate yourself so that you do not accidentally support this cruel and unethical business. Check references: You may be unknowingly encountering a puppy mill if a breeder does not allow you to see his facility, has several breeds or litters for sale at the same time, offers to ship you a dog without interviewing you in person, won't talk at length with you on the phone, or won't offer the names and numbers of owners who have purchased puppies from him in the past. Although some puppy mills are regulated, they are all inhumane and should really be avoided altogether.

You will need to do some research to locate good-quality breeders. If you are researching particular breeds, get to know people at local breed clubs, American Kennel Club (AKC) conformation dog shows, and dog obedience trials. Talk to veterinarians; perhaps they will be willing to offer the names of clients for you to interview as part of your research.

What the breeder charges may seem like a lot of money, but it is a small investment compared to what you'll pay to maintain your dog over his lifetime, and it is money well spent when you consider what a breeder provides you with: information about pedigree, detailed vet records, and a disclosure of all health issues. Most will microchip each puppy with an identification chip injected safely under the skin. Good breeders will tell you what and when to feed your dog; they'll inform you about any food allergies. Good breeders know how each puppy is developing. When you visit a good-quality breeder, everything about the dogs will appear to be happy and healthy: The puppies will be playful, well socialized, interested in visitors, and they'll be living in a clean and properly heated area. Also, a good breeder will not allow you to take the puppy until it is at least seven weeks old. This is important because puppies tend to be far better socialized and developed when they have those full seven weeks with their mother and littermates.

> **Good breeders will match you with your puppy.**

Good breeders will also expect as much of you as you do of them. They will interview you extensively: about your knowledge of and experience with dogs, the suitability and safety of your home, as well as your commitment to training and to the puppy's general welfare. They will likely match you with the puppy they believe has the right temperament for your family and fits your level of experience with dogs. They may ask for references from your veterinarian or others. Usually, they will want your whole family to visit their puppies, sometimes more than once, and some may also offer to let you meet the dam (mother) before she gives birth so she can be comfortable with you.

And there's more: You will be asked to sign a contract that requires you to return the dog to them if you decide you cannot keep him at any point, though most breeders offer a refund only if the dog is returned within the first year. Since you and your dog will become a living part of their reputation, your breeder will want to stay in touch with you regarding your puppy's development, as well as his health and behavior.

Once you locate the breeder you want to work with, be willing to wait. Good breeders do not always have puppies for sale. They specialize in one or two breeds and typically whelp the litter in their own home. This takes time, but in the long run, it will be worth the wait.

Your Training Goals and Plan

AS I SIT DOWN TO WRITE TODAY, Boz, a two-year-old Border Collie, is curled up at my feet. Last spring, I lost Saxon, my beloved Giant Schnauzer, to cancer. As anyone who has lost a pet knows, it's a devastating and heartbreaking experience, and I may never get over the loss of Saxon. But about eight months after he died, I found myself wanting a new dog for myself, as well as for my Ibizan Hound, Brieo. We both could use the additional companionship, especially because Brieo is a "low dog," meaning that he prefers to follow rather than lead. But, given that I was still mourning Saxon, I wasn't quite ready to make a lifelong commitment to a new dog. And I know how unwise it would have been to have gotten a second dog just as a companion for Brieo.

After much thought, I decided that I would become a foster mom to Boz, meaning that I've taken him into my home temporarily until he finds his forever home. Boz was given up by a family that could not keep him anymore due to personal reasons. Now I am giving him everything I would be giving a dog I was taking in permanently. Boz has his own crate, bed, bowls, and all the rest of his supplies, as well as a lot of affection and one-on-one time with me. Becoming a foster parent for a dog can be challenging—and it's not for everyone. But if you have experience with owning dogs, and are on the fence about adopting again, fostering may be the perfect option for both you and the dog.

> **Successful training starts with a good plan.**

Even though Boz will be with me only until we can find him a good, permanent home, I began training him from the moment I agreed to take him in. The same should go for you: Once you have chosen your dog, it's time to prepare *immediately*. While many dog trainers believe that there should be bonding time without training when a family first gets a dog, I urge you to begin training your dog immediately. When you use the positive reinforcement approach, training time *is* bonding time. It's showing your dog that he is being taken care of and being rewarded for doing well. If you don't train your dog early on, you are inviting future behavioral problems. An untrained dog will almost always learn how to get what he wants by doing the wrong thing, such as by jumping or barking, and then become confused and anxious when you try to untrain and retrain him later. A dog is happiest when he learns from the very first day in his new home that training is a natural and routine part of life. Simply be prepared to be consistent, firm, and fair.

Successful training starts with a good plan, and a good plan starts with clear goals. I actually post my goals and plan on my fridge as a constant reminder to focus on my long-term objectives. As countless students have also told me (and I've found), working toward dog training goals—and consistently meeting those goals over time—has given them (and me) more confidence about achieving goals in other aspects of life.

What Are Your Dog Training Goals?

MOST ELITE ATHLETES WILL TELL YOU that if they can envision themselves shooting a free throw or hitting a home run, they are a big step closer to accomplishing that goal. That's why I want to guide you in a short exercise about your dog's future . . . and *yours*. Imagine that your dog is fully trained. What is his behavior like at home? Do you enjoy each other's company? What is it like when you have other people visit your home? How do you play together and how does he play with other dogs? What is it like to take him on walks? What is it like when you take him with you for recreation or on visits to friends' homes?

Now you're ready for the next step: setting training goals that will ensure that you end up with the dog that behaves the way you envision. As you and your dog begin to meet your goals, you will see how much progress you're making, and how much closer you are getting each day to having the relationship that you imagined.

It takes five weeks to lock in a new habit, which is one of the reasons that I recommend a five-week training program: It works best for your dog *and* for you. (Your dog isn't the only one who has to learn new habits!) So, choose goals that you imagine will keep you inspired for five weeks . . . and beyond.

Setting Goals: A Checklist

HERE IS A CHECKLIST TO HELP YOU SET YOUR GOALS. Try picking only your top ten, so that you can get an idea of what is most important to you. The list doesn't need to be perfect or final; it's just a tool to help you get focused and specific.

AT HOME

❏ My dog is impeccably **house-trained**. My dog knows where to go potty and goes potty on cue. When she needs to go outside, she gives me the signal that I taught her.

❏ **The crate** is my dog's home. She enjoys her crate, goes to it when asked, and keeps calm inside it.

❏ My dog **settles down** when I ask her. Although I love it when my dog is enthusiastic, she doesn't jump up unless she's invited.

❏ **Suppertime** is enjoyable and calm. My dog sits to receive her food and does not guard it from people or other animals. She doesn't bother me when I am eating.

❏ **Grooming** my dog is a pleasant experience. She enjoys being handled while I brush her. She accepts bath time with ease and enjoys being handled and massaged.

❏ My dog obeys the **furniture rules and chews only** what is allowed.

❏ Although my dog likes being with me, she **isn't so needy** that she shadows me everywhere. When I leave the house, my dog relaxes. When I return, she is happy and mellow.

TRAINING

❏ My dog and I **love to train** for a quick minute when the opportunity arises. We also love doing our training homework daily and bond more closely while we train.

❏ **Sitting** calmly is my dog's way of saying please. He sits when asked and has learned the situations in which I usually ask him to sit.

❏ **"Down"** and **"stay"** are mastered. When I cue the command, my dog does it without hesitation.

❏ My dog **loves hearing his name** and is attentive when I say it.

❏ **"Come here"** is mastered. When I recall my dog, he comes to me right away.

❏ **Playtime** is fun for my dog and me. When others are invited to play, they are safe and so is my dog. When I ask him to give back a toy or let go of it, he does so right away.

❏ **Tricks** are now a fun part of our ongoing training. As my dog masters each trick, we are joyful and proud together. I love to show off his tricks to other people.

SOCIALIZATION

❏ When the **doorbell** rings, my dog is interested, but sits until cued to **greet a visitor.**

❏ **Walking** with my dog is joyful and relaxing. She loves walking on a leash by my side, and she responds when I ask her to finish sniffing and resume walking.

❏ When we **meet other dogs,** mine is well behaved regardless of what they do.

❏ When we encounter **strange noises or surprises,** my dog is mildly interested but doesn't freeze or try to fight or flee.

❏ When we go to the **groomer** or the **veterinarian,** my dog and these professionals are happy to see each other.

❏ When my dog is allowed to join me **inside a place of business,** she has impeccable behavior. I feel like I can take my dog anywhere.

❏ **Car rides** are peaceful with my dog. She loves to go in the car with me.

If you were able to narrow the list down to your top ten, good job; that will help you and your dog be successful together. Trust that whatever priorities you pick are going to be the right priorities, and don't worry about the others for now. Don't get stuck on trying to be perfect; perfection is not possible in dog training. If you follow the training program, and are disciplined about doing your homework, you'll go far. After all, if you make no choices, you will end up neglecting your dog's social and emotional needs. So make your choices and feel good about them. Post your list of goals on the fridge or somewhere you can see it. Be inspired by it.

From Goals to Plan: The Daily Routine

KEEPING TO A SCHEDULE tells your new dog, regardless of his age, that you, his benevolent leader, are in charge. It helps him learn the household rules and understand that he must "work" for his food and his privileges. Dogs respect and want that kind of safe certainty. In time, both you and your dog will find the daily schedule and routine . . . well, routine.

It's important to get your dog started on his routine as soon as you bring him home—each point on the daily routine represents an opportunity to train him—which means that you should begin preparing for a new schedule of your own weeks before you visit your shelter or breeder to choose your dog. While your dog's routine will ultimately depend on his needs and yours, every day must include time for feeding, potty, walking, and play.

Here's a sample routine for you to look over. But don't worry about it too much now: We'll cover every step in the course of our five-week training program, with detailed instructions.

MORNING ROUTINE

▶ **WAKE UP.** Greet the dog at her crate, ask for a sit before opening the crate, direct your dog out of the crate, and ask for another sit.

▶ **POTTY.** From the crate, go outside (with a sit at the door) to do a potty on cue. Give your dog a treat when she obeys you. A sit at the door, then back inside for breakfast.

▶ **BREAKFAST.** A sit as you prepare to give your dog her breakfast.

▶ **PUPPY POTTY.** If you have a puppy, go outside again to potty, using the potty-training protocol we'll discuss later (see page 55). Always give your puppy a treat when she goes potty.

- ▶ **BRUSH AND COMB.** Handle your dog all over as you brush and comb her coat.

- ▶ **WALK.** Use the walk training program (see page 80).

- ▶ **PUPPY POTTY.** Each time you crate and uncrate your puppy, take her outside to potty.

- ▶ **CRATE TIME IS NAP TIME.** Your dog learns to love her crate as you give her time in it when you go to work, go out on errands on which your dog cannot accompany you, or need time to do things around the house. As she becomes comfortable with these scheduled naps in her crate, the possibility of separation anxiety lessens.

AFTERNOON ROUTINE

- ▶ **GREET.** Each time you let your new dog out of the crate, continue the crate training protocol . . .

- ▶ **POTTY.** . . . and the potty-training protocol.

- ▶ **TRAIN.** Take time for your formal daily 10-minute homework practice. (Each week's suggested agenda is detailed in your five-week Fundamentals Training Program.)

- ▶ **PUPPY POTTY.** You know the drill.

- ▶ **SOCIALIZATION.** Depending on your dog's readiness, you may choose to go on a brief car ride or on a walk. You might visit a neighbor or neighboring dogs in a place where you can do socialization exercises. If you have children, this might be the right time to socialize your dog with your kids. (Socialization activities are spelled out throughout the book.)

- ▶ **RELAX AT HOME.** Brushing, petting, or engaging in other quiet activities that bond you and your dog.

- ▶ **PUPPY POTTY.** Should be familiar to you . . . and becoming more familiar for your pup.

- ▶ **CRATE TIME IS NAP TIME.** The purpose, again, is to help your dog love his crate and not associate crate time with exile or punishment.

EVENING ROUTINE

▶ **GREET.** Sometimes the afternoon crate time might be brief.

▶ **POTTY.** Notice how you're building your dog's association of getting out of the crate with going potty—all while practicing the *sit* cues on the way.

▶ **SUPPERTIME.** Similar routine to breakfast.

▶ **PUPPY POTTY.** It's that time again.

▶ **WALK.** Can be a socialization walk or a special time for you and your dog. It's your call.

▶ **PUPPY POTTY.** You're another day closer to having a potty-trained dog.

▶ **FAMILY TIME.** Rotate a variety of activities, keeping your focus on your dog for 10 minutes. This may be a good time to involve your kids in assisting you with her training. It's

9:00pm PLAYTIME.
"She got really excited when I showed her the new ducky toy. I think I'll save it as a speial training reward."

12:00am POTTY TIME.
"She woke me up at midnight. Fortunately, she went right to her spot the moment I cued her."

5:00pm SUPPERTIME.
"Hand-feeding is a joy. When I came home from work, I hand-fed at the front door and that seemed to calm her."

6:00pm TIME TO WALK.
"His focus is better today, although he still pulls on the leash every minute. He responds more quickly to the 'be a tree' technique."

important that the dog be socialized to your whole family. Remember that you must always supervise when kids are involved.

▶ **POTTY.** Build up your dog's understanding that potty time comes before good-night time.

GOOD NIGHT

▶ **CRATE.** Into the crate for rest. If you've exercised enough today, your dog is more likely to sleep better, and so are you. I like to express my daily gratitude and blessing to my dog.

MIDDLE OF THE NIGHT

▶ **PUPPY POTTY.** Your middle-of-the-night puppy potty routine will come to an end. I promise.

Your Training Log

I HIGHLY RECOMMEND THAT YOU record your dog's schedule, as well as her progress in meeting your training goals, in a notebook or logbook. It will allow you to chart your dog's progress, identify her strengths and natural body rhythms, and spot patterns and problem areas early. For example, you will potty train your dog more quickly and accurately if you know when your dog does her business, when she no longer needs certain puppy potty trips, and how she tells you with her body language and behavior cues that she needs to go out. Tracking small improvements will inspire you to patience and confidence. As your dog gets older and her natural patterns change, I recommend that you start a new log to help you identify those new patterns and routines.

Adapt the daily training routines on the previous pages to your own lifestyle. Perhaps another person helps with afternoon dog walks, or you use doggy day care (particularly if you have a puppy that needs to go to the bathroom every three hours). In any case, it will help everyone caring for your dog do a better job; no one will be confused about whether others did what they were supposed to do: The schedule and log will help keep that information in one place. With my family, I write out weekly assignments that need to be checked off.

WEEK 1

TRAINING LOG FOR _Bailey_   DAY _Wed._

SKILL	PROGRESS	NOTES
USING TREATS AS LURES. Practice luring your dog with treats.	🙂	Bailey enjoys following lure as we move around the house. First time practicing outside. Success!
LURING TO SIT. Touch treat to dog's nose, lure up (rump goes down), mark, praise, touch collar, treat last.	✔✔✔	Kids enjoyed luring Bailey to sit. We are having fun.
LURING TO RECALL, PART 1. Take 2 or 3 steps back, lure dog. Mark, praise, touch collar, treat last. If dog already sits, add it.	Needs work	Dog is not sitting when I lure him into me. Help! But at least he comes when I call him.
EYE CONTACT EXERCISE. Touch treat to dog's nose, then bring it to your eyes. Mark and reward for dog's eye contact.	Great!!!	Dog is staring at all of us all the time. Is that ok? We like it. Attention skills are better.
WALKING, "BE A TREE." When dog pulls leash, stop and hold leash firmly to your body. When dog looks back at you, mark, lure, and start again.	Maybe next	We are not getting anywhere fast, but he is looking back at us when we stop moving. I am patient!
LEASH TETHERING. Around your home.		st the clip so I bought a ger leash to go around my aist. He is more attentive.
HAND-FEEDING. Feed all meals by hand from dog's bowl. Your dog sees that you are the giver of food.	⭐⭐☆	Dog loves hand-feeding exercise. He doesn't care when the kids run by his food bowl.
CRATE TRAINING. Teach dog to love his crate.	Mixed	He loves his crate, but not ready for me to close door.
POTTY TRAINING. Keep track of input (meals and treats) and output (potty time). Note accidents.	Oops	Had 2 accidents, but it was our fault.
BITE INHIBITION, HANDLING, GENTLING, "OUCH" EXERCISE. Lots of gentle handling. Touch paws and all over body.	Needs practice	He stops biting when I say "ouch," but starts again. But his biting is all play and is getting gentler.
CHOOSE AN ACTIVITY/GAME. Peekaboo—played with kids.	🙂 🙂	Bailey did great and so did the kids. I reminded the kids to be gentle with Bailey's eyes.
CHOOSE A SOCIALIZATION EXPERIENCE. 1. Picked up kids from school. 2. Played with neighbor's puppy.	⭐⭐☆	1. He got excited so we hand-fed for sits, and he calmed down. 2. Neighbor puppy is a brat. Help!

SAMPLE LOG: Keep track of your dog's successes

You can write the schedule and log into a day planner book, or download free Daily Training Routine printouts at my website: lovethatdogbook.com. I recommend that you log everything, including sleeping and napping, waking up in the middle of the night, peeing and pooping, potty accidents, walking, playing, eating treats as well as meals, and even drinking water. If you know what time your puppy or young dog ate her meals or drank water, it becomes fairly easy to predict when she will need to go out to potty again. Write down your mistakes as well as your successes. Whether you have a puppy or an older, rehomed dog, log everything for at least the first 30 days, and ideally for the full five weeks of the training program.

Preparing Your Home and Family

I T'S SO MUCH BETTER if you can prepare your house and yard before your new dog comes home, but even if you can't— even if you already have your dog—consider this an opportunity to correct any setup and safety issues in your home, yard, or car. Now is also the time to have a discussion with all other family members about the new house rules. If you have regular visitors in your home, such as a babysitter or housekeeper, prepare them as well.

EQUIPMENT AND SUPPLIES

Y OUR DOG'S BASIC EQUIPMENT and supplies can be purchased inexpensively and resourcefully, or you can spend

YOUR DOG'S COLLAR

W hen you add dog tags to your dog's collar, it's his uniform. In addition to a flat buckle collar, you may use a harness or training collar.

FLAT BUCKLE COLLAR
This essential collar displays your dog's tags and is traditionally attached to the leash.

MARTINGALE COLLAR
Also called a Greyhound Collar, it hangs fairly loose around the dog's neck until the dog pulls, tightening the collar . . . without any strangling!

GENTLE LEADER
With the leash attached to the halter under the dog's chin, the dog will automatically turn back toward you whenever he pulls.

BODY HARNESS
Pick one that connects to the leash at the dog's chest (rather than on top of the dog's spine).

more outfitting your dog than you did buying her from a top-line breeder. How much you spend, I'll leave up to you, but here's your shopping list.

❏ **FLAT BUCKLE COLLAR.** When his collar is complete with dog tags, it's your dog's uniform. I recommend a flat buckle collar in either leather or webbed fiber. (You may need to start with a lightweight kitty collar, just to get your dog used to the feel of the collar while he's around your home, and use a heavier collar on walks.)

❏ **DOG TAGS.** One tag should display your name, the dog's name, and your phone numbers. Local laws may also require you to display a dog license tag that includes current vaccination data. If you have a second residence, such as a weekend house or a beach house, you should have an extra set of tags with local phone numbers made.

❏ **TRAINING COLLARS (OPTIONAL).** I am against the use of choke collars and prong collars, as they can be misused and can hurt a dog unnecessarily. I support the careful use of some head-collar training devices (the ones that look somewhat like horse halters), such as the Gentle Leader, as long as you follow the manufacturer's instructions, as improper use can hurt your dog. I'll tell you more about using the Gentle Leader in the chapter on behavior problems.

❏ **MARTINGALE COLLAR (OPTIONAL) (ALSO CALLED A GREYHOUND COLLAR).** If you have a dog with a narrow head, such as a Greyhound, you may want to use this collar, but only when taking the dog on a walk. It has an extra loop that tightens around the dog's neck if he pulls, but will not choke the dog if you fit it properly. I learned to always take off a Martingale when we're not out for a walk, because the collar may get caught on something. Many years ago, I woke up in the middle of the night to see my Irish Water Spaniel, Aisley, standing calmly next to the foot of my bed, her Martingale caught on my wrought-iron bed frame.

❏ **HARNESS (OPTIONAL).** Many owners find that they can walk their dog with more control when his leash is attached to a harness instead of a collar. I prefer harnesses where the leash attaches at the dog's chest, rather than on his back. I find that many breeds treat the top-of-the-back attachment as an invitation to pull, while the chest attachment causes the dog to turn toward you when he pulls. Make sure that the harness fits snugly and check your dog for chafing.

❑ **LEASH.** I recommend a six-foot leash (instead of a four-footer) so that your dog can get a little extra freedom, especially during exercises when you tether him to your belt. If you're thinking about using a retractable leash, such as a Flexi, wait until your dog has completed the five-week fundamentals program, has developed excellent recall, and can walk politely at a loose heel.

❑ **CRATE.** See the crate training section (page 58) to help you choose what's right for your dog and your decor.

❑ **X-PEN.** If your budget will allow it, get a collapsible exercise pen, often called an x-pen (see box at right), as your dog's movable playpen area. This lightweight, portable pen can be used to keep a dog in or out of an area. Set it up as a contained ring or divide a room like the Berlin Wall . . . to be taken down when your dog matures. You will find other uses for your x-pen while you go through this training program. To keep my dogs from moving ours, I tie dumbbell weights with bungee straps to the bottom of the pen.

THE X-PEN

Versatile, lightweight, and portable, these panels can be attached together . . .

. . . AS A PLAYPEN
Give your puppy or dog a little freedom to move or lie down.

DUMBBELL WEIGHTS
Dumbbell weights make it harder for your dog to move the x-pen.

. . . AND AS A ROOM DIVIDER
Protect part of a room as off-limits.

❏ **BABY GATES.** These movable gates help you close off rooms or keep your dog confined to a particular room.

❏ **BEDDING.** Since your new dog may chew his bed, choose an inexpensive option at first—towels and cheap blankets.

❏ **FOOD BOWL AND WATER BOWL.** Although I'm a fan of bowls that fit into a raised housing, you may want to go as simple and lightweight as possible at first, especially as you're mastering the hand-feeding protocol (detailed in the next chapter). Once hand-feeding has been mastered, you can switch to a more deluxe setup, including a metal or ceramic bowl that is easy to sterilize.

❏ **FOOD AND TREATS.** See the feeding section in the next chapter for guidance in making diet choices. Remember to set aside a portion of your dog's daily diet for training treats.

❏ **TOYS FOR PLAY.** Allowing a dog to "own" only a couple of toys that he can play with whenever he wants to will help create opportunities for training. Don't allow him to destroy or shred toys; blocked intestines can require surgery. Always supervise toy play.

CHEWING FOR REWARDS

My favorite chew toy is the Kong, because younger dogs love them and yet they are practically indestructible. A Kong can be stuffed with treats or dog food to slow down a dog that eats too fast; you can give it to him while he is in his crate or as a reward.

KONG TOYS.
Each of these toys is designed to have treats or soft dog food stuffed into its opening.

STUFF THE KONG.
Fill it with treats or pack it with soft dog food and put it in the freezer.

YUM!
You have directed your dog's chewing to an activity that rewards him and holds his attention.

❏ **TOYS FOR CHEWING.** Chewing is a dog's natural impulse. So, rather than tempting your dog to chew things he shouldn't, direct his chewing behavior positively by regularly giving him toys that are made to be chewed.

❏ **TOYS FOR TRAINING.** These are special toys that I "lend" to my dog as a reward during training sessions; after some brief moments of play, he has to give them back to me in exchange for a cookie, a training technique that I will teach you later (see page 123). They can be delicate rubber squeaky toys or special plush toys, and are always returned to me for safekeeping.

> ### TREAT POUCH
>
> **M**any dog owners use a treat pouch (often called a bait bag) to have treats ready during training. To help your dog focus on you and not on the pouch, clip the pouch to the back of your belt, not at your hip.

I also use tug toys and retrieving toys as training rewards. And then I always have a very special toy in reserve to trade with my dog when he has taken contraband, such as a shoe, or to stop unwanted chase behavior. For contraband trades, I recommend a plush toy that has lots of squeaky and crinkly features, and that can't easily be shredded. Avoid toys that would get chewed up if left with your dog for more than a minute.

❏ **SPECIAL TRAINING EQUIPMENT AND SUPPLIES.** As you go through the program in this book, I will discuss a number of special supplies, including a 50-foot leash for recall training (a rope tied securely to the end of your dog's leash can suffice), a clicker for trick training, and a treat pouch that clips to your belt.

❏ **COAT GROOMING.** Your basic list includes a brush that is right for your breed, plus a comb, coat rake, and shedding blade. If you bathe your dog yourself, use a dog shampoo and coat conditioner.

❏ **NAIL CARE.** Options include a nail clipper and emery board, or an electric nail grooming tool. I personally like the PediPaws. Also get some styptic powder or cornstarch to stop bleeding in case you accidentally cut too close.

❏ **ORAL HYGIENE.** Use only toothpaste that has been formulated for dogs, plus a soft-bristled toothbrush. Dental treats can help when they're used as an addition to toothbrushing, but not as a substitute. Bad dental hygiene can lead to infection, which, when it travels through the bloodstream, can cause heart disease and more. Brushing your dog's teeth regularly is as important to his well-being as good dental hygiene is to yours.

❏ **POOP BAGS/WASTE DISPOSAL SYSTEM.** If your dog uses a potty area in your yard, have a pickup tool or scoop and disposal container nearby. If he does his business on walks, make sure to pick it up with poop bags. I recommend biodegradable pickup bags; they're available at most pet stores as well as online.

❏ **FIRST-AID KIT.** You can buy a ready-made kit or assemble your own. At minimum, the kit should have a tick remover, cleaning solution such as hydrogen peroxide, antiseptic cream, gauze wraps, first-aid adhesive tape, scissors, and sterile eyewash. Some excellent first-aid kits, available at pet stores, contain upward of 60 items.

DOGPROOFING AND SETUP

YOU MAY FIND IT HARD TO BELIEVE, but having dogs in my home actually helps me be a better housekeeper. I am always looking for ways to keep the dogs out of trouble in my house and yard. Here is a dogproofing checklist to make you a better housekeeper, too.

❏ **SHOES.** Most dogs can't resist the temptation of the smell of your feet on leather or canvas. If you wear your shoes in the house, put them away in a closet and remember to keep the door closed. If you don't wear shoes in your house, put all shoes by the door in an area that your dog can't get to. If necessary, put an x-pen around the shoes.

❏ **TOYS.** Fuzzy shapes and easy-to-chew toys are too often a doggy delicacy. Put them away. Keep toy closets, toy boxes, and cabinets closed.

❏ **HOMEWORK, BILLS, IMPORTANT PAPERS.** "My dog ate my homework" may convince your child's teacher, but bill collectors tend not to accept that excuse. Recently, when I wasn't paying attention, Boz chewed some pages out of a dog training log. Yes, even the experts make mistakes; with some dogs it takes only a moment's distraction.

❏ **CLOTHES.** Don't hang clothes so low that they can be dragged away, and keep them off the floor, especially once they've been worn and have your delightful smell on them.

❏ **THE KITCHEN.** Counter surfing (when a dog jumps up to see what goodies are on the counters) is a favorite dog sport. Keep your counters clean of any traces of food, your cabinet doors shut, and objects that are dangerous or breakable well out of surfing reach. Also make sure that cleaning supplies (including sponges and gloves) are well beyond your dog's reach. In fact, it's wise to prepare your kitchen as though you were childproofing it: All potentially poisonous products should be stowed away, behind cabinet doors secured with childproof locks.

❏ **GARBAGE PAILS AND WASTEBASKETS.** Keep them out of reach, and empty them often.

❏ **THE BATHROOM.** Keep toilet lids down, especially if there are chemicals in the water. Beware of toilet paper getting unspooled or even chewed right off the roll. Soap bars look like dog treats, so keep them out of surfing range. It's a lot to control, which is why it is usually easiest just to keep bathroom doors shut at all times.

❏ **SHUT DOORS.** In fact, you may want to keep most doors shut when you can't supervise your dog. Especially make sure you shut any doors that open to the outdoors.

❏ **TOWELS.** Keep cleaning towels near the door; they'll come in handy when you come back from walks or rainy-day potty visits to the backyard.

> **TRAINING TIP**
>
> "Keep towels near the door so that you can wipe your dog's feet and coat. I suggest that you practice wiping your dog's feet and coat before he gets caught in his first rainstorm, so that he's comfortable when you need to dry him off quickly. Most dogs are more comfortable with your wiping their front paws first and then their hind paws."

❏ **TOXICS.** While most toxic substances are in the kitchen and bathroom, make sure that no stray sprays, cleaners, or alcohol are misplaced or stored within your dog's surfing reach.

❏ **BITTER APPLE SPRAY.** Most dogs don't like the taste of bitter apple spray. It works best when sprayed in advance to help teach the dog to keep out of a wastebasket, off a counter, or from chewing furniture. Another option is a hot-sauce-and-perfume mix. Test any sprays to make sure that they don't stain.

❏ **ELECTRICAL CORDS.** Tack them to baseboards; keep them out of sight. If you can't supervise a dog in a room where he can reach electrical cords, consider taking the dog out of that room. Dogs can be electrocuted or strangled by electrical cords.

❏ **CURTAIN CORDS.** If your curtains have dangling cords, install cleats high up and tie off the cords.

❏ **PLANTS.** Make sure that your house plants are out of reach. If you're not sure if a plant is toxic, the ASPCA website (aspca.org) has a good list of plants that are toxic to dogs and other pets.

❏ **CRATE SAFETY.** Make sure that your dog's crate is in a comfortable spot that is not too hot or too cold.

❏ **BABY GATES.** Use baby gates to block off rooms, especially if doors can't be closed. Some people don't like hiking over baby gates, but I have done it for years and don't mind. Some baby gates include swinging doors if hiking and hurdling are a problem for you.

MAKE YOUR FURNITURE RULES. Is your dog allowed on the couch or comfy chairs? Some trainers believe that allowing dogs on furniture undermines your authority, but I don't agree. I think it's an issue of personal preference and that whatever decision you make, you can keep your authority intact.

Of course, most dog owners have a furniture story to tell. My rule is no dogs on the couch, which my dogs obey when I'm at home . . . but sometimes disobey when I'm out. One evening I came inside the house quietly and saw Jock, Merit, and Saxon scatter off the furniture like cockroaches. One of the pillows had been shredded. Even though Saxon had pillow fuzz all over his beard, I couldn't do anything about it, since I didn't catch him in the act. For a while after that, I put the x-pen panels on the couch and furniture, and kept the remaining pillows out of reach. In the end, when it comes to setting furniture rules, it's important to stay consistent, and not to tempt your dog by leaving him alone in the room while you're still training.

YARD SETUP

WHEN YOUR DOG FIRST COMES HOME, you will always have to supervise him outside. Seal off access to areas underneath the house, porches, and decks. If fencing is allowed in your neighborhood, make sure that there are no gaps in yours, including gates and areas hidden by bushes. If you have a swimming pool, you should have a pool fence or, at minimum, a pool cover that the dog cannot squeeze under. Some people like so-called invisible fencing: electronic sensors that are placed or buried around the perimeter of the yard that trigger an electronic shock collar when the dog wanders near. I'm personally not a big fan of electric fences—if the dog endures the shock while chasing, say, a squirrel past the perimeter, he is less likely to return because he quickly learns that he will have to endure another series of unpleasant shocks.

I say that when your dog is outside in an unfenced yard, so are you. If you need to use an electric fence or shock collar, test it weekly to ensure that it's operating correctly—and at the correct voltage for your dog.

Many dogs love to play in gardens, which to them means digging and eating whatever they can find, wherever they find it, even things they shouldn't—like, for example, mulch, especially if it's made from wood or contains composted materials. Mulch and many plants can be toxic or impact your dog's bowels. Consider putting garden fencing around plant beds if you treasure their appearance. Refer again to the ASPCA website (aspca.org) for a list and photos of well over 350 plants that are toxic to dogs.

To reiterate the obvious: Remove any plants that are poisonous.

Fence off or remove any other temptations. If you have a septic tank, make sure that the cover is secure and can't be pried open. If you have a grill, keep it covered. Any bird feeders must be out of the dog's jumping reach, or moved where the dog isn't allowed to go.

If you don't want your dog doing his business everywhere he wants on your property (and who does?), establish his potty area from day one. If you have a yard, the ideal potty area will be located near the house for quick access, as well as within reach of a garden hose. It should be at least 10 feet by 10 feet, and about 3 inches deep, and layered with a bed of absorbent sand, covered with pea gravel or small river rock. Be prepared to clean the potty area often.

If you live in an apartment and have a patio, you can build or purchase a child's sandbox to use as a potty area for your dog, complete with artificial turf (that must be cleaned), actual sod, or high-tech grids. Make sure you have your poop equipment nearby, whether you use biodegradable bags, a garden trowel, or a long-handled scoop. If you live in a building or housing development with a common dog run, make sure to follow all the rules for cleanup.

CAR SETUP

AN IMAGE THAT PRACTICALLY DEFINES FAMILY LIFE is a car trip—complete with a dog. We'll get to that idyllic journey with the family dog in Chapter Twelve. Right now, let's set up your car for everyday trips: going to the vet, to a friend's home, on errands, or to the park. Your dog should ride in the backseat, ideally inside a carrier crate or strapped in with a dog seatbelt harness. You can protect the seat with a blanket or purchase seat covers. Some dogs need help getting into cars, so be prepared to lift yours or use a ramp or steps. Make sure she gets proper ventilation, either by air-conditioning or a fan, or with windows that are open just enough to get some breeze. Although another iconic image is that of a dog sticking his head out a car window, it's dangerous to let your dog do that. Countless injuries occur from flying debris.

PREPARING A HOME WITH KIDS

MY KIDS HAVE GROWN UP around a whole menagerie of pets, especially dogs. Although I have allowed them to have their own gerbils, snakes, and cats, all our family dogs have

SAFETY RULES EVERY CHILD MUST KNOW

When your dog or puppy first arrives at her new home, she may be frightened. But whether your family is adopting a shy dog, a carefree puppy, or a confident dog, explain to your children that everyone's habits and schedules will change. Ultimately, your job is to set the example; your kids will imitate what you do. It may also be helpful to discuss the following rules with your children before the dog comes. Remember that more than two million children have been bitten by dogs in the past year.

◆ You must ask me to play with the dog. I am the dog's supervisor.

◆ For the next few weeks, there will be no running or making loud noises in the house.

◆ If there is a problem with the dog and I'm not in the room, you must come get me immediately.

◆ All doors to the outside must stay closed when the dog is not in her crate. Never let the dog out of the house unsupervised. If baby gates and x-pens are up to keep the dog out of (or inside) certain areas of the home, those barriers must not be moved without my help.

◆ You must sit on the floor while handling the puppy.

◆ Never hit the dog when she makes a mistake. You could hurt her and she could hurt you back.

◆ When the dog is sleeping, don't touch her. You could scare her and she might bite you. If you must wake the dog, ask me to do it.

◆ You're not allowed to feed the dog or touch the dog while she is eating unless it is part of a training exercise I'm supervising.

◆ Never climb inside the dog's crate unless it is part of a socialization program that a grown-up is supervising.

been *my* dogs. I let my kids *help* with dog care, but I believe that dogs require too much hands-on effort to entrust their primary care to children. Over the life of a dog, your kids will go through many life changes, starting and stopping new fads and relationships more quickly than it takes to complete this training program—even if they promise with completely honest intentions that "this time is different."

Before your new family dog comes home, you must prepare your kids and set the rules. And if your dog has been in your home for some time, you can teach an old family new tricks. Rule number one for you: You must supervise kids when they play with the dog. Rule number one for kids: They must ask to play with the dog. As every parent knows, children don't always have reliable impulse control, especially with all the excitement that comes with getting a new dog.

Your children will learn impulse control, but right now you are training them as much as your dog. I supervised my kids around dogs until they were 11 or 12, but I'll leave it to you to determine when you feel that your child is skilled enough and mature enough to be left alone with the dog.

OTHER PETS IN YOUR HOME

WHEN MY DAUGHTER PAIGE WAS 12 and old enough to be entrusted with a cat, she did her research, saved her money, and bought a Siamese kitten that she named Isles. At this time, my Giant Schnauzer, Saxon, was seven years old, and had grown accustomed to being the king of the house. I knew that it was going to take a lot of time and patience before I could expect Saxon and Isles to coexist peacefully. Initially, they were kept apart with baby gates, and although they could see each other, no interactions were allowed. Three months later, I formally introduced them. Every day, Paige and I would put Isles in my lap and give him a treat. When Saxon sat perfectly, we'd also give him a treat. If Isles got nervous or if Saxon started to get excited, that would be the end of the session. Saxon graduated to "lie downs" and "settles" next to Isles and me. Over the course of an intensive week of supervision, Saxon and Isles could be around each other while I watched. Eventually they could be together without supervision. In fact, Isles grew to like dogs, started to play with Saxon, and a great relationship developed between them.

My experience is that with patience and positive reinforcement training, most dogs will coexist safely with other pets. It just takes time. Right now, I keep Boz mostly separate from Brieo and from the other dogs that are boarding with me. Boz works well when he's with me one-on-one, but when he's with other dogs, he gets overexcited and tries to herd them (this is natural behavior for a Border Collie). Before I decide to introduce Boz to the other dogs here, I want to get him used to Brieo. I started by feeding him upstairs and tethering him on a leash at all times—a training technique I recommend using when a dog first comes home, which we will discuss in the next chapter. I'm experimenting with different activities, erring on the side of caution always, such as feeding the dogs in the same room, separated by a chair.

Once you bring your dog home, it may take weeks, or perhaps even months, to get him comfortable with your other pets, and vice versa. With the right supervision and step-by-step progress, however, the transition should go smoothly. Just remember: When introducing pets to each other, be extremely patient. To repeat myself: Always err on the side of caution.

Your Dog's Health

YOUR DOG'S VET AND GROOMER will both play significant roles in her health over what I hope will be many, many years. My advice is that you interview a vet before you get your dog. Talk to other pet owners who have used the vet's services. Does the vet seem to have good bedside manner and make a thorough examination? Is the facility clean? Does the staff seem friendly and helpful? Do the costs seem reasonable for your area? Does the vet offer emergency services or have a relationship with an emergency pet hospital that is close by? Talk to other pet owners. And, of course, you'll probably want to find a vet who is reasonably close to home in case something comes up that needs attention right away.

You will also want to have supplies at home in case any emergencies arise. As mentioned earlier, home emergency preparedness includes having a well-stocked first-aid kit. You will also want to create an information sheet that lists veterinarian and emergency pet-hospital contacts and driving instructions, alternate contacts in case you are not reachable, feeding and medication instructions, crating protocol, directions about the use of treats, calming instructions, and details of any health problems. The information sheet is important for a pet sitter or for friends who are helping you, or in case something happens to you (God forbid) and you're unable to care for your dog. (See page 240 for a detailed checklist for your dog's caregiver.) It's a good idea to keep the list posted on the fridge or some other visible place.

If you decide to use a professional groomer, the groomer may encourage you to bring your dog by for a quick visit just to get some treats and praise before the first grooming session. When you see well-groomed dogs, ask their owners about their groomers. Find a groomer in your price range who has good rapport with your dog, who follows instructions, and who will take the time to look at sample pictures of other dogs with you. Some groomers will allow you to stay during the session to make your dog more comfortable.

It's taken a lot of preparation—and a lot of time and work— just to get organized to bring your dog home. But everything you've done was an important and necessary step to ensure that you are going to take great care of your new pet. And here's the good news. You're ready.

Now go get your dog . . .

THE
FUNDAMENTALS
PROGRAM

Feeding, Potty Training, and Crating

W E WILL BEGIN the Fundamentals Training Program (see page 67) this week, but first I'd like to discuss three essentials: feeding, potty training, and crating. Having protocols in place for these everyday routines will establish your authority and give your dog the security that comes from having a sense of routine. You should begin these protocols *at the same time* you begin to train your dog in the fundamentals—the minute she comes home.

If you have a puppy, think of her as a blank slate. Nature has programmed this little dog to know that her survival means adapting to her environment. She'll immediately begin searching for rewards, and learning by trial and error what is safe and what is dangerous. You are this creature's

This chapter covers the first things your dog will need to learn to become a part of your family: feeding, potty training, and crating. I'll discuss bonding with your new companion through close tethering, plus techniques for discouraging your puppy from biting. You'll also learn to treat loud noises or other accidents that might startle your dog as no big deal, through a game I like to call The Jollies.

most important influence, and the earlier you begin to shape her behavior, to teach her those lessons, the safer and more secure she'll feel and the happier you'll both be.

For an older dog that has been rehomed, like Boz, immediate training is an ideal way to short-circuit bad behaviors and replace them with new healthy behaviors. To borrow a concept from neurolinguistic programming psychology: Training a rehomed, older dog represents a "pattern interrupt," allowing the previous patterns of bad habits to be replaced by new patterns and good habits.

Your Week One Checklist

HERE IS A CHECKLIST of what you should have completed, and what you'll begin this week:

COMPLETED ACTIVITIES

❑ Made top 10 checklist of your training priorities.

❑ Purchased your dog's equipment and supplies, including a training log.

❑ Dogproofed and set up your home, yard, and car.

❑ Discussed the rules with your kids.

❑ Found a veterinarian.

THIS WEEK'S ACTIVITIES

❑ Start your dog's training log and establish a routine to follow every day this week (Week One Training Log, page 86).

❑ Begin leash tethering (page 49).

❑ Begin hand-feeding protocol (page 52).

❑ Play the Name Game while hand-feeding and handling your dog (page 53).

❑ Begin potty training (page 55).

❑ Begin crate training (page 58).

❏ Begin bite inhibition, handling, and gentling (assuming that there are no outstanding behavior issues).

    ❏ "Ouch" exercises: explore dog's mouth, count teeth and toes (page 65).

    ❏ Play Pass the Puppy (page 65).

    ❏ Play Peekaboo (see page 65).

❏ Begin Week One of Fundamentals Training Program (Chapter Four).

Tethering

ONE WAY TO BEGIN TO BOND IMMEDIATELY with your dog is through leash tethering. I use a mountain-climbing carabiner (usually available at hardware or camping stores) that clips to the leash and to my belt, so I can easily attach and detach the leash. You can also hook the leash through your belt. Some puppies don't like being tethered, so start tethering for brief periods—maybe only five seconds in the beginning. Give your dog a treat for exhibiting calm behavior when tethered, and slowly build up time. (For now, simply hand him the treat—using the same hand each time. You will learn more about the correct ways to give treats at the beginning of the Fundamentals Training Program.) Through tethering, your dog will learn to read your body language and literally feel more connected to you. Eventually you can graduate to walking on leash everywhere, before progressing to free roaming in certain areas (while still tethering in other areas, such as when you're doing the dishes and want your dog to settle down next to you). If your dog chews the leash, prevent that by spraying it with bitter apple or soaking it in unsweetened mouthwash such as Listerine.

If your dog jumps on you while tethered, back up a step and tether him to a doorknob or a sturdy table leg. If he jumps up as you approach him, walk away for a moment before stepping toward him again. With some patient practice, your dog will begin to understand that he is not supposed to jump on you, and you can try tethering him to your belt again.

When your dog is tethered to you, have your other family members or friends approach him to give a treat and then walk away. The goal is to have a calm dog that always follows your body language, which will lead him to turn, follow, or stop when you want him to. Right now, Boz is always on a leash, dragging it while I supervise him, or tethered to my belt so I have both hands free. When Boz is ready, we will take the next step: I will hold his leash in my hands. But first I need to let him learn about me—and understand that I'm in control.

TETHERING WITH A CARABINER CLIP

Tethering trains your dog to focus on you and follow your moves. The spring-loaded carabiner clip can be bought at many hardware or mountain-climbing stores.

The carabiner will clip easily on and off your belt loop—or to your belt if you have a strong dog that might tear your belt loop if he pulls on the leash.

Tethering also promotes bonding and helps you and your dog learn each other's body language as you move around your home.

Feeding

GIVING YOUR DOG too much food isn't a sign of love. My goal is to help you raise a well-fed dog that isn't fat; in fact, I prefer to keep a dog a little on the lean side. I do this by watching the amount of food I give her and by making sure she gets plenty of exercise. Weight can go on easily, but shedding extra pounds can take a dog many months. It's especially important to watch your dog's weight if she's of a breed that is prone to hip or joint problems.

A dog's metabolism slows down as she ages, so the amount of food you feed her will depend on her age. Because of their tiny stomachs, puppies must be fed three or four small meals a day. When most dogs are six months old, you can reduce the number of feedings to two, and from there, get your vet's advice on adjusting your growing dog's diet. Most adult dogs (I take the view that a dog is fully grown at age three) can be fed once or twice per day; my preference is twice for most dogs. I recommend changing the amount a dog eats depending on the time of year and your dog's activity level; more in summer, less in winter; more if she is active, less if she is sedentary. The amount of food a dog requires also depends on breed. Again, ask your veterinarian for advice on precise feeding amounts for your dog; instructions printed on dog food bags are not breed-specific. Your vet can also help you decide if your dog would be best served by a protein-rich diet.

The quality of commercial dog food has improved greatly in recent years. Some owners prefer to make their own dog food, or to use prepackaged raw ingredients that can be cooked and, in some cases, fed raw. (In fact, there is a raw dog food diet with the delightfully undelectable name BARF, which stands for Biologically Appropriate Raw Foods.) Whatever nutritional program you and your vet decide to follow, be sure to keep track of your dog's progress. One reminder: Whenever you adjust your dog's feeding regimen, taper off the old as you slowly change to the new.

FEEDING MORE THAN ONE DOG AT A TIME

IF YOU ALREADY HAVE other dogs in your home, start by feeding your new dog separately, as I have done with Boz and Brieo. Once you have completed the first week of hand-feeding and can easily pick up your dog's bowl while he is eating, you can graduate to having your dogs eat in the same room with a chair between them, or on opposite sides of the room while you supervise. This setup helps avoid both fights over food and situations where a faster eater takes away the slower one's food. (For more on what to do in a dogfight, see page 227.) If you don't have other dogs at home, you may consider feeding your dog at the home of a friend who has a well-trained dog that has already had positive social interaction with your dog. Having a variety of hand-feeding experiences will lessen your dog's territoriality and food-guarding behavior.

Be sure to allow for training treats when planning your dog's diet. They have calories, too.

VITAMINS AND SUPPLEMENTS

Some veterinarians and pet owners choose to add vitamin supplements (many of which are chewable) to the dog's daily diet. I think there's merit to supplements, but you should never use them without discussing them—and the proper dosage—with your vet. Supplements come in five categories:

▶ **VITAMINS,** especially A, various Bs, C, and E

▶ **PROBIOTICS** such as acidophilus and **PSYLLIUM,** which aid digestion and help skin and coat

▶ **OILS** for the skin and coat, such as flaxseed oil, olive oil, and fish oil

▶ **GLUCOSAMINE** and **CHONDROITIN,** which help maintain healthy cartilage, for joint support

▶ **ANTIOXIDANTS,** which can also be added to the dog's diet by simply mixing fresh sweet potatoes and fresh green vegetables such as broccoli, peas, and spinach into his food

HAND-FEEDING PROTOCOL

BEFORE YOU START FORMALLY TRAINING YOUR NEW DOG, it's best that you feed her all her meals by hand. Hand-feeding establishes you as the source of your dog's food, sending her the message that it's *your* food that you are, in your benevolence, giving to her. This wires her brain to see you as the friendly, higher-ranking person in her life who is also the source of her rewards, emotional comfort, food, water, and play. Hand-feeding also promotes safety; your dog becomes far less likely to guard her food. Food guarding can become a serious safety issue. While it may be a natural survival instinct in dogs, a pet dog that guards her food can be dangerous and unpredictable. This simple hand-feeding protocol is vital; it helps your dog mellow out when people are around her food while she is eating.

To begin, measure out your dog's food and put some of her meal in her bowl. Sitting in a chair (or on the floor if it's a puppy or small dog), scoop some food into your hand, and let your dog (who should be on a tether or leash) eat right out of your hand. Hand-feed the whole meal to her, and do it for every meal for a whole week. If you have a puppy, you will hand-feed small meals to her throughout the day. Don't wear rubber gloves and don't be squeamish. Have fun with it; hand-feeding is no messier than kindergarten finger paints. Just wash your hands before you start, and make sure you've rinsed off any soap or hand sanitizer.

While hand-feeding your dog, say her name in a loving way. This is called the Name Game, and I want you to do it whenever you hand-feed. As the week progresses and you and your dog get more comfortable with hand-feeding, touch her collar and pet her gently on the side of her body as you say her name. You're getting your dog used to being handled so that she will be better prepared for grooming and other times when you or the vet need to check her body or administer medications. If your dog stops eating when you touch her, stop petting her and keep offering her food. Alternate hands. When she gets comfortable with your touching her collar and petting her, try petting and touching a little bit between scoops. Then put another small portion of her premeasured meal in her bowl and hand-feed that until the bowl is empty. Let her see you refill her bowl and resume hand-feeding. Refill the bowl and hand-feed again and again, until her meal is complete. Pretty soon you will transition to feeding your dog from a bowl that you hold in your lap.

After she eats each small portion that you have scooped from the bowl, you want her to look at you before she gets more food; this will help your dog bond to you and respect you as her food source. If this process progresses well, begin, toward the end of the week, to alternate between hand-feeding small amounts and letting her eat out of her bowl directly (while you supervise her). When your dog seems comfortable (when she lets you touch her body and collar as well as her food and bowl without guarding her food or ducking away from you), use one hand to pick up her bowl before she has finished eating while you hand-feed her a scoop with your other hand. Get her used to being fed from different bowls and containers: metal, plastic, ceramic. You also want to begin hand-feeding her in various rooms of your home as you allow her access to these rooms. You can also hand-feed her in the yard and in the car. This will get your dog comfortable with your touching her and her food at any time and in any place. This concept—getting your dog used

> **TRAINING TIP**
>
> " Kids love to hold puppies, but they must be taught how to do this correctly. Sometimes a puppy will wriggle out of a child's arms and fall. Or sometimes a child will want to hold a puppy until the moment she actually touches it, and then back away or let go of the puppy. When a child drops a puppy, it can hurt the puppy and harm both the child's and puppy's confidence. Therefore, I never let a child stand while she holds a puppy. "

> Hand-feeding is a good opportunity for your child and dog to become comfortable with each other.

to performing activities in a variety of locations—is called generalizing. Generalizing is a fundamental concept that we will revisit throughout this training program, and it will be applied to every lesson you teach your dog.

Once you have completed your week of hand-feeding (including handling the dog and playing the Name Game), you can teach this practice to your children and spouse. Teaching everyone in your family the hand-feeding protocol will promote safety, family bonding, and generalized experience.

Hand-feeding is a good opportunity for your child and dog to become comfortable with each other. Have the child sit on your lap or on a chair next to you, and do the hand-feeding protocol beginning with step one. I started involving my own children in hand-feeding when they were as young as four months and able to sit up and balance in my lap. Before that, I used a lifelike baby doll to acclimate my dogs to having a small child hand-feed them. If you have young children, for safety's sake, please use your own judgment and consider involving a professional trainer to supervise hand-feeding. I prefer a chair to the floor, because the dog's mouth is at the height of the hand rather than level with the child's face. If you have a young or small puppy that has been exercised and is now calm, relaxed, and not mouthing (which means the puppy is not still using his mouth to explore you and initiate play as he did with his littermates), then it's okay to have your relaxed child on the floor during hand-feeding.

As you and your child have success with these initial steps, start feeding in other rooms as you did when you were hand-feeding by yourself. When your child and dog seem comfortable with each other, graduate to having your child pause for a minute, then remove and refill your dog's bowl while she's eating (in exchange for food in the other hand).

After your children master hand-feeding, recruit a few friends and run them through parts of the protocol, too. Getting your dog used to having people around her food bowl will prevent future problems. It's much easier than repairing them later.

As you'll see later in the book, hand-feeding will be used whenever you teach your dog skills and new tricks. I often return to hand-feeding to keep my dog fine-tuned, or if he seems to be regressing in behavior or gets stuck on learning a particular cue or skill.

Potty Training

THE MYTH THAT DOGS HOUSE-TRAIN THEMSELVES is just that—a myth. They won't. We need to teach our dogs *our* rules, which may strike them as completely arbitrary. As far as they're concerned, they should be "allowed" to go potty whenever they need to, and wherever they may be at that moment.

All of my dogs have been terrific at going potty when told to. My Border Collie, Jock, would pee for me in exchange for praise and kisses, a cookie, or a single ball toss. He would pee 10 times in a row if I asked him to! My potty-training motto is "Fun things don't begin until after we go potty."

Please allow me to give you some house-training don'ts. (And by the way, I prefer the terms *house-training* or *potty training*, which make us think of our goal, rather than *housebreaking*, which makes us think of failure and punishment.) These are common house-training mistakes—and at one time, some of them were even considered the "right way" to house-train.

Punishing potty errors after they've happened is perhaps the most common training mistake; it only aggravates the problem. Going potty is a natural behavior. When we punish this behavior—or any other unwanted behavior—after it has happened, to the dog it seems that she is being punished for what she is doing now (like coming to you when you called her name or sitting in front of you and wagging her tail), not the mess she made a minute ago. If our timing is off, there is virtually no chance that our dog will understand what is making us so angry. It used to be thought that swatting a dog with a rolled-up newspaper and rubbing her nose in her mistake would get the message across, but I assure you with complete certainty that it will not. Rubbing a dog's nose in her pee or poop is counterproductive and mean-spirited—and it can give her a bacterial infection. The only way to deal with a potty error is to catch the dog in the act and scoop her up and take her, or lead her, quickly outside to the potty area. Until your dog is house-trained, do not allow her to have free access to the entire house, and supervise her always, perhaps by keeping her tethered to you or by using baby gates, x-pens, and closed doors.

Let's take another moment to consider how a dog's mistake might be handled in aversive training. Assume you come home to find dog poop on your rug. At this moment, the dog is resting quietly on her mat and she hears you call her name. She comes to you right on cue, but instead of getting praised for that, she gets yelled at. Now the dog has to figure out why you are yelling at her while pointing to cold poop on the rug, and then why she's being swatted with a newspaper. That's too complicated, as well as unclear, uninspiring, and mean. Positive reinforcement house-training is better all around.

So, what's the right way to potty train your dog? First, it's important to understand that it will likely take several months to potty train your dog completely. Commit to patience; mistakes will happen. Learn to laugh at them, if you can.

Your schedule and training log will be the main tools you use in potty training. By having your dog visit the potty area many times each day, and by logging when she does her business, you will become better able to predict when she will next need to go out. Make a note in your dog's training log when she pees and poops—I use a simple "#1" mark for pee and "#2" for poop—and in time you will shape her habits like a champion. Whenever a mistake is made, I consider that *my* mistake. As in all areas of dog training, we learn at least as much from our failures as from our successes, so I log the mistake, hoping to pick up on my pup's pooping and peeing pattern. Success requires your own constant attention, predictive abilities (made much easier with your training log), and timely rewards for your dog's good business practices.

After you take your dog to what will become her designated potty spot, say the word you want to associate with going potty in an upbeat way, such as "Boz, go peeps, go poops," or simply "go potty." As she does her business, praise her along the lines of "good pee" or "good poo" or "good potty" in a calm tone so that you don't distract her, and then give her a treat immediately afterward. Your puppy will learn to associate the potty area with the rewards you will give her for each success, and she will begin to look forward to being rewarded for doing her business in "her" area. Other trainers like to use the cue "do your business," paired with the reward praise "good business." Some people get creative when naming the potty cue; one colleague named the dog's potty cue after an ex-spouse.

(He eventually grew tired of having to explain this joke and needed to teach his dog a new cue.) Whatever you name the cue, say it the same way every time, and realize that your dog may learn the verbal cue long after having learned the physical potty ritual.

If you live in a city building where your dog doesn't have her own potty area, you'll need to adapt this protocol. Surely there is an outside public "restroom," even if it's a hydrant (if that is customary and acceptable where you live) that your dog can be taken to. Just keep taking your dog to an acceptable spot and reward her for her success. If she starts doing her business on the way, quickly scoop her up and take her, or lead her, to the correct spot for her to finish.

Some of my clients prefer to paper train their dog indoors, using newspaper or pee pads. I'm not a big fan of this approach, because it's a two-step learning process. In paper training, first the puppy needs to learn to do her business on the paper or pad. Then she needs to unlearn that behavior, and learn that she needs to go outside and do her business at an entirely different spot—and one that doesn't even slightly resemble the newspaper or pee pad she has grown accustomed to.

But I also understand that not everyone has the option of training his or her dog outdoors. For instance, it can be dangerous for puppies that have not had all their vaccinations to go outside on a dirty sidewalk or street. If your vet recommends that you keep your puppy inside until she's had all her shots, use paper or pee pad training. Then when your vet says it's okay to take the dog out, have your puppy do her business on the pee pad or newspaper outside. Cut down the size of the pee pad, smaller and smaller, until you have eliminated it.

If you live in a city apartment and have a very small dog, you may prefer to set up a permanent litter box in the bathroom. That will work if you keep the rest of the house-training protocol consistent. Your challenge will come when you take your dog outside for a walk; you will have to teach her to generalize her potty behavior to this foreign environment. If she starts to go, scoop her up as if she were making a mistake in the house, get her to the nearest acceptable spot right away, name the cue as she does her business, and praise her for the success. Be patient and regard any mistake as a learning experience. Remember to write it in the training log to help you learn.

If your dog has already been potty trained but has started peeing in the house again, or if you have a rehomed dog that is said to be potty trained already but has regressed, then patiently act as though this is the first time in this dog's life that she is learning potty training. If your dog has persistent potty problems, it's possible that she has an underlying medical problem. Check with your vet.

If your dog pees when she gets excited—we call this glee pee—such as when you come home or when a guest arrives, take note and try to anticipate and avoid the situation. As soon as you enter your home, calmly greet your dog and take her immediately outside. Puppies are prone to glee pee whenever anything new happens, including simply moving to another room. They have little bladders, so take your new dog outside often to potty. As young as seven weeks, puppies are ready to start learning to potty outside. (But remember to check with your veterinarian if your dog hasn't gotten all her shots.)

Crate Training

THE CRATE IS YOUR DOG'S SANCTUARY, the place where he can get away from it all. It's where he sleeps at night and where he's confined at times during the day. The crate needs to be respected as your dog's safe haven, not his jail, and should be associated with reward, not punishment. Although most dogs naturally love a cozy den environment, the crate is obviously not found in nature, so most dogs need to be trained to love their crate.

Of all the good reasons to crate train your dog, the most significant is that crate-trained dogs tend to be better trained in general. Crating teaches a dog to settle down and have quiet time. It encourages him to chew only on acceptable things, because *you* provide him with those things while he's in the crate. A crate-trained dog tends to be better able to cope with anxiety and—if necessary—rehoming. When a dog travels, his crate offers security and comfort. Veterinarian staffers and groomers truly appreciate working with crate-trained dogs, and so will you. When I have guest dogs boarding in my home, I require that they accept some kind of confinement, preferably a crate, until I determine that they are sufficiently mature to be trusted with free access to my home. The Kennedys' dogs Splash and Sunny can be in my home without crates, but young Cappy (Bo Obama's littermate) needs to be crated. Even if you work at home, crate train your dog. Using a crate is similar to having a playpen for a toddler or a crib for a baby: It provides a safe area that allows you to take your eyes off your youngster for a moment. Never get your dog out of the habit of being crated.

Throughout the life of a crate-trained dog, he is likely to spend more hours inside his crate than in any other one place, so it's important to keep it comfortable and clean. Inside the crate is your dog's bed or mat, which should have a machine-washable cover. Many dogs like having a padded side or bolster to nestle up against.

Some people mistake crate training for potty training, so to be clear: The crate is not your dog's bathroom. Good crate training does facilitate good potty training, but if you insist on having your puppy potty inside your home, do not use the dog's crate as his bathroom. Instead, set up an x-pen adjoining the crate for your puppy's potty.

There are many types of dog crates. The wire-cage style can be covered with a blanket or fitted cloth cover as long as it gets adequate ventilation. Some crates are portable and made of lightweight fabrics and mesh, similar to camping tents. Crates can also be stylish, with finishes that include molded plastic, stamped metal, wicker, and furniture-grade wood.

CRATE STYLES

When choosing your dog's crate, factors to consider are cost, durability, portability, and style.

WIRE CAGE
Good ventilation and durability. Can be covered with fitted quilted padding or a blanket.

PLASTIC
Portable and durable. Some manufacturers have introduced stylish designs.

SOFT-STYLE
Portable and lightweight, these are good for trips as well as in-home use.

CRATE-TRAINING PROTOCOL

YOUR MAIN GOAL IN CRATE TRAINING is simply to help your dog love her crate. The majority of puppies accept the crate without complaint, associating it with the comfy coziness of naptime. But if your dog isn't immediately comfortable with going in her crate, don't force her. That would be unproductive. Instead, use the following exercises to train her to like it. And remember: It's best to do this training session before your dog's meal so that she will really want the treats that you will toss around (and eventually inside) her crate. Using treats that your dog enjoys, toss a few of them around the crate and leading toward the opening, and then take a step back. Don't toss any treats inside the crate just yet. If your dog looks at you and then at the crate where the treats are, say "good" and toss a couple more treats near the crate's opening. (Have a lot on hand.) When she finishes those treats and looks to you for more, try placing a few just inside the opening, and then step back again. Little by little, toss the treats a bit deeper inside the crate.

While you do these first trials, stay silent except to praise your dog for showing any interest in the crate: sniffing around it, moving toward it, daring to go inside it. Don't say "in your crate" or any other verbal cues. Don't bend down or step forward, as your dog may be uncertain and feel cornered, which could make her averse to the crate. If your dog is already averse to the crate as some rehomed dogs are, slow the progress down and do many trials tossing treats around the crate—you may need to feed her entire meals outside her crate at first. To start helping her trust going inside the open crate, leave the door open and put treats inside, but don't force her. Be content with feeding your dog just outside the crate near the door opening. Be sure to clamp the crate door open so that it can't accidentally swing and startle her when she goes near it.

Once your dog is comfortable going inside the crate, it's time to feed part of her meal in a bowl inside the crate. Since you will also be doing the hand-feeding protocol right now, use your judgment on how much she should be allowed to eat from a bowl without you touching her. If you have been hand-feeding your dog in different parts of your home and using different bowls (as I hope you have), it will likely be easier for her to trust that it's safe to go into the crate to eat. This slow, deliberate progress is called behavior shaping, which is a technique you will use to teach your dog many training cues. You can also start getting your dog comfortable with the idea of eating in her crate by stuffing a Kong with part of her meal and setting it inside.

Your dog's next step is to eat an entire meal there. Put a portion of her meal in a bowl inside the crate and back away, leaving the crate door open; later, you will teach your dog to accept being fed with it closed. Remain silent as she goes inside to eat. When she has eaten all her food and looks to you for a refill, praise her. Continue feeding the rest of her meal in small portions. If she does not eat, she may not be ready for this step, so proceed more slowly and make sure that she is hungry when you try again. Don't force her; just praise what she does right and write that note in the training log. My Brieo is so well conditioned that when he sees me touching his food bowl, or when he comes back in the house after going potty, he'll run into his crate, whether or not I happen to feed him in his crate for that meal.

The next step is to name the crate. Naming is another technique you will use to teach your dog cues. Select the name for the crate; I suggest the obvious: "crate," "bedtime," or "den." As you place a couple of treats in it and she goes inside, say "good crate." Notice that you're not teaching her to do something that she hasn't already done, but simply giving a name to something she has been doing. Repeat this about ten times throughout the day (for a few days), and make it a fun game by tossing kibble in and around the crate. Your dog is learning that good things happen there.

> **The crate is your dog's sanctuary.**

Now it's time to direct your dog to go in on cue. A *cue* is a word or action that gives the dog information about what you want her to do. Start with her outside the crate. Let her see you put a few treats inside and then close the door. Open the door and say "crate." When she goes inside, say "good crate" and close the door. While she is inside, offer a few treats through the crate and praise her. Wait a few seconds before you let her out. If she stays in the crate or she goes out and goes back inside, say "good crate." When she comes out, praise her, including the words *good crate*, and close the door. Repeat this step about six times throughout the day. If you've made the exercise fun, your dog may want you to do it even more, and that's great.

Next, hold a few treats in your hand for your dog to smell, but don't put them in the crate. Open the door, say "crate," and when she goes inside, give her the treats and praise her. Repeat this step about six times. If she doesn't figure it out or resists, back up to the previous step.

The next step is to introduce her to being inside the crate for a longer time with the door closed. Start by showing your dog that you're putting some of her meal in the bowl. Hold the bowl in your

A WORD ABOUT WHINING AND BARKING

Some dogs will whine or bark in their crates when you disappear from their view. If this happens, do not reappear when she's making noise, as you do not want to teach her that whining brings a reward (your return). Instead, wait until she settles down and stops whining, and then reappear quietly. Make notes in your logbook about how much time elapsed before she *started* whining, so that the next time you do this exercise, you can be sure to return more quickly, before she has a chance to get going.

If your dog barks or whines for a very long time, you may need to bring in a trainer or behaviorist to determine if it's the beginning of true separation anxiety, or simply part of your dog getting used to her new home. It's counterproductive to get your dog so worked up that she gets into a pattern of barking and whining. (For more on barking problems, see page 211.)

hand, open the door, say "crate," and when she goes inside, say "good crate" and put the bowl inside. You may want to put some of her food in a Kong (stuffed with a special treat, like peanut butter) and place the Kong in her food bowl. As she starts to eat, gently close the door and say "good crate" again. When she finishes eating that portion of her meal, wait a few seconds before you open the door, and praise her for staying in the crate quietly, so that she understands that she's safe. Say "good crate" as she comes out, then put more kibble in her bowl or a Kong. Let her see you fill her Kong or food bowl so that she knows you are the provider of all these wonderful things, and then put the container in the crate (or simply toss kibble inside). When she goes in again, close the door while she eats. After she has finished, wait a moment again, praise her, and let her out. It is important that each time you let her out of the crate, you act like it's no big deal: no excitement, no relief, just a calm greeting and praise.

Next, ask her to go into the crate, and when she's inside, close the door for a moment, and give her the treat through an opening as you praise her and name the crate. Then open the door to let her come out, praise her and name the crate again as she exits, and close the door once she's out. If she chooses to stay inside, that's great because it means that she is understanding the process: Good things happen inside the crate! Repeat this exercise six times, each time keeping her in the closed crate for one second longer. (You will eventually add other cues, like *sit*, *down*, *settle*, and *off*, to crate training. But wait until you're into the Fundamentals Training Program before adding any of that.)

Now comes the hard part: getting your dog used to being in her crate while she can see you doing something else in the room. With your dog inside the crate, and the door closed, start by letting her see you take a step away as you put a treat through the closed door. Then return, pause a few seconds, and tell her she is a good dog in a very low-key, calm tone of voice. Then repeat the process and drop a special treat (like a piece of hard cheese) into her crate. Get up and turn away from her. Return and pause a few seconds before letting her out. Next, repeat the process, but this time give her a special toy to chew on or a stuffed Kong while she is in the crate. Increase your number of steps each time. Add some business in the room that she can see you doing, even if you're just shuffling papers, opening a bag, sitting down and watching a little TV, or getting her food ready, as you add time with each repetition. Each time you let your dog out of the crate, remember to treat it as an ordinary, almost boring moment. The goal is to teach your dog that she gets something really great in the crate when you leave (not when you return).

> Associate your dog's crate with rewards and positive experiences.

The final stage in crate training involves your leaving the room. Some dogs will accept this step without complaint right away, but others may take many weeks to get through this stage, so don't press your dog to progress faster than she is ready or you may add to her anxiety and set her back in her training. Start by leaving for literally one second, returning, and letting her out. Build up time on each repetition. While you do these final-stage exercises, give your dog a Kong stuffed with treats and/or peanut butter. On each subsequent repetition, leave the room for a second or two longer. The hope is that your dog will become so engrossed in the Kong that she will barely register that you're leaving. Walk into an adjacent room and go about some business that your dog can hear, occasionally reentering to just check in on her and praise her; then leave again. When she's comfortable with that, practice keeping her in the crate when you leave your home. At first, leave as quietly as you can. Stay outside for a few minutes, and make a little noise as you reenter (but don't make a big deal). Subsequently, you can build up to being gone longer and making a little more noise as you leave. Eventually, go out and run a short errand. If your dog shows anxiety when you return, or there are signs that she was anxious while you were away (her pillow is shredded, for example), you may want to ask another person your dog already likes to stay in the room while you do these sets of exercises, and then start removing that person, too.

I also recommend moving your dog's crate to different rooms. Many years ago, my Irish Water Spaniel, Aisley, loved the crate when it was upstairs in my bedroom, where I also have my office. But during Aisley's training I moved her crate downstairs to the kitchen and she barked her head off. We took a few steps backward on her training, but I continued to move Aisley's crate around to different rooms, playing crate games (such as tossing kibble in and around her crate) as we went, and she adjusted beautifully.

Throughout this training program, I recommend returning to the crate exercises if your dog's behavior backslides at all. This is not a form of punishment. Rather, it is a way to get her refocused on success. After Saxon died, Brieo understandably backslid: He didn't eat well, paced and looked for Saxon, and chewed on himself and developed a rash. I rebuilt Brieo's comfort and confidence by going back to basic crating and hand-feeding protocols; that helped a lot.

Bite Inhibition, Handling, and Gentling

ALL PUPPIES PLAY-BITE WHEN THEY ARE with their mother and littermates; it's natural behavior in the canine world. When a puppy bites too hard, a yelp or return bite teaches him to play more gently. Although dogs use their mouths to play and explore, they also need to learn that hard biting is not okay—ever. That's why we use handling and gentling exercises to teach them bite inhibition from the very start. Some dogs catch on right away, while others can take more than a month to get it. Merit, my Flat-Coated Retriever, took 45 days to stop biting. Ouch.

Bite inhibition protocols are different for puppies and adult dogs. For example, when a foster dog that is more than six months old comes to me that has been labeled aggressive or mouthy, I observe his behavior, body language, and eating habits to help me determine how I will approach these issues safely. The average dog owner may want to use a professional trainer or behaviorist who uses positive reinforcement methods to assess mouthing and biting behaviors, and help develop protocols for that particular dog. (For more information on aggression, see page 217.)

Start bite inhibition training by sitting down with your puppy and putting a finger or hand in his mouth. If he mouths on you, say "ouch!" Say it loud enough so that your puppy gets the message, but not so loud that it frightens him. Let your hand go limp; do not pull it out of your puppy's mouth. When his bite slackens, say "good dog." Another technique is to tether your dog to a doorknob while you touch his mouth; if he bites, say "ouch" and walk away from him for a moment. (Remember, his punishment is that you've taken away the reward of playing with you.) Keep at this "ouch" exercise, building up to massaging your puppy's gums and counting his teeth. When he starts to lick your hand, gently praise him. Don't punish him for biting you, don't clamp his mouth shut or force your fingers down his throat. In this case, you *want* your puppy to figure it out.

Your dog will need to have his teeth examined and brushed. Once he allows you to touch his mouth freely, wrap gauze around your finger and wipe his teeth. Once he allows you to do this, you can graduate to a toothbrush. One time, Saxon wouldn't eat his food, so I examined his mouth and found a small twig stuck in a back molar, and I removed it. If Saxon hadn't learned to be comfortable with my hands in his mouth, it could have become serious.

It's equally important that your dog be comfortable with being handled on the rest of his entire body, not just his mouth. Begin to help your puppy become accustomed to this by cradling him on his back while you rub his tummy to calm him. When he is calm, count his toes, touch his eyes, his ears, and as much of his body as he will allow. I have my students play Pass the Puppy, to get the pup used to being handled by others, and Peekaboo,

THE THREE TYPES OF MOUTHING

Before you start teaching your dog to develop a "soft mouth," it helps to know the three situations in which mouthing often occurs:

1. As a prelude to play; seen in puppies who mouth in order to encourage another dog or human to play;

2. During play; and

3. Unexpectedly, which usually indicates that the dog wants to play, or sometimes that she is feeling pain or physical discomfort.

> Biting is a natural behavior in the canine world.

by covering the puppy's eyes gently for a moment to get him used to being vulnerable. Also pretend to clip his nails with the clipping tools before you actually start using them or having a groomer do it. Ultimately, you are preparing your dog to tolerate new situations.

If your dog isn't comfortable with a particular handling or gentling exercise, try to discover the point at which he begins to get uncomfortable. Stay within his comfort range for the time being; then, at your next training session, repeat the exercise, again within his comfort range and moving on to the next step only if all goes well. If you push your dog faster than he is ready, he may shut down or become frightened. So stay alert to the limits of his comfort zone—and make sure to take play breaks between exercises.

Handling Mistakes with The Jollies

YOU WILL MAKE MISTAKES that scare your new dog. You will drop something that makes a loud noise, or perhaps even accidentally falls right on her. You will stumble over your dog. You will get caught in her leash. You will turn on the TV set without realizing that the volume is cranked all the way up. These loud noises and unexpected commotions frighten almost all dogs that are new to a home.

When you accidentally frighten your dog, it's best to laugh it off immediately and play a quick round of The Jollies. Basically, you want to act as if you're having fun, in effect saying, "That is so cool that I tripped over you and dropped the groceries and now there's a broken glass jar that we all get to stay away from. Wow!" This is not unlike responding to a child who's taken a tumble. Children and dogs look to us to see if they should be upset or not. Have fun while you move your dog to safety, and continue doing The Jollies while you clean up the mess and give her a treat or two. If she's hiding, just keep doing The Jollies. Don't try to pet her or lure her out, though you may leave a few treats for her to take when she is ready. You're trying to teach her that the world is filled with unexpected and startling events, but we don't have to fear them.

CHAPTER

4

Week One: Fundamentals Training Program

EVERY YEAR, I TRAIN HUNDREDS OF DOGS—from puppies as young as seven weeks to rehomed older dogs. Many clients come to me for general training, while others seek to correct specific behavioral problems, such as poor house-training, chewing, jumping, and concerns about dominance and possible aggression. Later, in Chapter Eleven, I will discuss some common behavior problems and ways to address them, but for the next five weeks, I want you to focus on your Fundamentals Training Program.

I want to emphasize once more that training—including the potty training,

This is where the real training begins. Early on much of your training will involve luring your dog with treats. In this chapter, I'll teach you how to *lure* your dog to *sit, recall* (come), and start to walk on a leash. You'll also begin to socialize your dog by letting her play with others—under close supervision, of course. Do your homework (training activities and games), and be sure to track your—and your dog's—progress in your Week 1 Training Log.

crate training, and handling and gentling exercises discussed in the previous chapter—begins the moment your new dog comes home. Instead of letting your dog learn by trial and error (mostly error), help him learn what you want from the very start.

Clients often ask me how old a dog should be before training starts. My own puppies start class at seven weeks of age. Anything younger than that is too early—puppies need to remain with their mother at least that long to maximize their natural socialization skills.

This program will help you and your dog master these ten basic skills: 1) sit, 2) recall, 3) leash walking, 4) down, 5) stay, 6) settle, 7) release, 8) standing pose, 9) off and take it, and 10) boundary training. When you use a system of positive reinforcement training methods and techniques, you will see how easy it can be to motivate your dog to learn, and to train him to follow your cues.

By the end of this five-week program, I expect that you will begin to notice a wonderful change in your dog. I call this delightful change *spiriting*, or the process of unlocking your dog's personality. The words "inspiration" and "spirit" stem from the same root, and I believe that when you spirit your dog, you inspire his best personality traits. In my classes, I get a lot of pleasure from watching that relationship form over the time I work with my students. Sometimes it seems to happen all at once: An owner who has done the homework consistently but hasn't experienced much success with his dog will come to the last night of class with a suddenly spirited dog. I love it when a dog "gets it" and wants to train. Maybe you've seen such a dog in your neighborhood: a well-trained, confident dog that loves to socialize—his owner has taught him how to be successful in our human world.

This week, we will focus on three specific skills: sit, recall (your basic "come here"), and leash walking. Dogs learn better in short bursts of time rather than in a long training session, so I recommend that you spend no longer than five minutes practicing any one exercise. At the end of each exercise, take a break and allow your dog playtime before moving on to another.

Also remember to vary the location where you practice the exercises. As we discussed with the hand-feeding protocol, dogs' brains are not naturally wired to generalize cues. Your dog may think that he needs to obey a certain cue only when he's in your kitchen facing the window on a sunny day with that bag of treats on the kitchen counter. By making sure to practice the exercises in a variety of places, at different times of day, both indoors and outdoors, you will help your dog begin generalizing every cue to different locations.

That said, expect your dog to regress when you move to another location. For instance, even if he responded brilliantly to the *sit* cue in the living room, he may have no idea what you are asking him to do now that he's in the kitchen. Be patient as you start again from the beginning.

Throughout this training program, and with each new skill you'll learn, I want you to follow three basic ground rules:

▶ **GROUND RULE #1: HAVE FUN.** You and your dog will be more motivated if you approach these lessons expecting to enjoy yourself. There should be an air of recreation to the proceedings—it's all part of building the important habit of playing together.

▶ **GROUND RULE #2: DO THE HOMEWORK.** Spend at least 10 minutes (and more, if possible) each day doing the homework assignments. Even if your dog has already learned a skill, or if he seems like he'll never learn it, practice it again and again. And be patient!

▶ **GROUND RULE #3: YOU'RE ALWAYS TRAINING.** Every interaction is a learning opportunity. That includes every walk, every meal, and every time you pet your dog. And one key thing to remember: Your dog will learn better with many short bursts of training activities than with one long session.

Mind Your As and Ps

FOR EACH SKILL that you and your dog learn, you will progress through four stages together. My colleague, Dr. Pamela Reid, who is vice president of the ASPCA's Animal Behavior Center and a certified animal behaviorist, calls these stages the "Four As of Learning."

▶ **STAGE 1: ACQUIRED.** The *first* session in which your dog successfully completes a new task.

▶ **STAGE 2: AUTOMATIC.** You and your dog can *fluently* do the skill at least 80 percent of the time.

▶ **STAGE 3: APPLICATION.** The two of you have *generalized* the skill so that you can apply it in a variety of places, including some real-life situations outside of training.

▶ **STAGE 4: ALWAYS.** The two of you maintain the skill so that it's a natural part of *everyday* life together.

This approach gives you a quick way to evaluate how you and your dog are progressing with each skill, and it will guide you to your next step. Think of each stage as a building block.

As you train, you are building a strong, benevolent relationship with your dog. In fact, dog training is also your Relationship Training System. This system emphasizes "Three Ps":

▶ **POSITIVE.** A good relationship is positive and supportive. When you use positive reinforcement, dogs enjoy learning. Unlike aversive training, my program will show you how to focus on the positive with every step.

▶ **PLAY.** Dogs enjoy people who are fun. It is essential to integrate play into training. I will show you how to get your dog hooked on positive play.

▶ **PALS.** To a dog, being a best friend means receiving loving care, sharing valuable rewards, having fun, and being a member of your pack who is valued because he follows your rules. I will help shape your relationship into one where obedience is tied to being best pals rather than adversaries.

Okay, your orientation is complete. Let's get to work.

Lures and Rewards: How to Use Training Treats

TREATS ARE A CRITICAL COMPONENT IN TRAINING, so it's important that you not overfeed your dog before a training session. Hunger motivates a dog to perform. Also remember when portioning your dog's meals that training

BASIC LURING EXERCISE

U se treats as lures to train your dog to follow your hand motions and focus on you. Hold the lure in your fingertips. The treat should be soft and small enough to be eaten in one bite. Say your dog's name, then praise (say "good"), and touch her collar as you allow her to eat the treat.

START AT NOSE LEVEL

Move your hand slowly to teach your dog to follow the lure. At first, move just a few inches before you let her nibble the treat.

MOVE THE LURE

As your dog follows the lure consistently, begin moving it up, around and through your legs, and take a step or two.

treats—some of which can be high in calories and fat—count as part of his daily diet. You will probably find that your dog likes certain treats better than others, so experiment. Ideally, like good-quality dog food, treats should be rich in protein. Treats should be tasty and as small as possible (without cheating the dog) so the dog can swallow it quickly and not lose focus on you and the next training moment. Likewise, soft treats are better to use than crunchy ones; since they can be swallowed more quickly, your dog can refocus on you right away. Anything your dog enjoys can be used as a treat reward and for luring: pieces of hotdogs, cheese, carrots, or any number of commercially available dog treats.

You will use the treats as lures, or as a tool to direct your dog to follow your hand for each cue. Since you're also hand-feeding this week, luring will be easier; your dog will be accustomed to the idea that good things are at your fingertips. Once this act of following your hand comes naturally to him—which it will, in time—you will be able to phase out the use of lures for each cue or trick.

To use a lure, hold a training treat in your fingertips and let your dog smell it. Move your hand slowly near his face, and watch as his head follows your hand. Continue to move your hand and watch as he follows with his nose, keeping it close to the treat. This is called luring. As you lure your dog, say his name, praise him, and touch his collar as he tries to eat the treat. As long as your dog stays interested in the lure—he tries to nibble at the treat and hopefully not too much of your fingertips—move your hand away from him very slowly so that he follows. If your dog starts to lose interest or gets distracted, bring the lure closer to his nose and do something different: Try moving to a slightly different spot or move your hand a little more slowly or quickly. Joyfully say his name and be so interesting and emotive that he can't ignore you. After a few minutes—or whenever you feel that he has had enough—reward him by praising him verbally, petting his collar, and letting him eat the lure.

> **Dogs learn more easily when you are consistent.**

Repeat this basic luring exercise many times a day during Week One with activities like Follow the Lure, which you'll find detailed in Chapter Nine. Keep track of your dog's progress by making notes in your logbook.

Whenever you reward your dog by allowing him to eat the treat, I want you to also get into the habit of touching him, especially around his collar. Getting your dog comfortable about being touched around his collar is important for a number of reasons. It helps with safety, especially if you need to urgently control your dog, or if he gets lost and a stranger needs to read his tags. It will also make it easier for the veterinarian and groomer to handle him, which they'll most definitely appreciate. Frequently touching your dog's collar will also help when you're ready to recall him to you. If the only time you touch your dog's collar is to put his leash back on, he may come to think that touching his collar (and recalling, by association) means that "fun is over." If that's the case, he may think that he should prolong his fun by running away from you or starting a game of Keep-away rather than coming when you call.

Each time you teach your dog a new skill or cue, use the same hand. Dogs like consistency, and they learn better when the things they're being asked to do look the same every single time. Get into the habit of being as consistent as possible with every lesson. I prefer to use my left hand because that's how I was taught. I give treats with my left hand, and I always have my dogs walk on my left side. In many training programs the left side is considered the correct side—you'll see that in dog shows almost all dogs are on the handler's left side—but either side is okay, just as long as you make a choice and stick with it while your dog becomes fluent (learning stage #2) for each new skill. After that, you can experiment with using either hand to lure and signal your dog, which will help him generalize.

Although many trainers like to put the treats in a pouch that clips onto the belt, I find that dogs often become so focused on the treat pouch that they don't focus enough on you. When I first started training Ebony, I forgot to take the treat pouch to class one evening, and she simply refused to work! I stopped using the pouch altogether after that, and now put training treats in my pocket. If you walk your dog on your left side, you should put your training treats in your left pocket. Remember to clean out your pockets before you put those pants in the laundry or you'll get grease stains. If you're intent on using a treat pouch, I recommend clipping it to your belt in the middle of your back where your dog can't see it, rather than at your hip where he may be continually tempted and distracted.

The Dog That Doesn't Respond to Food as a Lure

NOT ALL DOGS INITIALLY VALUE FOOD as a reward. If you have such a dog, try experimenting with different kinds of treats, including fresh meats that require refrigeration. I sometimes use human food as treats, because that way I can put a treat in my own mouth so the dog will stay focused on my face and body language. Also be careful not to overtreat your dog. If you give your dog treats throughout the day, and not just in response to good behaviors in training, it's likely that she will very soon stop valuing the treat.

What do you do if your dog simply won't respond to treats as a reward? Work to find out what she does value, and give that to her. Some dogs like to be touched, or prefer a brief round of play with a special toy. Some like soothing verbal praise the best, although I find that to be quite rare, occurring mostly in dogs with anxiety problems or a history of neglect or abuse.

If your dog works for the reward of playing with a special toy, then you need to limit the amount of time she plays with that toy, or use it exclusively for training purposes. Look ahead to Off and Take It Trades (page 123), because you'll need to adapt those techniques to trading for another toy; otherwise, your dog may be reluctant to give up the toy when you need her to. This can lead you to play "chase the dog," which will undermine effective training. Sometimes you can create desire in your dog by "selling" her on how great a toy is. For example, offer to play short games of fetch and then put the toy away before she gets bored and stops playing with you; you stop the game while she is eager to continue. Be careful not to oversell a toy that she doesn't like; I'm pretty sure you'll discover that your dog is too smart to fall for that one very many times!

It's a trickier situation if your dog works primarily for affection, because you certainly don't want to withhold affection from your beloved dog. In brief, you need to give your dog a clear signal that tells her that training has now begun and that she will get affection from you when she does what you need her to do. Such signals include petting a special toy (or petting the ground near her) while you make happy sounds, and as soon as she focuses on you, lure her to sit. In time, she will recognize that consistent happy "ritual" as a fun time for her to earn your extra affection.

If none of these techniques works, consult a dog behavior specialist or experienced trainer to determine if there is some problem that needs to be addressed. (Remember: Always choose an experienced professional who uses positive reinforcement training.) Talk to your veterinarian to rule out any underlying medical issues that may be affecting your dog's behavior.

Luring to Sit

SINCE *SIT* IS THE MOST FUNDAMENTAL DOG TRAINING cue, let's begin with that. Your dog will learn many other basic behaviors—such as *come*, *stay*, *down*, and *standing pose*—from the sit position. You should think of *sit* as your dog's ready position. If this were military training, *sit* would be like standing at attention. If this were a ballet studio, *sit* would be first position. My dog Brieo, foster dog Boz, and all dogs that board with me are required to sit for everything from the moment they get up in the morning to the moment they go to sleep at night. They sit when I open or close doors, when I come home and greet them, at mealtime, when it's time to go on a walk, when they get in and out of the car, and before and after playtime and training. Having your dog sit for everything emphasizes that you are your dog's benevolent leader, and that he takes his direction from you. Your dog will also learn that sitting is how he says "please," for which he is often rewarded with a treat. I don't like to anthropomorphize dogs, but in this case it's instructive to put words in your dog's mouth. "When I sit, the food bowl appears and I get to eat," he might say, or "When I sit, the door opens and we go for a walk."

As you teach your dog to sit, use only the lure at this stage, and don't say anything at all, like "sit" or "sit, Brieo." This may be challenging at first, because language is, of course, the primary tool we humans use to communicate. But the natural canine orientation is not verbal, it's visual. Verbal cues will just sound like noise to your dog and will get in the way of his acquiring the lure concept. You will be tempted! But, for the time being, your focus is on getting your dog used to following the motion of the lure. Also, if you have a rehomed dog that already understands verbal cues, I want you to stop using them, and retrain him, starting by luring with your hand signals. This will encourage him to watch you. I want your dog's attention focused on you while he is acquiring each new skill. In later lessons, we will add the verbal cues (a process we call naming the behavior).

To begin, hold a lure in your fingertips. Touch the treat to your dog's nose and let him sniff it. Now raise the lure slowly, straight up above his head. When his head begins to tilt up, continue slowly raising the lure. As he continues to follow the lure, his head will tilt up and his rump will lower to the floor. It's simple physics.

The moment his rump touches the floor, say "good" as you feed him the treat and pet his collar with your other hand. Give him five seconds of joyful verbal and physical praise. I typically say "What a good puppy, good Brieo, what a good dog." I want your dog focused on you and, ideally, staring at you. You're also teaching him to make eye contact with you, which will further strengthen your bond and keep him highly focused on you. If he seems distracted, increase your enthusiasm: You need to be the most interesting thing in the world to your dog.

LURING TO SIT

Sit is the most fundamental dog training cue. Teach your dog to sit for everything. Start teaching him to sit by luring, and without saying any verbal cues.

GET HIS ATTENTION

Your dog has already begun learning that when you're holding a treat, good things happen. You taught him that in the basic luring exercise (see page 71).

LURE HIM TO YOU

While holding the lure at nose-level, take a step toward your dog and let him sniff the treat.

RAISE THE LURE

As you slowly lift the lure straight up, your dog's head tilts up, causing his body to tilt down. When his rump touches down, mark (say "good"), praise (pet him, touch his collar), and treat last.

Some dogs will get this cue right away. Not so for others. If your dog seems to have trouble figuring out what you're asking him to do and won't sit for you even after several training sessions, you want to dissect the whole action into smaller parts. We call this breaking down a cue, or rewarding for the smallest successes, even for simply lifting his head. If his nose goes up in the air, treat him. Little by little, get your dog to move his nose a half inch higher on each subsequent repetition. Once you get his nose pointing toward the sky, his rump will automatically start to lower. Treat him as his rump starts to move down. On the next rep, reward him when his rump is a half inch lower. Eventually he'll touch down.

Be patient. Assume that it will take 10 repetitions of this exercise before your dog connects putting his rump on the floor with getting a treat. To your dog, getting the treat the first time probably seems like an accident; the second time, it becomes a coincidence. Once he makes the connection—sitting and treat go together—it becomes a learned pattern.

Even if it takes your dog 15 to 25 reps to make the connection, believe me, the more repetitions and practice time you put into this exercise, the easier it will be each time you work with your dog. You are giving him a very important foundation in teaching him to follow your lure. If you or your dog is bored because it's too slow, or you're frustrated because he isn't getting it, take a break before the dog totally loses interest. Do another quick activity the dog enjoys, such as a brief game of Follow the Lure. Make notes in your training log, and try a different activity for a while. If you're going to train for more than two minutes at a time, add some variety with one of the homework games or activities in Chapter Nine after each two-minute training exercise. If training is not mixed with playtime experiences, you may undermine your dog's confidence level and enjoyment of training.

Timing and Voice Marking

D OING MANY REPETITIONS WILL HELP TRAIN *you* to have good timing: delivering the positive feedback at exactly the right moment to mark the behavior you want your dog to do. For example, when you say "good" the moment your dog's rump touches the floor, you are letting her know she has completed the task you were asking her to do. You're using the word *good* as a marker; if your timing is off, your dog will accidentally learn the wrong lesson because you marked the wrong moment. For example, if you mark "good" too late, your dog may understand that

WHAT ABOUT THE CLICKER?

P erhaps you've heard about trainers who use clickers to mark a dog's good behavior. Basically, you click instead of saying "good." It's simply easier to click precisely at the right moment.

Personally, I love the clicker. But in my work with families, especially when children are involved, I prefer voice markers. Particularly during the five-week fundamentals course, it's very important that your dog focus on you as much as possible—and that

means the sounds you make as well as your physical motions. Also, because you're trying to coordinate so many new gestures, I think that learning the clicker right now can get in the way.

But if you can't wait to start working with a clicker, flip ahead to Chapter Ten, where I introduce clicker training, before moving ahead to the next exercises.

it's good when she tilts her head or opens her mouth or wags her tail. You want her to associate "good" with her rump touching the floor. So, as you repeat each exercise, make sure that you mark your praise precisely—in this case, the moment your dog's rump touches the floor.

You can use other marker words besides *good*. Common markers include "thank you" and "yes!" Whatever marker word you teach your dog, use it consistently, including how you pronounce the word. Try to say it the exact same way each time: at the same volume, in the same tone, and with the same level of emotion. Learning to give your dog well-timed markers is essential to *your* training, so work the program by doing many sets of reps with the intention of learning to give well-timed feedback markers consistently.

Luring to Recall, Part One

RECALLING MEANS that your dog comes to you when you signal him. Recalls are initially important for your dog's safety, but they eventually allow you to give your dog more freedom; a dog that develops excellent recall skills can be granted more liberties and has more opportunities to socialize. Since recall can be a challenging behavior for many dogs to master, I have found it most effective to break down the cue and teach the last part of the cue first. That's right, this week you will teach your dog only the *last* part of the cue: sitting when he gets to you.

You'll need a partner for this exercise; if you have children, this is a wonderful training exercise to include them in. Ask your partner to hold your dog's leash. Put a treat in your hand and take three steps back. Lure your dog by holding the treat toward him, and then bringing it toward your knee. Have your partner release the leash. As your dog arrives, lure him to sit, using the hand motion I described earlier (page 75). Once he sits, mark it (say "good"), praise him, and reward him with the treat.

If your dog comes to you but doesn't sit, praise him but don't treat him. Then back up another three steps and repeat the exercise: Lure him by drawing the treat from his nose to your knee. If your dog doesn't sit on the repeat try either, do it once more:

A NOTE ON SAYING YOUR DOG'S NAME

If you're using the hand-feeding protocol from Chapter Three, you're already playing the Name Game (page 53); now make it part of your day, playing it at random intervals or as an easy break between exercises. You want your dog to get used to hearing her name, and associating it with good things and affection. Unless she is uncomfortable on her back or with being handled, end a training session by cradling her between your legs and calmly rubbing her tummy and touching her all over as you say her name. Play the game the same way you do during hand-feeding: Say your dog's name and if she responds, say "good dog," touch her collar, and reward her with a treat. Think of this exercise as a massage that relaxes your dog.

One important note: Never say your dog's name when you're trying to correct her behavior, such as when you tell her to get off the couch, to stop mouthing your hand, or to drop some contraband. For example, while I often say "good Brieo!" I never say "no, Brieo, get down" or "drop that, Brieo!" You don't want to inadvertently train your dog to associate her name with punishment. That can delay bonding and slow the learning process; some dogs may stop responding to their names.

Remember: Use your dog's name only in the course of praise and reward.

I can almost guarantee that you will make a mistake at some point and call your dog by name in a negative association; everyone, including me, makes that error sometimes. When it happens, make a note to yourself to play a round or two of the Name Game as soon as possible.

Praise him (no treat), back up three steps, and try it again. If he is still not sitting on the third try, give him the treat and praise anyhow, to reward his good recall. This means your dog isn't quite ready to link the sit with the recall. That's okay. Just continue to teach him to sit using the luring exercises above, and practice the recall/sit again in your next session. You may choose to decrease the distance to help him gain confidence and understand that he is being rewarded for following your instructions. This is known as building a positive reinforcement history.

If your dog is consistently coming to you and sitting on cue, try backing up a few more steps each time. Remember to use the same hand to cue and treat your dog.

Eye-Contact Exercise

NOW FOR THE FUN PART: I'd like you to end this recall exercise by spending a few minutes training your dog to look at your eyes. Once you've got this simple and fun exercise down, do it several times a day, at random intervals. Eye contact is crucial for bonding and for focus, so start practicing this with very young puppies. Pretty soon they'll be watching your each and every move.

To begin, touch a treat to your dog's nose, and allow her to sniff it. As soon as her interest is established, bring the treat to your eyes, say "good," and silently count off two seconds. If she stays focused on the treat for two seconds, feed it to her. On the next rep, add one extra second. On each successful repetition, add an additional second.

Continue to silently count the seconds, and to say "good" in a happy, rewarding voice. Take a small step to the side before you begin the next rep so that your dog begins to generalize the behavior to slightly different locations.

If your dog turns her head or breaks eye contact, move to another position and try again for a second. Do not reward her if she breaks eye contact, or you might accidentally train her to look away from you. If your dog is a jumper, step on her leash so that she can't jump up while doing this exercise. I find that some breeds naturally do this better than others. For example, in my experience, Jack Russell Terriers are generally more easily distracted than German Shepherds; but I've also seen the opposite. Remember: All dogs attain success at their own pace.

Leash Walking: The First Steps Together, or "Be a Tree"

ONE OF MY FAVORITE THINGS in the world is taking my dogs for long walks, which I generally do twice a day. We'll often wander down one of the horse trails on my property. Not only are our walks great exercise for them and for me, but they help keep the dogs curious and engaged.

I can tell you, though, that the walks would be no fun at all if Brieo and Boz pulled on their leashes. We've all seen it: the dog that appears to be dragging its owner down the street, from fire hydrant to lamppost to garbage bin. You want to train your dog to walk on a loose leash, fairly close to your side. The goal isn't the perfect *heel*—that's unrealistic for any but the most focused animal. Even in elite dog shows, those highly trained dogs stay perfectly focused on the handler for only the brief moments when the spotlight is on them. I tell you that so that you'll have more patience and confidence as you teach your dog to walk on a leash. If he's the rare exception that doesn't pull, this is your lucky day and my only advice to you is to count your blessings and buy a lottery ticket.

If you walk your dog on your left side, hold the leash handle in your right hand and grip the middle of the leash in your left, so that the leash crosses in front of your body. If you prefer to walk him on the right side, do the opposite. Even though I sometimes loop the handle over my wrist, be careful: You want to avoid injury if your dog pulls too hard. If you use a Martingale collar, a head halter, or a body harness (preferably one that clips to the leash at the dog's chest rather than his back), your position when you hold the leash is the same.

The point of this training session—which should last no longer than five minutes—is to get your dog used to walking on the leash the way you want him to. I recommend that you use a six-foot leash and come prepared with lots of treats. Hold one in your left hand and lure your dog in the direction you want to walk. If you have a small dog, get ready to bend down a lot. Start walking forward, allowing a lot of slack in the leash. When your dog starts to pull, stop walking, hold the leash tight to your chest, and stand

LEASH POSTURES

Your first walks together will be brief exercises designed to teach your dog to focus on you.

FOCUS FIRST

Before you take your first steps together, make sure that your dog is focused on you.

"BE A TREE"

Whenever your dog walks ahead of you, stop, hold the leash tight to your chest, and stand like a firm tree. The moment he looks back at you, say "good" and lure him toward you as you step backward.

still and firm, like a tree. The moment he looks at you, say "good" and lure him toward you with the treat as you take two steps backward. Praise him, touch his collar, and reward him with the treat. Your timing needs to be precise, so watch for that moment when he looks at you, even if for only an instant at first, because that's when his attention is returning to you.

If your dog doesn't look at you, break down the lesson and reward his tiny improvements. If he continues to lean forward against the leash without trying to take a step, look for the moment when he slackens the leash and praise that. If he still doesn't give you attention, make a slight sound to attract him. If that doesn't work, silently "reel yourself in" to your dog (don't pull him toward you, but go hand-over-hand up the leash as if you were pulling yourself up a rope), and then lure him to start walking in the opposite direction. If he looks at you as you reel yourself in, praise, stop reeling, and lure. Remember that this isn't a walk for distance or heeling; it's a five-minute walking exercise to teach you how to hold a leash and to manage pulling. Be patient.

As you practice this exercise throughout the week, try to change it up to keep your dog interested and to generalize the behavior. Change directions as you walk. If you prefer to do this indoors, walk around objects, like chairs or tables. Try increasing the speed at which you walk, and practice making abrupt turns—not to trick your dog into making mistakes, but to see if you can use your lures and a fun voice to keep him completely focused on you.

In later weeks, we'll add distractions, such as another dog or an interesting human, but don't intentionally add them just yet. I want your dog to experience as much success as possible. If you are practicing this exercise outdoors and you encounter a person who wants to greet your dog, stop walking, step on the leash, and clutch the handle to your chest, to keep your dog still. If he is able to sit, request a *sit*, mark it, and praise and reward him. If he doesn't sit yet, manage the situation by stepping on the leash so he can't jump up while you meet the person. Stepping on the leash allows your dog to sit, stand (pose), or lie down, but he can't jump. Say a brief hello and calmly let the person know that you need to focus on training.

For now, it's best to try to anticipate and avoid distractions as often as possible.

Socialization Exercises

FAR TOO MANY DOGS are surrendered to shelters or rescue organizations because they are not well socialized. This is far more often the fault of the owner than it is a reflection on the dog. As owners, it is our responsibility to take the time to socialize our dogs—with people, as well as with other animals—from the very beginning. That's why you should spend at least one session this week (as well as throughout the five-week program) training in the presence of other people, and, if your dog is fully vaccinated, with other dogs. If you know people with dogs, set up an indoor or outdoor playdate or playgroup. If not, ask your vet or groomer for names of people with well-behaved dogs. As your dog first socializes with other dogs, you may want to consider choosing dogs about the same size as yours, especially with teacup-size puppies.

> It is our responsibility to socialize our dogs.

Here's an exercise I like to do when I train with another person and his dog. Begin by allowing just two minutes off leash (within a fenced area if outdoors) free playtime. Then recall your respective dogs. Because your dog is still learning the *recall* cue, you may need to physically interrupt her playtime by approaching her and luring her with the hand signal we practiced: treat to her nose, then to your knee. Spend at least 10 seconds praising your dog, and take a few moments to practice the *sit* cue. Treat her, and then release her for another round of play. It is important that you interrupt the play for three reasons: 1) to help build successful recall, 2) to teach your dog that recall does not mean the end of playtime, and 3) to remind your dog that she needs to keep you as her primary focus. Do this play-and-recall exercise for four rounds. This exercise can be used on dogs of all ages, although young puppies usually learn it more quickly than older untrained dogs. If your dog doesn't recall well from these play rounds, you may need to rely a bit on your training partner's ability to lure (or at least distract) the other dog, and then step between the dogs to lure yours.

If at the end of those four rounds your dogs seem to want to continue to play, try another activity, such as training your respective dogs near each other. But don't force the playdate to go any longer than is comfortable, and try to end on a positive note, ideally with both dogs (and both owners) wanting to play again next time.

A few tips on being around other dogs: During these brief, off-leash play periods, observe whether your puppy hides or exhibits any aggression. If she needs to get away from the other dog, don't pick her up or you will teach her to want to jump up when she feels uncomfortable or feels a desire to be rescued, which could make her more fearful. Instead, let her move between your legs if she feels more comfortable there, and then have the other owner redirect his dog's attention (ideally, by luring and then having the dog sit to regain focus). I urge caution on taking your dog to a dog park at this stage, and I talk more about dog parks in Chapter Twelve. If you have a rehomed dog, you will probably want to socialize her for briefer periods as you discover her comfort zone and behavior triggers and issues.

Okay, class dismissed. Remember to make your homework fun.

Orientation to Homework

IN CHAPTER NINE, I have detailed 26 activities and games designed to help you and your dog have fun while you master the lessons in each chapter. I strongly suggest that you spend at least 10 minutes a day doing a few of these activities and games, and I've indicated which ones best coincide with each week of training. The games are also good to shift to when your dog doesn't succeed at behavior you're trying to teach.

Why is doing your homework so important? In training your dog, you are engaging in a process called conditioning—you are modifying your dog's natural behavior to do what you want. Simply put, conditioning means learning through association. The more repetitions you do, followed by a reward, the more he expects that the next repetition will earn him the same reward. Eventually, he will become fully conditioned: He will perfect each cue (perform each behavior) without a treat or other reward. But that's only going to happen if *you* put in the time and effort.

As I've stated, dogs learn better with many brief lessons than with one long one, and you can turn 60 seconds into a mini-lesson. Having many short lessons throughout the day will help keep your dog in an always-learning attitude.

As you begin doing homework this week, I want you to focus on the fun of it. Celebrate the successes, laugh at the failures. Your dog loves fun and will be more confident when he's having a good time with you. Establish a pattern of having fun in your first week and it will carry with you throughout this course. In my classes, I often refer to homework as "funwork," especially when kids are in attendance. When a kid hears me say the word "homework," I can see his enthusiasm deflate quicker than a leaky balloon, and then fill right back up when I say that it's actually funwork. I'd like you to bring that attitude to homework this week.

Recommended Games and Activities

ADD VARIETY AND FUN to the training experience by playing these games (see details in Chapter Nine):

▶ Name Game

▶ Eye-Contact Exercise

▶ Follow the Lure

▶ Home Visit

▶ Supervised play: find a training partner

▶ Pass the Puppy and Peekaboo emphasize bite inhibition, handling, and gentling (assuming that there are no outstanding behavior issues)

▶ "Ouch" exercises: explore dog's mouth, count teeth and toes

WEEK 1

TRAINING LOG FOR _____ DAY _____

SKILL	PROGRESS	NOTES
USING TREATS AS LURES Practice luring your dog with treats.		
LURING TO SIT Touch treat to dog's nose, lure up (rump goes down), mark, praise, touch collar, treat last.		
LURING TO RECALL, PART 1 Take 2 or 3 steps back, lure dog. Mark, praise, touch collar, treat last. Extra: If dog already sits, add a sit before the treat. Be animated and happy when you lure.		
EYE-CONTACT EXERCISE Touch treat to dog's nose, then bring it to your eyes. Mark and reward for dog's eye contact.		
WALKING: "BE A TREE" When dog pulls leash, stop and hold leash firmly to your body. When dog looks back at you, mark, lure, and start again.		
LEASH TETHERING Around your home.		
HAND-FEEDING Feed all meals by hand from dog's bowl. Your dog sees that you are the giver of food.		
CRATE TRAINING Teach dog to love his crate. Many treats and meals in and around crate.		
POTTY TRAINING Keep track of input (meals and treats) and output (potty time). Note accidents.		
BITE INHIBITION, HANDLING, GENTLING "Ouch" exercise. Lots of gentle handling. Touch paws and all over body.		
CHOOSE AN ACTIVITY/GAME.		
CHOOSE A SOCIALIZATION EXPERIENCE.		

For free training log downloads, visit lovethatdogbook.com.

CHAPTER 5

Week Two: Training in Everyday Life

FOR THIS WEEK, and each subsequent week, we are going to build on the skills that your dog learned the previous week. If your dog can't keep pace with any of the lessons, that's okay. This isn't about getting a grade or comparing your dog to other dogs. It's about helping her have a great life with you. Proceed at the pace that works best for her.

This week's program builds on last week's skills. After practicing tethering and the "sit" command, you'll introduce your dog to the concept of the jackpot: the ultimate treat payoff. I'll show you how to start cueing your dog without the promise of treats, plus how to add a verbal component to the recall cue. You'll also lure your dog into a down position, and teach her to release with a verbal cue. Homework includes more games and training activities, plus keeping up with your training log.

If this means that you have to spend a lot of time this week reviewing last week's exercises, do that. In my classes, I always have dogs that can't do certain cues during the week I teach them. I remind those owners to continue to help their dogs be successful, not to push them too hard, and to stay committed to the exercises—their dogs *will* get it. Trust me on that.

This week we begin to integrate your dog's training experiences into her daily life. For example, the tethering exercise will prepare her for anticipating your body language during walks. We will also continue to work on the *recall* cue, and begin to teach the *down* position.

Tethering

ET'S BEGIN WITH A QUICK AND SIMPLE tethering exercise that you can practice for about 5 to 10 minutes every day—you'll find it a nice break between more difficult exercises. Begin by tethering your dog to your belt (see page 49), and be sure to have a few treats ready. Start moving around, adding a few distractions along the way. If you're training inside your home, walk around tables and chairs, go into various rooms, sit and watch TV, talk on the phone. Do a few simple acts like filling your dog's water bowl, touching the outside of his crate as you walk around it, reaching into his crate and touching his sleeping mat (straighten it up or fluff his bed). If you're training outside, move around a small area in a somewhat random pattern: Take out a few objects (like a brush, toy, or towel), set one on the ground and move away from it, set down another object, and another, then pick them up in a different order and put them away. As you do this exercise, notice every time your dog looks at you, mark it by saying "good," touch his collar, pet him for a moment, and reward him with one treat.

BITE INHIBITION, HANDLING, AND GENTLING

We won't introduce new bite inhibition exercises this week, so please continue to practice the ones we learned in Chapter Three (page 64). After you explore your dog's mouth, massage her gums, count her teeth, or do whatever she's ready for, be sure to log her progress toward having a softer and gentler mouth. Be prepared for at least a few nips to your hand—remember that it took my Flat-Coated Retriever, Merit, 45 days to stop biting hard. Next week, we will take bite inhibition to a new level by introducing the *off* and *take it* cues.

When you move, don't try to trick your dog with abrupt turns. In fact, try to give him hints as to your next move by shuffling your feet as you turn, bending down a little, swinging your arms around smoothly, or clapping lightly. The more success your dog has (and the more he's rewarded), the more likely that he will want to continue doing that behavior.

I want to remind you of some general reasons to practice tethering that we introduced in Chapter Three. When you tether your dog to your belt loop, you are literally keeping him close to you, helping him learn your body cues as you turn, change speeds, pause, and start again. Tethered to you, he learns, with practice, to pay close attention to you and walk at your pace. And vice versa—*you* will learn to anticipate *his* body language: how he starts to drift away from you and explore something, or tries to go toward a room or object that's off-limits. If he misbehaves in some manner—say, he begins to venture toward something off-limits (perhaps, that special couch), or to go potty inside—you will be so close that you can immediately direct him to stop pulling, drop contraband, or move away from an off-limits area or object.

Sit: Your Dog's Real-Life Rewards System

I WANT YOU TO BEGIN to ask your dog to sit for everything, including her meals. Because you're still hand-feeding this week, ask her to sit before every scoop of food you offer. Once she sits, it's okay if she stands up to eat, as long as she doesn't jump on you or at your hand. Once she's finished each portion, ask her to sit before feeding her again. Remember to practice this exercise in different places, including in her crate if crate training has progressed to that level.

Asking your dog to sit for everything (and not just during a training exercise) is what I call a real-life rewards system—a way to teach your dog the relevance of what *sit* actually means throughout the day. Your dog will understand that when she sits she gets a reward: to play with the toy that you are showing her, or to eat the food in the bowl that you are holding, or to go through the door that you are ready to open for her. She also will understand that when she does not sit, she gets a punishment: She doesn't get to hold the toy, eat the food, or walk through the door. As we began learning last week, the *sit* is your dog's ready position, and it should become her way of saying "please, may I?" In addition, you want to generalize the cue by training your dog in various locations and while out on walks.

Remember that we still haven't introduced the verbal cue for *sit*. My students are constantly forgetting this: They really have to concentrate on not using the verbal cue at this stage. The same will hold true for you: The more you practice your homework, the more natural it will become for you to use only the luring motion for *sit* at this stage. We'll introduce the verbal cue later.

Withdrawing Treats: Slot Machine and Jackpot Psychology

ONCE YOU HAVE REACHED that 80 percent automatic threshold for *sit*, meaning that your dog sits on cue 8 out of 10 times, stop rewarding him with a treat at the end of every success. An interesting thing happens when you begin withdrawing treats that your dog has come to expect: He tries harder to get the treat, which keeps him interested in training.

Withdrawing some of the treats uses what I call "slot machine psychology." Ask yourself, Why do humans gamble? Because we know there's the possibility of a payoff but we enjoy the uncertainty of not knowing if or when it's going to come. The same thing holds true for your dog. Behaviorists have discovered that once a dog first acquires a skill (learning stage #1), the most effective way to reinforce that skill so that it becomes an "always" behavior (learning stage #4) is by using unpredictable and random rewards. It's just as psychologist Edward Thorndike posited about a hundred years ago in his trial-and-error theory of learning (now a cornerstone of modern behavioral psychology): Once they've been rewarded, dogs will try to figure out how to get that reward again. And *you* are the dog's slot machine.

An important component of this technique is a reward called jackpots—a virtual puppy bonanza. Instead of rewarding your dog with one treat, you give him 7 to 10, one at a time. (This will feel like a much bigger reward than if he eats them all in one gulp.) Be sure to say "good" with extra enthusiasm each time you dole out a treat in the jackpot. Awarding jackpots will increase your dog's curiosity, self-confidence, and enjoyment of training. Getting 10 treats is fun!

Let me illustrate how this works with an example. Imagine the first time your dog starts to sit even though your lure barely moved above her nose. This means she probably understands that your hand motion is asking her to sit. Now, *that* is worth a jackpot. Of course, her sitting may have been an accident, but that's okay. If she sits a bit quicker on the next trial after the first jackpot, I like to award another, smaller jackpot (a couple of extra treats rewarded one at a time). Here's what your dog may be thinking after two jackpots in a row: "That first jackpot may have been an accident, but, hey, maybe that second one was more than a coincidence; possibly there was a correlation between my sitting and that yummy food." Okay, your dog isn't thinking in that vocabulary, but psychologists like Thorndike, Ivan Pavlov, B. F. Skinner, and others have established that dogs like to figure out the cause of their successes and how to win repeat rewards.

It's not uncommon that a dog's success rate momentarily drops off after a jackpot; her own excitement may distract her and cause her to lose her focus. That's okay. The drop will most likely be temporary. If, however, the success rate drops below the 80 percent rate after a behavior has been learned, it may mean that your dog is bored or temporarily burned out, and needs to move on to another activity, such as a fun game of Peekaboo (page 65) or one of the other activities that your dog can already succeed at.

As your dog continues to master each cue, you will withdraw treats. When your dog achieves total mastery for a cue (which may take a number of weeks, so be patient), you will have withdrawn treat rewards altogether for that cue. We've introduced that mastery stage as learning stage #4: always. As you withdraw treats for one cue, it is important to begin another cue with treat rewards so that your dog stays interested in training. This technique builds her desire for lifelong learning.

SIT: THE HAND SIGNAL

Notice in the images below that the hand signal for *sit* looks just like the luring motion when holding a treat. Begin using the hand signal (without the lure) once your dog has become fluent with your luring.

GET YOUR DOG TO FOCUS

Cup the position of your cueing hand as if you were holding a treat. You may need to bend over a little to "sell" your dog on the illusion. After enough reps, you will be able to start with a flat (uncupped) hand.

MAKE THE HAND SIGNAL

Raise your hand just as you did when you held a treat. When the dog sits, mark, praise, and then treat with your other (non-cueing) hand. As your dog becomes fluent, flatten (uncup) your cueing hand.

Modifying the Sit Hand Signal: From Lure to Cue

ONCE YOUR DOG HAS MOVED to learning stage #2, automatic, for the *sit* cue and you have begun to introduce the slot machine techniques of withdrawing and jackpotting treats, it is time to modify the lure motion into a hand signal. Using a hand signal will allow you to gesture to your dog to sit when you stand a little farther away from him.

Notice in the photographs above that the starting hand position is the same in both the luring movement and the modified cue: The hand is upturned and the fingertips hold a treat. Even though you've started to phase out treats, bring them back as you teach this (or any) new skill. The way to teach your dog this modified signal is by putting your hand into the starting hand position and then raising your fingertips just above his nose, then slowly and deliberately straight up into the air. The moment his rump touches down, stop signaling, mark, praise, touch his collar, and treat him. If he succeeded in responding to this cue on this first attempt, that is worth a jackpot. The speed with which he responds to your modified cue becomes the new baseline for how high you raise your hand on the next rep.

Sit Cue: Withdrawing Treats

NEXT COMES A BIG LEARNING STEP: Will your dog sit when you give the hand cue and are *not* holding a treat in your fingertips? Start this step by palming a treat in the hand that you use to give the visual hand signal, and palm another treat in your other hand. Try the hand signal cue as you had been doing previously, touching your fingertips lightly to your dog's nose, sliding the cue straight up above her nose, slowly and smoothly. The moment her rump touches down, mark it by saying "good," praise her, touch her collar, and finally, reward her with the treat in your cueing hand followed by the treat in your other hand. You may also put a few treats in your other hand to anticipate that first jackpot success. If she doesn't succeed, that's okay. Just turn around with her and try again. If she doesn't succeed on the next trial, go back to holding the treat in your fingertips for another few reps before trying this step again. It's okay to help your dog win this next jackpot by repeating the step she already knows a couple more times before returning to try this new step again.

Once your dog consistently succeeds at this step for about five trials, on the next rep, don't palm a treat in your cueing hand; instead palm a jackpot in your other hand. If she sits on your cue, mark it, offer praise, touch her collar, and finally, reward that jackpot. Continue for a few more reps like this, and then bring in the slot machine: Make the rewards unpredictable.

To prevent boredom, be sure to mix some playtime into the learning phase by working on other behaviors that she knows, or experiment by tossing a ball or toy, or simply pet her. These brief play breaks keep you and your dog in the spirit of learning. Also, remember to generalize to different locations; as your dog gets it, try locations that are slightly more distracting—how about a random *sit* during a walk? Little by little, she will recognize the starting hand-signal position and will watch your every move. As you continue rewarding her successes with treats, play breaks, games, and your affection, you are likely to discover that she gains confidence and starts to offer behaviors that you didn't even ask for, such as a paw shake or bringing a toy to you. When that happens, thank your dog with all the excitement of having just won the lottery yourself, and give her a jackpot.

Recall: Luring at a Distance and Adding the Verbal Cue

L AST WEEK, we learned the end of the important *recall* cue: that moment when your dog arrives in front of you. This week, we will acquire the whole cue by increasing the recall distance, still keeping a *sit* at the end. Start by practicing your dog's current baseline distance, whether it's three steps with a *sit* or one step without a *sit*. If he doesn't yet sit at the end of the recall, I want you and your dog to acquire that behavior before you add the distance. You may need to adapt the techniques in last week's *recall* exercise, such as starting with the *sit* exercise and then, once it has been acquired (learning stage #1), add a half step *recall* and acquire that. Add slight generalizations, such as moving a half step to the side. Then gradually increase the distance, even if it is only by inches at a time.

Once your dog has acquired the *recall* with the *sit* at a distance of three steps, you can practice this exercise with a partner. I recommend doing it indoors, ideally in a well-lit hallway with all doors closed. This will keep your dog from becoming too distracted, and help him stay focused on you more easily.

Your partner will hold the dog by the leash. Act very excited as you touch a treat to your dog's nose, tease him for a moment without giving him the treat, then turn and run four feet away. Stop and turn to face your dog. If he pulls on the leash, that means he is paying close attention to you! In that case, I recommend that your partner gently hold him in place bodily; you don't want the dog to pull harshly (which could hurt his neck) or learn a bad habit. Now you'll add a verbal cue. As you turn, happily say your dog's name and add, in an upbeat tone, "come here!" At this point, your partner lets go of the leash.

A NOTE ON VERBAL CUES

Since *come here* is the first verbal cue that your dog will learn in this training program, let's take a minute to consider the whole notion of verbal cues. If I were calling Brieo, I would say in my happy voice, "Brieo, come here!" The tone is not commanding; it is excited and playful. I prefer the cue words *come here* over a simple *come*, because the word *here* helps your voice to sound excited and happy, while the word *come* by itself can sound too commanding.

Add your dog's name to the beginning of any positive cue (including *recall* and *sit*), but remember not to add your dog's name when it is a negative or boundary cue (such as staying off the furniture). Also, be sure to say the cue only once. For example, don't say "Come here, Brieo, come here. Come," or "Sit-sit-sit-sit" even if your dog doesn't sit.

Repeating a cue can cause what behaviorists call learned irrelevance: When we repeat a cue (to sit, for example), our dog learns that the first time we say "sit" is irrelevant, and that she needs to wait until we say the word five times in a row and with a certain tone before she is supposed to sit. Don't accidentally teach your dog to think that the sounds coming out of your mouth are irrelevant. This is why it's very important to pay attention to your verbal cues, consistently offering them only once and always in the same tone of voice. If your dog doesn't get the cue, simply turn around and start over again with the lure. When she succeeds, remember to mark and reward.

Do all you can to attract your dog to come to you: Crouch (or even kneel on the floor for a puppy or small dog), pat your hands together (don't clap loudly if your dog startles easily), and lure him to come right in front of you (not to your side, but facing directly at your knees). As he arrives, cue the *sit*. When his rump touches down, praise him with extra excitement, touch his collar, and give him the treat. I call this exercise the Lassie Recall in honor of the TV show, because Timmy petted and praised Lassie each time she returned after having been lost.

If your dog is successful at this distance, add a little more distance on the next repetition; if not, shorten the distance a little. On subsequent reps, change it up: Sit, crouch, stand, switch ends of the hallway, or move to another spot entirely as you lure your dog to you.

If he isn't coming right to you when you call him, try these techniques:

▶ While your partner holds the leash, run back and forth between your dog and the spot, making playful sounds and

THE DOWN CUE

Begin teaching your dog to lie down by luring her from a *sit*. Continue practicing with a lure as she becomes fluent. Do not use a verbal cue, yet.

❶ START AT SIT

With your dog in a sitting position, let her sniff the lure, then turn your palm down, slide the lure down her chest and downward.

❷ MARK EACH SUCCESS

Move your hand smoothly toward the ground, staying close to her body. As her belly and elbows touch down, mark the success (say "good").

❸ PRAISE, THEN TREAT LAST

Touch your dog's collar as you say her name, and finally let her eat the treat.

movements. Each time you return to your dog, touch the treat gently to his nose so that he can smell it.

▶ Try running with your dog to the destination, then put him in a *sit* and treat him.

▶ Have your partner let go of the leash as you begin running away. This is called a *chase recall*, because the dog will try to catch up to you. *Chase recalls* are fun for most dogs, thus they increase the dog's desire to catch up to you and come when called.

Down: Luring Your Dog into a Down Position

IF YOU EVER NEED to control your dog in an urgent safety situation, such as avoiding an aggressive dog or a distraction that makes him either fearful or overly excited, you will be grateful that the *down* cue is part of his repertoire. *Down* is also a building-block cue when you get to *settle down* and relax, which you'll learn in Week Four.

With your dog in the *sit* position, hold a lure in your fingertips with your palm turned down. Slide the lure toward your dog's chest. Just before you touch his chest, lure straight down to the floor, staying close to his body. If he drops straight down, mark it (say "good"), praise him, touch his collar, reward him with the treat . . . and count your blessings, because your dog is already well on his way to mastering the *down*. Practice a handful of reps and begin to generalize by moving a step to the side and turning around and moving to a different spot. In subsequent home-work sessions, generalize into different spaces. If your dog is a really fast learner for the *down*, begin to modify your lure motion into the actual hand signal cue by shortening the slide into his chest and then moving your palm downward slowly and smoothly to the floor. Remember to jackpot him and start to withdraw treat rewards using slot machine psychology as he becomes fluent for the cue. On subsequent reps and in future training sessions, generalize this behavior to various other places in your home and on walks.

Many dogs need help learning *down* because they tend to stand up out of the *sit* when the lure is offered. If your dog stands up, don't worry about it; she is trying to figure out what you want her to do. Let her work it through. Just take her back to *sit* and try again. The *down* will come with time, patience, and practice.

Another option for helping your dog learn *down* is to shape the cue by using a temporary breakdown learning step: Sit on the floor with your knees bent. Lure your dog to crawl under your legs. The only way she can get the lure is by dropping all the way down and crawling a step or two under your leg. This temporary breakdown step helps your dog become familiar with moving toward the *down* position. Some dogs are not naturally comfortable doing a *down* because the position may seem too vulnerable, or they may not understand what you're asking them to do. Once you have succeeded with this temporary breakdown shaping step, continue to work it over and over as you see her become more comfortable. By breaking it down, you make it eas-ier for her to figure out what you want her to do, which decreases failure, which is always good.

Once she becomes comfortable doing the *down* this way, begin luring her under only one leg. As she succeeds with this step, you can withdraw this leg, too. When she begins to respond more quickly without having to crawl under your legs anymore, that tells you that she is getting it and trusts you to be in this vulnerable position. Remember to give your dog plenty of successful trials even if you have to proceed more slowly than you would like. Your patience will be rewarded.

Release: The Verbal Cue

YOU WANT TO BE ABLE to tell your dog that she has done a good job and is now free to take a recess from training and be on her own for a while. That's where *release* comes in. Begin to teach the cue as you finish practicing each exercise and transition into a brief play period mixed with behaviors that your dog already knows well. Mixing the total freedom of the *release* with some practice cues will keep her focused and happy to do or try out just about anything you request. If you're not at the end of a training session, but sense that your dog needs a break, limit each *release* recess period to about a minute. If your dog has too much playtime, she may lose focus and forget about you. If you're training with a partner who also has a dog, release your dogs at the same time so that they can play together.

The simplest way to teach *release* is to drop your dog's leash—assuming that you're indoors or in a fenced area so that she can't run completely away—and say "release" or "go play" with a happy voice as you pat her side, then point her to the play area. Most dogs will naturally start to play or wander around until they find a play partner or a toy. Patting her and pointing let her know that it's okay to do something else now. She may not associate the verbal cue right away, but dropping the leash and patting her serve as her cue. Eventually she will also associate the verbal and physical cue that tells her it's playtime.

We'll learn more about the *release* next week. But for now, class dismissed. In other words, "Release!"

Homework

THIS WEEK I WANT you to emphasize fundamentals that you've learned already, especially as you work with your new training partner and the partner's dog, which can be very distracting to a dog that is just learning. You'll also emphasize fundamentals in the troubleshooting exercises below. *Sit* will become an important fundamental building block as you now use real-life rewards—your dog should sit for *everything*.

SUPERVISED PLAY Find a training partner.

TROUBLESHOOTING

▶ **TETHERING** Treat your dog for focusing on you.

▶ **HAND-FEEDING** Have your dog sit to start hand-feeding.

▶ **BITE INHIBITION, HANDLING, GENTLING** Practice so that you're ready for next week.

▶ **CRATE TRAINING** Expand crate comfort with feeding and treats.

SIT Luring for real-life rewards for everything: meals, crating, going out, walks, training.

SIT Withdrawing treats and truncating the hand signal.

RECALL Luring with added distance and verbal cue *come here*.

DOWN Luring.

RELEASE Verbal cue.

Recommended Games and Activities

IN ADDITION TO REPEATING some or all the games your dog already knows, add these new games and activities (see details in Chapter Nine) to expand his interest in the fun surprises you bring.

▶ Which Hand?

▶ Supervised play with *recall* and *release*

▶ Come and Go with a partner: practice *sit* and *down*

TRAINING LOG FOR _____ DAY _____

SKILL	PROGRESS	NOTES
REAL-LIFE REWARDS SYSTEM Cue your dog to sit for everything, including all meals, at start of walks and training, before going into and exiting crate, playing.		
SIT: HAND SIGNAL, FROM LURE TO CUE Try to increase your dog's speedy response to your hand signal (visual cue) without causing failure.		
SIT: WITHDRAWING TREATS Put the treats in your other hand while cueing *sit*. Then withdraw treats slowly by using slot machine techniques.		
RECALL: INCREASE LURING DISTANCE, ADD VERBAL CUE Add *sit* at end of recall. Increase distance one step at a time. Add "[Dog's name], come here!" verbal/visual cue.		
DOWN: LURING Start from sit. Slide treat toward dog's chest then lure straight down. When dog begins following *down*, mark, praise, collar, and then treat last.		
RELEASE: VERBAL CUE Drop dog's leash, point to toy or playmate as you say "release" or "go play." Make sure that you're in a contained/fenced area.		
LEASH TETHERING At home, add random pattern walking. Help your dog anticipate your moves with your own body language and gestures.		
CRATE TRAINING & HAND-FEEDING Teach dog to love his crate. Hand-feed all meals in and around crate.		
POTTY TRAINING Keep track of input (meals and treats) and output (potty time). Note accidents.		
BITE INHIBITION, HANDLING, GENTLING "Ouch" exercise as you explore dog's mouth. Lots of gentle handling. Touch paws and all over body.		
CHOOSE AN ACTIVITY/GAME.		
CHOOSE A SOCIALIZATION EXPERIENCE.		

For free training log downloads, visit lovethatdogbook.com.

Week Three: Advancing to Verbal Cues

MY HOPE IS THAT you're seeing some progress: that your weekly training sessions, your playtime activities, and your daily repetitions of *sit, come here*, and *down* are beginning to pay off. However, it might also be the case that you or your dog are feeling completely lost. That is not uncommon in early stages of dog training; don't give up! Stick with this program and your reward will come. Time and time again, I have watched many student dogs "get it" for the first time in the final week. Review your training log and I am confident that

Now that your dog is becoming familiar with hand signals, you can begin to add the voice component to some of your cues, including *sit, recall*, and *release*. Next you'll learn about Puppy Pushups, Cookie Sit-Stays, and the first phase of the Off and Take It Trade. At the end of the chapter I'll introduce you to informal heeling, a walking exercise, plus how to tackle a common leash-walking problem: pulling. Review the games and training exercises from this chapter and previous ones, and, as always, record your progress in the log.

you'll discover small improvements that you may have overlooked: slightly faster reaction times, higher percentages of correct trials, or increased generalization. It's important that you acknowledge these small successes—they are your rewards for practicing the exercises consistently and patiently. If you're feeling overwhelmed, remember that you can always break down a behavior into smaller parts that you can string together into a full cue when you and your dog feel ready.

> Remember to acknowledge the small successes.

This week, we'll continue to build on what we've learned. We'll begin to combine *sits* with *recalls* and add the *release*. Your dog will learn to alternate between *sits* and *downs* by doing Puppy Pushups. We'll work to make walking more controlled as you learn to change direction and walk side by side in an informal heeling formation. You will also learn two new cues this week: *cookie quick sits* and the *off and take it* trade.

This week you will also add verbal cues to hand signals. Even when adding the verbal cue, I want you to maintain the hand signal so that your dog continues to focus on you. We are just naming the cue, not replacing the hand signal. As a further clarification: Add the verbal cue only if your dog is already fluent in responding to your hand signal. If she can't do that, be patient and keep practicing before you add any verbal cue. I promise, she'll get it.

Troubleshooting: Leash Pulling

IF YOUR DOG HAS ALREADY STOPPED LEASH PULLING, that's great news (and very lucky for you). But my guess is that your dog's leash walking skills are still inconsistent and you're probably itching to go on a "real walk" without his pulling. I'll take a further guess that you've given in to his demand and have allowed him to pull every once in a while. I don't blame you. Going on a walk is one of the simple joys of owning a dog, and I know the frustration of having to spend the time focusing on training rather than on just enjoying a nice stroll.

However, you must continue to be steadfast, and follow the "be a tree" activity you learned in Week One (page 81). If he starts to pull, stop moving and wait for him to focus back on you. When he turns to look at you, mark it by saying "good" and lure him as you walk backward until he returns to you, then have him sit for his reward. Then you may start walking again; all walks start with a sit and a treat while your dog is learning. Right now, walk time is about teaching your dog that the only way he walks with you is if he's on a loose leash. Allowing him to pull you just rewards him for doing so.

As you become accustomed to your dog's walking behaviors, you should also try to anticipate when he is about to pull, so that you can lure him to turn and walk in a new direction with you. Your first hint that your dog is about to pull is that his focus has drifted away from you. The second hint comes when he starts to wander too far ahead of you or turns in a direction of *his* choosing. When you anticipate this and lure him in your own new direction, his focus will return to you, even if it's just for a few seconds. This exercise will help your dog become accustomed to keeping his focus on you, even in a highly distracting environment. Play a game with yourself: See how often you can anticipate and redirect your dog's focus before he actually starts to pull. When you get back home, write down those results in your training log and see which techniques work best for your dog: "being a tree," luring, or changing directions.

This week, to practice luring your dog to follow your lead, I want you to play the Follow the Lure game that you learned about in Week One (see Chapter Nine for details). Adapt the game for walk time by palming a treat in the hand on the side where you walk your dog. I walk dogs on the left side, so I palm the treat in my left hand. The other hand holds the leash handle. Move your dog-side hand, with the palmed treat, toward your dog's nose to get his attention. Allow him to sniff the treat before luring him to follow you in a new direction. Change directions often, luring him in circles and weaving between obstacles. Make it fun with *start-stop-sit-and-turn* routines. As you learn more behaviors and cues, mix those in, too.

It will probably take a few sessions to teach your dog to follow you and the treat instead of the great smells and distractions that you're competing against. If your dog is too distracted, try this exercise indoors or in an isolated spot outside. Over time, you will build up his focus on you.

Assume that for now your walks will be not much more than glorified pacing back-and-forth, wearing a groove in the concrete if necessary. Patiently build up to a 30-second walk without pulling, even if you have to start with a 3-second walk before turning into a tree. If you chart the progress in your training log, you'll be able to appreciate your patience even more.

You may also try to solve the leash-pulling problem by using certain types of training collars, such as the Gentle Leader head harness or a no-pull body harness (the leash attaches at the dog's chest). I am opposed to using choke chains or prong collars. (See Chapter Eleven, Behavior Problems, for insights into how to use training collars with positive reinforcement dog training.)

Supervised Play: Recall and Sit Combination with Release

THIS WEEK I WANT YOU AND YOUR DOG to become fluent with the *recall-sit* combination, because we're preparing to add more skills, such as *stay*, onto this foundation. You can practice this alone or during a socialization activity with another dog. Begin by allowing your dog to play for about a minute. Then recall her by saying her name and adding the verbal cue "come here." Using a lure, have her sit in front of you. Then touch her collar as you praise and handle her, and reward her with the treat.

Next, cue *release* (see page 98). If she understands and bounds off to play for another round, then she's getting that cue. If she continues to sit, the good news is that she's obviously getting used to remaining highly focused on you, and you'll need to guide her back to playing. As you learned last week, have your dog sit, say "good dog," pat her gently on the side, and point to the play area as you say "release" or "go play." Remember to be consistent because, as you already know, dogs don't generalize very well.

Repeat this *recall-sit-release* combination at least four times in each supervised play session. The *release* part of the combination is important because your dog needs to understand that being recalled doesn't mean that playtime is over. You want her to associate recalls with just one part of her play experience, as well as with things she values, like treats, praise, and your attention and affection.

Introduce the Sit Verbal Cue Paired with Hand Signal

I T'S TIME TO PAIR THE VERBAL CUE to sit with the hand signal that you already know. As mentioned earlier, always maintain the hand signal when adding any verbal cue. It's crucial that your dog continues to focus on you. Typically, people who use choke chains are attempting to teach their dogs to rely on verbal cues and physical rebukes in order to get the dogs' attention and make them follow their commands. My opinion? If your dog is not yet fluent with your hand signal, then wait until he is.

To help him focus on this one word, do not say his name. For example, do not say, "Brieo, sit." Since you are back at learning stage #1 (acquiring a new skill), don't use the slot machine; treat him on every trial and generalize as you did previously. The moment his rump touches down, mark it with the praise "good sit."

After about six to eight repetitions like this, reintroduce the slot machine (remember, that means you'll slowly withdraw treats), but don't award any jackpots yet. Most dogs won't regress when the verbal cue is added; if yours does, it's likely that he's bored and you're not making it fun enough from his point of view. To keep your dog's interest, you can try various things: Move to a different location for each rep, spin around (most dogs love to spin), take his leash and run back and forth happily to get his spirit back up before the next rep, or simply do the reps more quickly. You may also move on to another exercise that he already knows and enjoys, and after a minute return to this one.

Remember to set your dog up for success when you pair any hand signal with its verbal cue. Once he responds with fluency to your hand signal and verbal cue together, reintroduce the slot machine to start withdrawing treats. It's okay if he tries harder to get his reward, but if he starts to lose focus and begins to fail trials, go back to a behavior that he already knows well and enjoys. Reward him for that and end the training session on a positive note, and go log it.

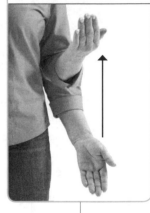

SIT HAND SIGNAL

The signal for *sit* should be very clear— you'll be using it a lot!

Puppy Pushups

PUPPY PUSHUPS ARE A QUICK SEQUENCE of *sit* and *down* and *sit*, followed by a one-treat reward. The purpose of the Puppy Pushup is to phase out food rewards while improving your dog's ability to keep her attention focused on you in all kinds of distracting environments. My colleague, Dr. Ian Dunbar, first taught me this technique a decade ago, and I have been using it in my classes ever since. I use this exercise whenever I want my dogs very focused on me: at the dog park, on the street, around people who are unfamiliar to them, or while waiting at the veterinarian's office. Success at Puppy Pushups gives your dog a familiar ritual to get her focused on you in potentially uncomfortable settings.

Your dog is ready to do Puppy Pushups if she is already fluent with both *sit* and *down* hand signals. As she repeatedly performs *sit-down-sit*, she is learning to anticipate what cue you will give next and will respond more quickly. Have several treats ready in your hand so that you can reward her immediately. Once she has become fluent with Puppy Pushups in familiar settings (having succeeded on at least 10 reps in a row), start doing them in different, less familiar settings. You may need to reteach the Puppy Pushup sequence in each new setting. But even if your dog happens to learn this skill slowly, at some point she will suddenly get it, as if to say, "Oh! I know this one. We're in a different place, but what you want me to do is always the same." Once your dog learns more behaviors, add them to the Puppy Pushups sequence. At one time I would have my Border Collie Jock sit, pose (stand), down, roll over, shake paws, wave, back up, and do an *off* cue before I would give him his dinner. Jock loved it; dogs love earning their rewards.

Stay: Cookie Sit-Stays

A CRUCIAL CUE, *STAY* BUILDS your dog's impulse control, teaching him to stay focused on you even in the face of distraction. But to get there, you must be patient and your dog must have some maturity. The first step to master the *cookie sit* (more on that in a second), because it teaches him to remain seated and always focused on you in the face of a distraction (a cookie).

COOKIE SIT-STAY

Use the *cookie sit-stay* to teach your dog to focus on you while staying (and sitting). Having your dog's complete focus will help you to calm and control him during distractions. The *cookie sit-stay* is one of two techniques you and your dog will learn for staying on cue during this five-week Fundamentals Training Program (turn the page for the Conventional Stay). It is important to learn both techniques; they can be lifesavers.

ESTABLISH EYE CONTACT

Touch a treat to your dog's nose, then bring the treat to your face. Place the hand that holds the leash on your hip.

TOSS TREAT

Toss it about three feet in front of your dog, depending on his size.

HAND GLUED TO HIP

Tense that arm tight so your dog won't be able to reach the treat. Don't yank the leash, just stand still.

DOG REFOCUSES

When your dog finally looks at you, mark it (say "good").

TAKE IT!

Point to the treat and say "take it." Slacken the leash so your dog can reach the treat; mark and praise when he takes it.

To begin this exercise, start with your dog on his leash, sitting at the side on which you walk him. Hold the leash an arm's length from where it clips to your dog's collar. Place the hand that holds the leash on your hip.

CONVENTIONAL STAY

In addition to the *cookie sit-stay* (see page 107), the Conventional Stay technique helps your dog acquire the hand signal for this important cue. Start with just this visual hand signal; add the verbal cue "stay" once he becomes fluent.

❶ AS YOUR DOG SITS . . .
show him an open palm (hand signal) as you touch a treat to his nose and then bring it to your face.

❷ MARK, PRAISE, REWARD
Mark your dog's stay (say "good") as you praise him, then reward him with the treat.

Now, do a set of Puppy Pushups (*sit-down-sit*) using *both* verbal and visual cues. Next, touch a treat gently to your dog's nose to get him focused on it, then toss it about three feet in front of him. If you have a small-ish dog, toss it a bit nearer; if you have a big dog, a bit farther. As your dog jumps for the treat and tries to pull the leash, tense that arm tight against your hip (and use your body weight to keep steady) so that he will have only that arm's length of leash play. Don't yank the leash; just keep your hand glued to your hip. After one second, cue *sit* (both verbal and hand cue). As soon as he sits, say "take it" and let go of the leash (you may pick up the handle with your other hand). Your dog will probably dash right for the treat. Mark and praise that, and do another trial.

On these reps, pay particular attention to your dog's focus on you. When your dog understands the importance of focus, he will sit more quickly and wait for you to send him. You'll notice his body language calm down as he realizes that he'll get the reward as soon as he sits. If he does not take the treat, step forward to help him take it successfully, then try another rep.

If your dog doesn't sit right away, don't give the *sit* cue again. Remember: Saying "sit-sit-sit-sit-sit" only teaches a dog not to pay attention until the fifth cue. Instead, after a few seconds, watch for your dog to look at you and then request the *sit*. When that happens, mark it (say "good"), and send him to *take it*. (Make sure there's enough play in the leash for him to reach the treat without pulling.)

After a few days of practice, your dog will probably be sitting quickly and consistently (for at least a full second before you cue *take it*). It's now time to add the *stay* hand signal and verbal cue (see the next section for more details), and wait three to five seconds before you send him to *take it*, and then mark and reward that. With the hand that is not gluing the leash to your hip, gently touch the treat to your dog's nose, and then toss it. Then cue your dog to *sit* (mark it "good"), and then gently put an open palm toward your dog's face and calmly say "stay." Count silently for three seconds, tell him quietly and calmly "good stay," wait another second, and then cue him to *take it*, using your hand signal to point him toward the treat along with the verbal cue.

If that succeeds, count silently for four seconds on the next trial. Add another second for each successful trial; subtract a second for each mistake. Find the amount of time that your dog can *stay* comfortably without failure, and increase the time slowly from there.

If your dog is highly motivated by toys, then once he has built up his *cookie sit-stay* to about 30 seconds, change to throwing a ball or a special squeaky toy instead of a treat. Also use the *cookie sit-stay* at mealtime to teach your dog to sit when it's time for him to be fed, which decreases jumping and teaches good manners.

Stay—Another Way to Teach the Cue

SOME DOGS LEARN *STAY* quickly, but if yours is having trouble, you can try two additional approaches. First, start with her sitting in front of you. Touch a treat to her nose and then to your eyes, to encourage her to keep looking at you. After a second, calmly mark "good" and reward her with the treat. While she is still sitting, take out another treat and repeat the exercise. On subsequent trials, add the verbal cue "stay," while using the hand signal of an open palm close to your dog's face (or alternatively, wave your hand in front of her eyes) before you give her the treat. Little by little add an extra second until you reach 10 seconds, and then add 2 seconds for each successful trial until you reach 20 seconds, ultimately building up to 1 minute. Beyond 1 minute, add 10 seconds to each trial. Beyond 2 minutes, add 20 seconds to each trial until you reach 3 minutes. At the end of a training session (after you mark, praise, and reward the final successful *sit*), release your dog and reward her with lots of high-energy praise for sitting so still. Then switch to another training game (see Chapter Nine) that your dog enjoys and can do successfully.

If your dog starts to fail a trial by getting up out of the *sit*, resist the urge to force her back into the *stay*, especially if she fails just a few seconds shy of a longtime success. Instead, reduce the amount of time that she is in the *stay* position to a time frame in which she can be successful, and then practice reps in that time frame until she shows you that she is ready to stay longer.

To keep your dog interested in succeeding on those long stays, do a couple of short stays as warm-up trials, and again after the long trials. Be sure to jackpot your dog as she completes these longer trials. In your dog's training log, record the times—the failures as well as the successes—to help you know how long to have her stay on the next trial.

A *stay* is a great exercise to throw in randomly during evening hours to teach your dog not to beg at your dinner table and to relax while you watch TV or read this book. You might want to prepare a stuffed Kong, request that she lie down, and give her the Kong when she follows through on your cue. After a few minutes of chewing, interrupt her by taking away the Kong. Cue her to *sit-stay* (for about 10 seconds if she can reliably already do at least that much time), and then mark and praise her and give her the Kong again. After another couple of minutes, interrupt her and take the Kong away again, cue her to *sit* and enjoy about 10 seconds of fun together, such as a good belly rub if she likes that, or a quick round of Which Hand (see Chapter Nine). Then praise her again and cue her to *sit*. As soon as she sits, give her the Kong again, and resume enjoying what you were doing. Each time you take away the Kong, do something a little different or change the sequence of cues to have her earn it back.

Off and Take It Trades: Phase 1

THE *OFF* CUE MEANS "DON'T TOUCH." It teaches your dog to stop a certain behavior, such as sticking his nose in the garbage, carrying your favorite shoe, trying to cross the threshold of a door that you just opened, or hoarding the Kong you gave him a couple of minutes ago. *Off* is a clear way to communicate to your dog that certain boundaries are not to be crossed without your permission.

When your dog is first learning *off*, the cue must be paired with the *take it* cue (except for boundary limits, which I'll discuss in the next chapter). The combination is based on the trade concept: that giving something up will get him something of equal or greater value in return. So, in this exercise, you'll be teaching your dog two cues: *off*, which means "don't touch," and *take it*, which gives him permission to come forward and take the item. Next week, we'll take this activity a step further to the trading stage. The trade will teach your dog not to run away and try to get you to chase him when he has stolen some contraband, by showing him that if he lets go of the illegal object, he'll be rewarded with a trade for something that he values just as much or even more.

Let's begin with the basics: the *take it* part of the lesson. With your dog in front of you (I prefer that he stand, but sitting is okay), put about six treats in your closed hand. Shift one treat to your fingertips and steady your hand against your knee at your dog's nose level, and say "take it." Let him come forward and take the treat, as you mark it (say "good" or "good take it"). Do another rep right away by shifting another treat to your fingertips (your hand stays against your knee), and repeat the *take it* and marker steps. Then repeat again with a third treat.

On the fourth repetition, you'll begin teaching your dog the *off* command. Shift a fourth treat in your fingertips (keep your

OFF AND TAKE IT

Begin teaching your dog to keep *off* something by pairing it with the *take it* cue. This communicates that certain boundaries cannot be crossed without your permission.

① SAY "TAKE IT"
Place your closed hand (holding six treats) on your leg. Shift one treat to fingertips and say "take it." Mark and reward. Repeat sequence two times.

② KEEP QUIET
On the fourth sequence, don't say "take it." Keep quiet for just a moment as your dog sniffs the treat.

③ SAY "OFF!"
Speak loudly and sharply, to be slightly shocking. When your dog backs off and looks at you, happily say "good, take it" and offer her the fifth treat. Repeat, and treat her again.

CATCH YOUR DOG DOING SOMETHING THAT YOU LIKE

This is an exercise for *you*, not your dog: Your job is to reward good behavior that your dog offers on his own. When your dog does something that you like without being asked, joyfully mark it by saying "good sit" or "good down" or "good stay" or "good heel." Add praise and, on occasion, a treat or other reward such as a great ear or belly rub. Encourage his good manners now and you will get a spirited, curious dog that volunteers even more good manners in the future. It is simple psychology: What gets rewarded gets reinforced, what gets ignored disappears . . . Yes, it works on humans, too.

Your dog may start to offer *sit* or another behavior in hopes of getting a reward. This is his way of saying "please." Remember, the more often you catch him doing something that you like, the more likely he is to offer that behavior again. If he develops a habit of offering one particular behavior, continue to praise it, but offer treats randomly. Some breeds get bored easily and want to do something—anything—with you or they become demanding, so you need to recognize and encourage the good things that they do. Jot down these volunteered good behaviors in your training log and you will begin to observe your dog's patterns.

hand against your knee), but this time close your hand around the treat and do not say "take it." Almost all dogs will attempt to get that treat before you say "take it." When your dog tries to take the treat, say "off" in a firm and deep voice. Imagine you're a singer hitting a deep bass note when you say it. You want the *off* command to be sudden and loud enough to be slightly shocking, so that it interrupts your dog's focus on the treat without scaring off his whiskers. Typically, the dog will back away and look curiously at you as if he is thinking "What happened? Why didn't you give me the treat?"

The moment he backs away, mark it by saying "good, take it" in your soothing happy tone of voice and praise him while giving him the treat. Once he has a couple of successful *off* and *take it* trades, do another repetition, adding one additional second before you say "take it." As he continues to succeed, increase the time between *off* and *take it* up to five seconds. If, on the other hand, your dog doesn't try to take it on the first try, then say "good" and cue him to *take it*—there is no sense in teaching him the *off* yet. You'll need to get some really great treats that your dog can't resist and entice him even more with extra rounds of *take its* as you lull him into the pattern before you teach the *off*.

To help your dog distinguish the *off* and *take it* verbal cues, mix the pattern: Sometimes use just the *take it*, other times add the *off*. Once your dog has acquired these basics and is progressing toward fluency, it is time to begin teaching him to generalize this valuable skill by doing *offs* and *take its* with toys and his food bowl.

Don't underestimate the importance of this exercise; it's a necessary step toward becoming a well-socialized dog. It helps prevent food guarding and resource guarding, the potentially dangerous behavior in which your dog may bite any hand that comes near his food or things he tries to "own," such as toys or food bowls. *Off* skills also provide you with an opportunity to reinforce your dog's bite inhibition skills. If he mouths your arm or hand, for example, you can say "off" and know he will eventually mouth more gently to the point of not mouthing at all. Throw in a startled "ouch" if your dog mouths you.

Walking Exercise: Informal Heeling

AS YOU KNOW, I don't think most dogs need to perform an extended, perfect heel; it's a fairly advanced skill that requires more concentration than most dogs can successfully muster at this level of training. But you do want to start practicing *informal* heeling, an advanced form of walking by your side that will keep her closely focused on you while walking in typical real-life situations: around your neighborhood, town, city, and in stores and work environments.

Teach your dog the informal heel using your regular walking leash, held across your body. Your dog will learn to anticipate your

THREE WAYS TO WALK YOUR DOG

Enjoy walking with your dog in a variety of situations.

FORMAL HEEL
Advanced technique; you and your dog are fully focused on each other. Used when there is traffic or significant distractions, and in competition.

INFORMAL HEEL
Your dog walks at your side, but focus is not full. Leash is slightly slack.

LOOSE LEASH
You started loose leash walking in the "be a tree" exercise (Week One). Loose leash walking can be used as a reward for good heeling. It allows your dog to sniff, roam a little, and be a dog.

walking changes by your changing body language, and you will learn to anticipate her changes, such as when it's time to sniff, go potty, or explore the world as a dog. The tethering exercises you've been doing at home will help a lot with this.

Start practicing the informal heel indoors, where there are few distractions. First, ask your dog to sit at your side. Say "ready" to cue her to look up at you, and mark and treat her when she does. Then walk forward four steps, marking and praising her if she follows and stays focused on you. Stop and immediately lure her to sit, then mark and reward her. Repeating this sequence (*walk-stop-sit, walk-stop-sit*) over and over will teach your dog to focus on you with a heads-up heeling gait as you walk together.

Next, practice this *walk-stop-sit* exercise while you're outside. Walk two or three quick steps, stop, and lure her to sit. Once your dog is focused enough to do the exercise fluently, start changing directions, adding *downs* and *cookie sit-stays*, doing a round of Puppy Pushups, or any other skill that your dog has already acquired. Do not teach new skills during heeling; keep your dog successful at this level by combining skills that she has already acquired.

If you're consistent in rewarding her for heeling, she will try to figure out how to get more treats and will learn that it happens when she walks at your side. When you reward your dog for staying close to you, she will, over time, be less likely to forge ahead of you to rush into the doggy park, chase the squirrels, greet another dog, or just pull on that leash for no apparent reason. Heeling also promotes good bonding.

Homework

ALTHOUGH YOUR DOG has learned a couple of new skills this week, most of your homework should emphasize strengthening the foundation that you already have. These fundamentals are building blocks for the new skills. Almost every elite athlete and coach emphasizes practicing fundamentals over and over again. That is also true for dog training. If you spend all your training time learning new skills, your dog can easily forget what he already knows, what you have already put so much effort into teaching him. As you practice these new skills, make your fundamentals consistently excellent.

WALKING (FUNDAMENTALS) "Be a Tree," play Follow the Lure.

WALKING (NEW SKILL) Informal heeling with *walk-stop-sit-walk-stop-sit* exercise.

SIT (FUNDAMENTALS) Luring and hand signal.

SIT (NEW SKILL) Verbal cue combined with hand signal (don't give the verbal cue without also giving the hand signal).

PUPPY PUSHUPS (FUNDAMENTALS) Keeps dog's focus on you and sharpens cues.

COOKIE SIT-STAY (FUNDAMENTALS) Use *cookie-sit* fundamental as building block for new *sit-stay* skill.

SIT-STAY (NEW SKILL) Build up *sit stay* time with lots of rewards.

OFF AND TAKE IT TRADE, PHASE 1 (NEW SKILL) Practice this completely new skill.

Training Games and Activities

SO THAT PRACTICING FUNDAMENTALS doesn't become boring for your dog, make it fun. Keep her focused on the lure with games like Follow the Lure (see page 153), and focused on you with the Eye-Contact Exercise (page 151). Rather than introduce a new game to your dog, see how you can adapt existing games to strengthen both her fundamentals and her new skills. For example, play Come and Go (page 152) with the added requirement at each lap of doing a set of Puppy Pushups that starts and ends with a *sit*. Play Find Me (Hide-and-Seek) (page 150) with some more difficult hiding places, using your partner to hold your dog. If she is able to remain sitting and staying while you leave the room without using a partner, try playing Find Me without a partner—as long as you hide quickly in easy-to-find hiding places. Remember that *staying* while you're out of sight may be too advanced for her maturity level and training history, so do your best to set your dog up for success.

WEEK **3**

TRAINING LOG FOR _____ DAY _____

SKILL	PROGRESS	NOTES
WALKING Add informal heeling with walk-stop-sit-walk-stop-sit exercise. Troubleshoot leash pulling with "be a tree," leash tethering, Follow the Lure.		
SIT: ADD VERBAL CUE Combine the verbal cue with hand signal throughout this training program. Continue giving clear hand signals.		
PUPPY PUSHUPS *Sit-down-sit.* Mark each *sit, down,* and *sit.* Praise, touch collar, and treat at end of each cycle. Sharpen dog's response to cues and focus on you.		
COOKIE SIT-STAY "Glue" leash hand to hip, touch treat to dog's nose, and toss it beyond dog's reach. Cue *sit* (then mark). Then send to *take it,* mark and praise.		
SIT-STAY (ALTERNATIVE METHOD) Dog sits, touch treat to dog's nose, then hold between your eyes. Increase dog's focus on you. Increase time when successful.		
OFF & TAKE IT: PHASE 1 Hold six treats, shift 1 to fingers, say "take it." On 4th rep keep quiet: If dog tries to get it, say "off" sharply. As dog looks at you, say "take it."		
RECALL & SIT COMBO WITH RELEASE After each minute of supervised play, *recall* ("come here") and *sit* (mark, praise, touch collar, reward). Release to play again.		
CATCH YOUR DOG DOING SOMETHING YOU LIKE Evaluate yourself. How well do you recognize and acknowledge your dog for offering behaviors without being asked?		
POTTY TRAINING Keep track of input (meals and treats) and output (potty time). Note accidents.		
BASELINE BEHAVIORS Crate training, hand-feeding, bite inhibition, handling and gentling.		
CHOOSE AN ACTIVITY/GAME.		
CHOOSE A SOCIALIZATION EXPERIENCE.		

For free training log downloads, visit lovethatdogbook.com.

Week Four: Completing the Foundation

THIS WEEK MARKS THE LAST WEEK of the Fundamentals Training Program in which your dog will learn new skills (next week we'll review). With this solid training foundation, your dog will have good manners in the vast majority of typical real-life situations, and will be prepared to move into more advanced training and activities.

Before you begin this lesson, take a moment to remember that a well-trained, spirited dog is given plenty of opportunities for success and acknowledgment in everyday situations. Make it a habit to catch your

In this chapter you'll learn the final key components of the Fundamentals Training Program, all of which have major real-life implications. By adding distractions and distance to what your dog has already learned, you'll test his focus while solidifying his understanding of his new skills. You'll add a verbal cue to *down*, learn the *standing pose*, and follow up with the second phase of the *off and take it* trades. Teach your dog to navigate the stairs carefully and confidently, to react calmly to the doorbell and the arrival of visitors, and to respect the boundaries you set for him. Practicing with the training games and activities is important as always, as is keeping a record in your training log.

dog offering behaviors that you like, and then mark that good behavior. Keep treats ready so that you can reward those spontaneous moments. (I keep airtight cups filled with treats around my home so they are always ready, placed high enough on shelves so that no dog can reach them.) Treating your dog for volunteered behaviors will add to his reinforcement history and encourage him to offer more good behaviors without being asked.

Be mindful: Lead your dog with spirit.

Remember to praise your dog's improvements during socialization opportunities, such as when he reacts more calmly to other dogs and people.

Please remember to keep your dog on the real-life reward system, in which you consistently ask him to sit for everything he gets from you: food, water, toys, playtime, and walks. The more consistent you are with this approach, the more quickly your dog will understand that his good manners are more than a training exercise—good manners earn him things that he values. With the real-life reward approach, you'll soon have a more self-confident dog that will offer and repeat behaviors because he knows that there is a reward in his future.

These first weeks of dog training are like building a house: The foundation is mostly invisible when you look at the finished product, but without that foundation the house won't stand. Regardless of how well you think you and your dog are doing, you both deserve to be acknowledged for all the hours you have put in. Keep in mind that your dog *is* making progress even if he doesn't always show it. If you review your training log, you'll appreciate the strong training foundation you have built.

In Chapter Four I shared with you some thoughts about "spiriting" the relationship with your dog. A spirited relationship is confident, trusting, consistently growing, and vibrant. This week, I want you to be mindful to lead your dog with spirit. In those moments when you feel that spirit's joyful warmth in your heart, please express it to your dog. If a blessing is something you already do in your life, bless your dog, your relationship with him, and yourself for being such a spirited dog owner who is making a difference in the life of one of God's marvelous creations. If blessing is not something you do, then take this opportunity to appreciate your dog's special gifts—every dog has them. Many people discover their own special gifts through good relationships with their loved dogs. My hope is that this mutual appreciation you and your dog have for each other will uplift both of you.

Recalls: Adding Distractions and More Distance

THIS WEEK, we'll advance your dog's recall skill by adding distractions. Let's also generalize your dog's experience by practicing recalls in a variety of places, including outdoor locations (if you think that your dog is ready). You'll still need to work with a partner. When you practice outdoors, train only in fenced-in areas, or with your dog on a leash that is at least 20 feet long or is tied securely to a long rope. (You don't want your dog running away!) Choose a location free of other dogs, traffic, or people; the new smells will be distracting enough at first.

In this exercise, while your partner holds your dog's leash, joyfully tease her with a treat for a moment. Turn your back to them and run away. When you get about six to eight feet away, turn around quickly, get down on your knees, open your arms wide, and joyfully call out "come here!" (This is the Lassie Recall we learned in Chapter Five; see page 95.) If your partner observes that your dog remained focused on you as you ran away, he releases your dog. As she runs toward you, continue to act extremely excited. When she arrives, praise her and touch her all over, especially on the collar, as you reward her with the treat. On subsequent recalls, add a *sit* or *down* before your dog actually catches you; she will learn to control her impulses—and you'll be safer if an excited dog isn't jumping all over you or tugging at your clothing. As you build up the distance, keep in mind that the ability to do this exercise at *any* distance with new distractions is more important than doing it at a longer distance. When you practice at a new location with new distractions, decrease the distance. It will increase upon successful practice.

If, however, your partner observes that your dog looked away as you ran from her, you need to keep working to train her to stay focused on you. The first step: Your partner doesn't release her. Instead, he happily runs her to you for your reward and praise.

There are a number of reasons your dog may initially "fail" this exercise: You're not acting excited enough, she isn't focused in the moment (and may need a short play-training break that you know she'll succeed at and enjoy), or there are too many distractions in the environment. Try a less distracting location, such as a long hallway indoors. Or try using a favorite squeaky toy instead of a treat. If even that doesn't work, then continue the earlier recall exercises from Week Two, or try the Come and Go game described in Chapter Nine.

Once your dog becomes fluent with this recall exercise, it's time to add a game of Hide-and-Seek. While your partner holds the leash, run away and let your dog see you duck behind a hiding spot. Then *recall* her. When she finds you, jackpot and praise the heck out of her. After all, not only did she *recall* successfully, but she made an extra effort to find you. Dogs love surprises like this. Once yours succeeds in finding you in those easy hiding spots, you can add to the fun, and the challenge, by making your hiding places a little more difficult to find.

Stay: Adding Distractions and Distance

ANOTHER WAY TO IMPROVE your dog's impulse control is to add distractions as you keep him in a *stay*. Start teaching this skill by having your dog *sit* and *stay* as you move a step away from him. Allow him to *stay* for a moment, and then return to him with praise and a treat. If your dog can't sit still for even one step, just lift your foot off the ground (as if you are about to take a step) and put it back down, and continue doing that until you can make that first step without his moving.

On the next trial, take a step in a different direction. Once your dog understands that your little movements aren't worth getting excited or anxious about, add a couple more steps, making an arc around your dog. As you move around, watch him carefully; most dogs have difficulty sitting still when they can't see their owners. Get to know your dog's body language; that will help you know instinctively if he is losing focus and about to move. For example, if he turns his head, that could be a sign that he is about to move his body. Before he moves, mark it ("good") and return to him. If he has moved, ignore it and realize that you need to break it down into smaller steps (and log it). Eventually, with practice and good timing, you will be able to circle all the way around your dog as he remains seated without turning around. Help him generalize this skill by practicing in a variety of places around your home, and then add outdoor locations with distractions when you feel that he is ready.

Down: Naming the Behavior

I'M HOPING THAT last week's Puppy Pushups helped you modify both the *sit* and *down* hand signals. This week, please continue practicing Puppy Pushups as we add the verbal *down* cue to the hand signal.

To begin, pretend to hold a treat in the hand you use to cue your dog, and lure her into the *down* position. As soon as she begins to commit to going down, say "down," praise her, and reward her with a treat that you have hidden in your other hand. This technique teaches your dog two things at the same time: First, she begins to understand that the food doesn't need to be in the luring hand in order for her to get the treat. Second, she is beginning to learn that this behavior is named "down." Learning two things at the same time challenges your dog, building her confidence and positive reinforcement history.

When your dog performs the *down* as you give both hand signal and verbal cue, award a jackpot. The other option, and one of my favorites, is to do another series of Puppy Pushups. Instead of asking your dog to sit, as you did last week, bring her to the *down* position and back to the *sit* using both the visual and verbal cues. You will find that this quick rhythm of pushups helps teach her to work more behaviors for less food.

Standing Pose

IT'S IMPORTANT THAT YOUR DOG LEARNS the *standing pose* (on all four legs) for a number of reasons (some of which I have mentioned)—for grooming, veterinary checkups, wiping muddy feet, tick checks. (During dog shows, dogs are required to hold still for the judge's examination in the *standing pose*, which is also called a *stand* or *stack*.) Teaching your dog to *pose* also takes training up a notch, because having a third position in his repertoire (along with the *sit* and *down*) means he can't as easily guess which cue is coming next. In the Puppy Pushup pattern, he knows that *down* always follows *sit* and *sit* always follows *down*. By adding the *standing pose*, he has to focus more intently on your instructions; he no longer knows for certain which cue will come after *sit*, *down*, or *pose*.

I prefer the verbal cue "pose" because it sounds much different from the other verbal cues your dog is now learning, while

LURE TO STANDING POSE

Posing (also called *standing*) is important for your dog to master for grooming, vet checkups, tick checks, and wiping muddy feet. The *pose* also adds a third posture (the others being *sit* and *down*), which makes your cueing sequence less predictable for your dog.

SHOW THE LURE

At your dog's heel side, start with her sitting. Hold a treat in front of her nose and lure forward so that (like the puppy in the photo) her natural movement is to stand up and sniff the treat.

MOVE IT FORWARD

Slowly move the lure forward so that your dog stands up all the way to sniff it. Don't let her eat the treat quite yet.

WATCH HER POSTURE

The moment your dog stands up fully, mark it (say "good"), praise her, and then let her eat the treat.

the verbal cue "stand" sounds too similar to "sit" and "stay." But before you teach the verbal cue, start by luring your dog to *pose* from the *sit* position. Stand at his side and hold a treat in front of his nose. After he sniffs it, slowly move the lure away from him in a forward direction, keeping it level with his nose so that his natural movement will be to stand up in order to sniff the treat. Once he's up on all fours and sniffing the treat, stop moving your luring hand and mark it (say "good"), praise him, and let him have the treat. As you repeat this exercise, your dog will perform each *pose* a little better and with a more relaxed posture than the last rep. As he does so, modify your motion into a hand signal by luring with an open palm (use your thumb to hold the treat in your palm). When he poses, mark it (say "good"), move the hand toward him, and reward him with the treat. He will learn that the open palm moving forward is his signal to pose, and will wait in anticipation of getting a treat as you move your hand toward him. With this technique, you can now increase your dog's ability to hold the *pose* by delaying your hand movement toward him as he waits for the treat. At first, delay giving him the treat by just one second, and then build up time on subsequent reps as he becomes successful. He doesn't need to hold the *pose* position for more than 30 seconds, which is just enough time to inspect him or go through a brief grooming ritual.

Once your dog has acquired a consistent lured *pose* with the new hand signal, retrain the whole cue while positioned on the other side of him. Once he becomes fluent with what you're asking him to do from both sides, it's time to add the verbal cue. Introduce the verbal cue—the word "pose"—once you have lured him all the way up and he is standing in front of your hand. At that point, mark the behavior, praise him, and give him the treat. Practice that sequence until he approaches fluency.

Your final step is to reteach the *pose* starting at the *down* position. My experience with most dogs is that once dogs become fluent at the *pose* starting from the *sit*, they tend to understand the same hand signal and verbal cue from the *down* fairly quickly.

Off and Take It Trades: Phase 2

THIS WEEK I WANT YOU TO BEGIN conditioning your dog to give up items without resistance, by using the *off* cue. When you cue your dog *off*, remember to pair that cue with a valuable *take it:* Offer something of equal or greater value than what you're asking him to give up. This is not just a learning exercise but a real-life lesson. One time, my Flat-Coated Retriever, Merit, brought me a whole cooked chicken carcass that he had stolen off the kitchen counter after dinner. Most dogs would have gobbled it down right there. But not Merit. He was so well conditioned to bring contraband to me for *off and take it* trades that he proudly dropped the carcass right in my lap. I was afraid that Merit might have eaten some of the chicken bones, which are dangerous to dogs, but I shouldn't have worried. He brought the carcass fully intact and his mouth betrayed no sign of chicken bones or chicken breath. Immediately, I thanked and praised the heck out of him as he proudly wagged his tail and followed me back into the kitchen, where I prepared a great stuffed Kong for him. Had I trained the *off* without the *take it* trade, Merit would have had no incentive to bring me the chicken in the first place. Instead, he would have eaten it all, leaving no traces behind. There are two morals to this story: (1) teach your dog to trade *off* for *take it*, and (2) don't leave contraband on any table or countertop that your dog can jump to and surf.

By the way, it may seem as if I rewarded Merit for stealing the chicken carcass, but let's think it through. I rewarded Merit's *last* behavior, which was bringing me the contraband. If I were teaching him to steal an object from the countertop, I would need to have been in the kitchen to mark and reward the steal the moment he got that bird in his mouth.

You can also use the *off and take it* trade to eliminate some bad behaviors. Here's another example. I had a client dog—we'll call him Sneezy—that liked to chew tissues, especially used ones. Yuck. I showed Sneezy a tissue and told him "take it." Sneezy took it. The moment he started to chew on the tissue, I held a treat on his nose. Sneezy dropped the tissue and took the treat without any cues. Although Sneezy liked the tissues, he didn't like them as much as really good dog treats. Later, we worked an *off* into it by doing the *off and take it* trade. Sneezy not only stopped chewing tissues, he took tissues to his owner if he found them in a wastebasket.

To get ready to teach your dog the *off and take it* trade, gather one or two things that she values, such as a really good treat or a special toy. Start with *off* at her food bowl. The hand-feeding exercises have been teaching her not to guard her food; now it is time to take away her food bowl while she is eating. First, drop some really good food (such as small cuts of hard cheese) near her food bowl. As your dog moves away from the bowl to eat the cheese, pick up the bowl. When she finishes eating the cheese and looks up at you holding her bowl, say "good," then put it back down for her. Practice this a few times to make sure she is comfortable with your taking away her food bowl.

Next, offer your dog a handful of food; if she leaves her bowl to eat from your hand, mark it by saying "good" and praise her as she eats from your hand. When she finishes, drop some extra food in her bowl to show her that when your hand reaches toward the bowl, it means that you are giving something good, not taking away her food. Once you practice this enough to see that she is very comfortable with your hand reaching toward her bowl, try saying "off" while you hold a stuffed Kong for her to see. As she focuses on the Kong, cue "take it." As soon as she takes the Kong, pick up her bowl and let her see you put more food in it. Now cue *off* again and show her the bowl. As she drops the Kong and focuses on the bowl, cue "take it." Continue switching between her food bowl and the Kong for the rest of the meal, and allow her to finish the goodies from the Kong, too.

Practice *off and take it* trades often, because you are conditioning your dog to be comfortable with you and your hands around her food, toys, and bowls. It is easy for all animals (including humans) to slip back into impulsive behavior or to guard items they cherish. Make sure also to experiment with *off and take it* trades using special toys and other objects that can be chewed safely, so that when your dog gets hold of something you prize dearly—such as your new shoes—or a yucky tissue, she'll be willing to make the trade for something other than food.

CONTRABAND TRADES

When your dog has gotten hold of some contraband, such as a shoe, teach him to let go of it by trading for an object that he values equally or greater. I recommend a special toy or maybe a stuffed Kong that's ready in the fridge or freezer.

CATCH HIM IN THE ACT

Put the valuable trade object behind your back as you calmly approach your dog chewing on contraband.

GET EYE CONTACT

Say "off" sharply; when your dog releases the contraband, mark it (say "good"). When he refocuses on you, mark that, too.

OFFER THE TRADE

Let your dog sniff the trade object. Typically, he will drop the contraband, and you can put your foot on it as you make the trade. Praise, touch his collar, and give him the object.

Climbing Stairs with Confidence and Safety

IT'S NORMAL FOR A PUPPY TO BE UNSURE or even fearful about climbing stairs. I advise teaching your puppy to climb up before climbing down: Looking upward is generally not as scary. The best way to teach a puppy to climb up is to start at the step just below the top, and lure him up. Praise him profusely, because this is literally a big step for him! After your puppy has mastered one step, place him on the second step from the top, then three steps from the top, then four, and so forth. Start close to the goal at first so your puppy can have success reaching the top right away. That will build up his confidence for increasing the distance to that goal.

Once your puppy has mastered going up three or four steps at a time, start teaching him to go downstairs. Attach some netting to keep a puppy or small dog from slipping between stair posts, if you're cautious like I am, and make sure you have lots of treats on hand. Begin at the step closest to the bottom, then increase one step at a time, as you did when you taught your puppy to go upstairs. If the stairs are open-backed (without risers), which can make some dogs fearful, then build your dog's confidence by teaching him first on stairs that are closed-backed (with risers).

Until you're sure that he has confidence and coordination to climb stairs in both directions with your supervision, prevent an accident by blocking off all stairs with baby gates. And even once he has become more sure-footed, use baby gates to keep him off the stairs and from wandering into rooms unsupervised.

If you want your dog to have access to the stairs, he must learn not to bound up or down ahead of you. For safety and control, he must climb stairs safely at your side; otherwise, he may push or trip you. Both have happened to me. Ouch.

To teach safe stair climbing behavior, try this exercise: Attach your dog to a short leash so that he can't get ahead of you or lag behind (but make sure the leash isn't so short that it pulls his collar). Keep him on leash and position him between you and the wall. Use your leg to cross in front of his chest area, taking one slow step at a time to maintain his pace and block him from rushing ahead of you. On most staircases, this means that in one direction you will need to walk with him on the side opposite to what you have been teaching him. Take the stairs one step at a time, marking, praising, and rewarding for each step. If he tries to get ahead, immediately close the space with your leg (unless it's unsafe). Pause after each step. To let your dog know that you'll now take the next step together, give him a hand signal such as patting your leg gently or pointing ahead.

When you reach the top (or bottom) of the staircase, always request a *sit;* that will slow him down. Once he has good impulse control and can take the stairs by your side one step at a time, increase to two steps at a time, and so forth. Move slowly! Remember that your leg is keeping your dog from rushing ahead, so you need to move deliberately—and with good balance—in case he gets rambunctious. In time, add the verbal cue "slow" for each step as you continue stair training.

When you're about to take the first step onto a staircase, I also recommend adding both visual and verbal cues if your dog already focuses well on you. To add these cues, begin by asking him to sit. Then say "stairs" and proceed as mentioned above.

Until your dog is fluent with your stair-climbing protocol, cue him for *every* step, using the visual signal (patting your leg or pointing), and then add the verbal cue "slow" when he is ready. As your dog masters this skill, you'll be able to withdraw the visual cue and verbal reminder for each step.

Boundary Training: Doors

FOR YOUR DOG'S SAFETY and the comfort of your visitors, it is essential that she obey your boundaries: no

SAFE STAIR CLIMBING

Climbing stairs together is safest if your dog stays by your side. Otherwise, she may push or trip you.

GET HER FOCUS
Before you take a first step, have your dog sit and focus on you.

ONE STEP AT A TIME
You step first, blocking your dog from going ahead. Mark, praise, and reward for each step. Move slowly!

SIT AT THE END
This extra *sit* at the bottom (or top) teaches your dog not to dash at the end.

jumping on guests, no dashing through open doors or up stairs, no going into rooms or onto furniture that are off-limits, no paws on the kitchen floor just after you've cleaned it. The *off* cue is one tool in boundary training. Let's begin to use this cue to train your dog to sit and wait at the front door while you open it to go outside, or for visitors to come in. You should be very consistent with this: Whenever you open a door, your dog must wait for you to go through it before she follows you. It is important that you cross the threshold ahead of your dog so that you can prepare for and manage her for what is going on in the next room (or outdoors), such as another dog, a child, or something in the environment that might trigger her to jump or try to dash ahead of you.

You will start door training by teaching your dog to mind your directions at interior doors, and you'll graduate to exiting your own front door. Begin by having your dog sit at a doorway inside your home while on leash. After she sits, say "off" and then open the door slightly. If she moves out of the *sit*, immediately close the door and wait a second or two before trying again. Keep doing this exercise until she remains sitting as you open the door, even if it's just slightly ajar. When she does so, tell her "good" and open the door all the way so that you can lead her through the doorway, with the same signal you use to begin a walk: Perhaps it's a hand pointing the way or a pat-pat to your thigh as you take the first step.

Now that your dog has had her first taste of success, challenge her on subsequent trials by requiring her to wait for you to open the door a little wider before you mark "good," praise her, and open the door the rest of the way and lead her through. Remember to cue *off* before you start to open the door on each rep. The goal is to have your dog remain sitting in front of the open doorway after you have told her "off" and opened the door all the way, until you lead her through with you. If she hesitates to follow you, try luring her over the boundary by saying "come here."

Once your dog has become fluent with sitting on cue before you lead her through a variety of interior doors, it's time to allow her to remain standing until she follows you through those same doorways. Start by saying "off" the moment before you open the door a little bit. If she stands still, take one small step across the threshold, mark it (say "good"), open the door all the way, and allow her to follow you (by using your signal when you start walking). As soon as you've both gone through the doorway, cue her to *sit* (then mark, praise, and reward when she's successful). Deleting the *sit* before going through the door helps her understand that *off* always means "don't go there, don't touch it" in any generalized situation. Improve your dog's focus on you by using hand signals without verbal cues; when you are consistently her focus, add the verbal cue (I recommend "let's go") along with the hand signal.

Doorbells and Knocking

AFTER YOUR DOG HAS MASTERED waiting at doorways, you have an additional skill to teach: how to respond to the doorbell and door knocking. While many dogs go a little nuts when the doorbell rings, you should condition yours to stay settled. It will take a patient partner to help you and your dog master doorbell training. Start with a closed door, and use the same kind of training technique that we learned with the *cookie sit-stay* (see page 106). In other words, with your dog sitting at your heel and your hand holding his shortened leash tight against your hip, have your partner ring the bell (or knock) and then stay silent. If your dog doesn't respond to the bell or if he looks at you, jackpot him. More likely, however, your dog will bark and rush to the door, so brace yourself and keep that hand glued to your hip as you wait for him to look at you. The moment he looks at you, mark it (say "good") and lure him backward and away from the door to follow you as you say "come here." Right now, don't even open the door, just continue to practice the *come here* routine each time you lure him away from the door after your partner rings the bell or knocks. Say "come here" only once; if that doesn't succeed, lure him to another cue such as a *down* or *sit*.

Another way to condition your dog to pay no attention to the doorbell sound is for you to show absolutely no reaction when you hear it. Your dog feeds off your reaction, so if you ignore the bell, he will learn to do the same. My dogs don't pay much attention to doorbells, door knocks, or phones ringing, especially since Maude (my African Grey Parrot) imitates all those sounds. If you don't have a trained parrot, you can ask your child or a friend to ring your doorbell while you watch television or read this book. When the bell rings, just keep doing whatever it is you're doing, without looking at the door or your dog. Your dog may go crazy for a while, but eventually he will figure out that reacting to the doorbell doesn't benefit him; he'll eventually settle down and quietly forget about it. Oh, and I almost forgot . . . it's okay to let your child back inside at the end of the session. She may have earned a treat of her own for her assistance!

Here's another exercise. Have your child or a friend ring the doorbell over and over again. Ignore the bell—as well as your dog's barking—until he settles down. When he finally quiets down, wait about three minutes and then casually answer the door to let your child or friend in. You and your human ally should have a calm conversation while walking around your home, ignoring your dog even if he gets excited again. If he tries to jump on either of you, turn away abruptly and keep your back to him as you continue moving away. When he settles down, calmly praise him in a low-key manner, then practice a few *sits* and *downs*, staying calm. Next, have your child or friend calmly cue him to do a *sit* and a *down*. Watch your dog's body language, and when he is calm, remain calm yourself and give him a stuffed Kong or a special toy that you have reserved for this occasion. While he chews or plays, resume conversation with your partner, remembering to keep your tone quiet. This training exercise is a very challenging waiting game and may take time (not to mention an ample supply of aspirin!).

Boundary Training: Furniture and Rooms

THE EASIEST WAY TO keep your dog out of rooms and off furniture is by using baby gates and x-pens to block those areas as off-limits. Little by little, you can experiment with removing the barriers for longer and longer stretches of time. But before you do that, be sure to reinforce your dog's enjoyment of her crate; make staying in the crate a habit. Then, at a moment when you can supervise her constantly, start experimenting with keeping boundaries without using physical barriers. The best way to do that is to keep your dog in a *settle*, which I'll teach you later in this lesson.

The first step, though, is to take your dog out of her crate and to give her attention and rewards, such as a chew toy that will keep her occupied. If she wanders into off-limits areas, *recall* her right away. Lure her if necessary. Use the *off* cue only if you catch her taking her first step or two onto or into the off-limits space, or else you may not make it clear what exactly it is that you want her to stay off and out of.

Settle Down

A SLIGHTLY DIFFERENT BEHAVIOR from the *down* and *down-stay*, *settle down* or just *settle* tells your dog to rest in place; as a more relaxed version of *down-stay*, it can be maintained for longer durations. In the *settle*, your dog can be in any position as long as he lies quietly: on his side or back, sprawled out, or chewing on a toy. The *down-stay*, by contrast, requires a dog to stay down without moving. Once he has mastered *down*, use *settle* to give him a bit more freedom and relaxation while he's "confined" to the *down* posture. You may use *settle*, for example, if you are okay with your dog being in the same room with you for a prolonged wait while you are eating, watching TV, reading, or working. You can also use *settle* when you are out in the world with him, such as while standing in line at a store or sitting on a park bench. Some of my students have named the *settle* behavior "chill," which is fine as long as you are consistent.

To teach your dog to settle, start with him in the *down* posture. Have plenty of treats handy. While he stays down, hold an open palm slightly above his head, wait a few seconds, and then with your other hand silently reward him with six to eight treats, one at a time. I call this the vending machine technique, and it's important to keep vending the treats as you watch his posture. As soon as you see him relax into the *settle*, mark that by saying calmly "good settle" (or "good chill"), and feed him the remainder of the treats. After the last one, count silently to five, show him that you have no more treats in your hand and, with a soft voice, *release* him briefly. Then repeat the *settle* behavior. It's important to keep that vending machine doling out the treats or your dog might get up. If he

SETTLE DOWN

The *settle* is a more relaxed *down*, and can be maintained longer.

① START WITH DOWN
Hold six to eight treats behind your back and establish good focus.

② VENDING MACHINE
Feed treats one at a time. When you see your dog relax, mark it calmly ("good settle") and dispense the rest of the treats.

does, stop dispensing treats until he lies back down. Most dogs pick up the *settle* cue fairly quickly if they've already mastered the *down-stay*.

Another way to teach and reinforce the *settle* is by combining it with hand-feeding. Slowly hand-feed your dog his entire meal, putting a few pieces of kibble at a time (or the equivalent amount if you don't use kibble) between his front paws and close to his body while he stays down. Stop feeding when he doesn't relax. By the end of the meal, he will probably be lying comfortably, enjoying being fed like royalty.

Homework

EMPHASIZE SUCCESS THIS WEEK. As you're nearing the end of your dog's Fundamentals Training Program, you may think that your dog is getting it so well that he doesn't need to be rewarded; or that he isn't getting it fast enough, so he doesn't deserve rewards. Both those judgments are easy to lapse into at this stage, so keep your dog's success in mind. Make whatever level he has achieved seem like the pinnacle of success.

RECALLS Add distractions by practicing at outdoor locations and with people around, especially kids, as well as adding distances from different directions.

HOMEWORK REMINDER: RELATIONSHIP TRAINING

When you do your homework this week and in all weeks to come, I want you to keep your good relationship with your dog in mind. The more your dog is focused on you, the more she will want to follow your cues and learn from you, especially as you reward her for good behavior and build up a wonderful reinforcement history together. Make it your mission this week to see what you can do to get your dog more focused on you, and make note of that in your training log. For example, practice the eye-contact exercise (see page 151),

being especially mindful to show your happiness when she looks at you. When you're walking, notice her focus on you and how that might also be improving her informal heeling without pulling.

Even as you have your dog sit for everything—which is the cornerstone of the real-life reward system—show your gratitude a little more when she does whatever you may request. Pay attention to her body language and reward all those great behaviors she offers naturally—and she will offer them a hundredfold.

STAY Add distractions and distance as your dog is ready. Remember to take your time: Good *stays* come with a lot of patience, practice, and your dog's maturity.

DOWN Add the verbal cue (name the behavior).

STANDING POSE Lure, try to advance all the way to the hand signal without lure, and then to add the verbal cue.

OFF AND TAKE IT TRADES Practicing the food bowl exercise also reduces food guarding.

DOOR TRAINING Start with interior doors before progressing to doors that lead outside.

STAIRS TRAINING Assuming that your dog can already climb stairs, teach stair climbing safety (your dog walks on stairs next to you, neither in front of you nor behind).

SETTLE Practice the vending machine technique, and also with hand-feeding.

Training Games and Activities

ADD SOME NEW WRINKLES to the games and activities that your dog already knows. See Chapter Nine for details.

▶ Integrate Find Me with Come and Go by doing *recalls* back and forth between you and your partner in separate rooms.

▶ Add *pose* to Puppy Pushups. When your dog is able to pose from your hand signal or verbal cue, start with a predictable sequence: *sit-pose-down;* then mix it up with combinations like *pose-sit-pose* and *sit-down-pose.* Remember to make it fun and keep your dog interested as you try to improve her fluency without causing her to fail.

▶ Fetch / Retrieve. Introduce the game, but don't insist that your dog get it or like it yet. Just assess where she is with this right now and reward her for any success.

TRAINING LOG FOR _____ DAY _____

SKILL	PROGRESS	NOTES
RECALLS: ADD DISTRACTIONS & DISTANCE Generalize to outdoor locations. With training partner's help, practice the Runaway and Lassie Recall exercise.		
STAY UNTIL RECALLED: ADD DISTANCE, DURATION & DISTANCE Add steps and time gradually, generalize to new locations. Circle around dog as he sits and stays.		
DOWN: NAMING THE BEHAVIOR Practice Puppy Pushups *(sit-down-sit)*, adding verbal cues to hand signals.		
STANDING POSE As dog sits at your side, lure forward so that he stands to follow treat. When fluent, add to Puppy Pushups sequence, and add verbal cue ("pose").		
OFF & TAKE IT TRADES: PHASE 2 Practice trades for items of equal or greater value. Trade special treats for portions of meal in food bowl.		
DOOR TRAINING Cue a *sit,* then say "off" before you open door and lead through with hand signal. Then mark, praise, reward. Later, add verbal cue "let's go."		
SETTLE DOWN From *down-stay* position, offer treats one by one (vending machine technique). When dog relaxes, say "good settle." Also, hand-feed in *settle* position.		
CATCH YOUR DOG OFFERING BEHAVIORS THAT YOU LIKE Also, use Real-Life Rewards System.		
POTTY TRAINING Keep track of input (meals and treats) and output (potty time). Note accidents.		
BASELINE BEHAVIORS Crate training, hand-feeding, bite inhibition, handling and gentling.		
CHOOSE AN ACTIVITY/GAME.		
CHOOSE A SOCIALIZATION EXPERIENCE.		

Week Five: Reviewing the Basic Skills

YOU'VE DONE IT. This is Week Five—the final week—of the Fundamentals Training Program. Congratulations!

In my classes, I spend this final week reviewing the 10 basic skills my clients and their dogs have begun to master. Use this chapter the same way—as a quick guide for assessing your dog's progress. Then let it guide you to the next level of training in the following chapters. If your dog has acquired each of the

This chapter provides an overview of all the skills you and your dog have mastered thus far: the Sit, Recall, Leash Walking, Down, Stay, Standing Pose, Settle Down, Release, Off and Take It Trades, and Boundary Training.

10 skills and does a few of them fluently, you've made tremendous progress. If not, don't worry; just keep working. As I've mentioned, it's not reasonable to expect that every dog will be able to master every one of these skills in just one month. Some take a little more time, and others seem to get it all at once, after several weeks.

If we were in class together, I would ask that you spend some time showing us what your dog can do, and how well she performs the following activities. You might consider hosting a fun "Family Night" (or "Fun Night with Friends"), where your spouse and children (or friends) gather, and you and your dog show off the progress you've made. You both have worked very hard these past five weeks, and you certainly deserve to be acknowledged and celebrated for your effort.

The Quick Guide

THE PURPOSE OF THIS quick guide is to help you assess your dog's current skill levels, see what's next for him to learn, and tune up any behaviors that may have become rusty. For example, at this point in the training he should be fluent in most (if not all) of the basic household manners protocols that you learned in the fundamentals program. At the very least, your dog should sit wherever and whenever you request him to do so. If his *sit* needs more work, remember to incorporate the behavior into the real-life rewards system: Have him sit for everything.

Whatever skill level you and your dog have reached during this training course, remember that sitting is *always* important, although it is usually the first behavior that a dog owner will take for granted. Sitting easily puts an end to most behavior problems: It is simply impossible for your dog to sit and jump on you at the same time.

One reminder before we get started with the review (and your dog's assessment): When doing any repetitive exercise, stay positive and have fun. Continue teaching a repetitive exercise only as many times as your dog stays interested. If he loses interest or fails too many times and gives up, switch to an exercise that he knows so that you end the training session on a positive note. Do your best to leave your dog wanting more and looking forward to the next session.

Even the youngest puppy wants to please—you just have to keep her focus.

Skill 1: The Sit

▶ **LURING.** Touch a treat to your dog's nose, then with the treat in your fingertips and your palm facing up, lure up above her nose. As she looks up, her rump touches down. Marker: "good." Do not use the verbal cue. Praise her, touch her collar, and then offer the treat last. See Week One, page 74.

▶ **YOUR DOG'S REAL-LIFE REWARDS SYSTEM.** Lure your dog to sit for everything: before meals, walks, playtime, and socialization. For example, when it's time to take her for a walk, before you put the leash on her and go out the door, request that she sit. This teaches her that when she sits, good things can happen for her; it becomes your dog's way to say "please." See Week Two, page 89.

▶ **MODIFYING THE HAND SIGNAL:** from lure to cue. As your dog achieves 80 percent success when luring, introduce the slot machine (slowly withdrawing treats) and reward jackpots for the best behaviors. Keep your eyes focused on her so that you don't miss a thing. See Week Two, page 92.

▶ **WITHDRAWING TREATS.** Use the hand signal cue without treats. Hold the treat in the non-cueing hand. See Week Two, page 93.

▶ **ADDING THE VERBAL CUE.** Once your dog is fluent with the visual cue (using only your hand signal), you may name that behavior using the verbal cue "sit." In this Fundamentals Training Program, always continue using the visual hand signal at the same time you say any verbal cue, because the repeated pairing helps your dog understand the link between the two. See Week Three, page 105.

▶ **GENERALIZED SITTING.** Use the cue at random moments on walks, in crowds, and in situations and environments that are more distracting than your dog is used to. *New skill.*

▶ **EVERYDAY SITTING.** Withdraw treats altogether in places that are familiar to your dog. Add new places, new distractions, and more distance so that he understands that although the setting and situation have changed, the behavior you're requesting is the same. Keep up the everyday habit of the real-life rewards system where your dog sits for everything. *New skill.*

Skill 2: Recall

▶ **LURING, PART ONE.** Lure your dog to move toward you from a few steps away. Have a partner hold your dog by a leash as you lure by drawing the treat toward your knee, and then have your dog sit. Reward on the *sit*. If your dog doesn't sit, just reward on the *recall*. Once that skill has been acquired, add the *sit*. No verbal cue. See Week One, page 78.

▶ **LURING, PART TWO, WITH AN ADDED VERBAL CUE.** Continue the *recall* lure you learned in part one, adding the verbal cue "[dog's name], come here." Once your dog is fluent with this step, increase the distance one foot at a time (as long as the dog continues being successful), up to 10 feet. As you get farther away, make sure you are the most interesting thing in your dog's view, because he may not notice the treat. Be happy and animated (crouch and pat your hands together without frightening your dog) as he runs to greet you. See Week Two, page 94.

▶ **RECALL-AND-SIT COMBINATION WITH RELEASE.** During supervised play, interrupt with a *recall* after about one minute. Use the recall cue that is currently most fluent for your dog: ideally, his name plus "come here," plus a hand signal (bring hands together and crouch). *Release* him back to another minute of play. This exercise works best when your dog has a human or dog partner to play with. See Week Three, page 104.

▶ **ADDING DISTANCE AND DISTRACTION.** Practice luring with a verbal cue and *recall-sit-release*, adding distance up to 10 yards. Add mild distractions, such as a toy held by a partner, or a partner walking in the other direction. Do the turn-and-run exercise described in Week Four, page 119.

▶ **GENERALIZED RECALLS.** Practice the cue outdoors, in a location with minimal distractions. Arrange supervised play dates in a backyard or park (inside a fenced area) to practice on a leash. Gradually increase the distance at which you recall your dog every minute or two, starting at a distance of a few feet and increasing only as your dog proves fluency with the shorter distances. Adding distance requires careful supervision so that your dog doesn't run away. *New skill.*

▶ **RECALLS EVERY DAY AND EVERYWHERE.** It is important to incorporate recalls into your dog's daily routine to help keep him focused on you throughout the day. I don't recommend withdrawing treats altogether for quite some time—even many years—as *recall* cues are typically among the most difficult for dogs to maintain in generalized situations. It's best to be careful and safe. Don't expect your dog to have *recalls* mastered for every situation every day. *New skill.*

Skill 3: Leash Walking

▶ **FIRST STEPS TOGETHER: "BE A TREE."** Whenever your dog pulls on her leash, stand firm, draw your hands to your chest (as you hold the leash handle), and wait. When your dog looks back at you, mark "good" and recall her as you did in the "puppy come here" recall. If you lure her to sit in front of you, it blocks her ability to run around you. When she arrives, praise, treat, and walk in the opposite direction. Assume that these walks will not be for distance, but just back and forth. If your dog stays close to you without being asked, reward for that. See Week One, page 81.

▶ **TETHERING.** Tether your dog's leash handle to your belt as you walk around your home and go about your business. Reward your dog for staying close and focusing on you. See Week Two, page 88.

▶ **TROUBLESHOOTING: LEASH PULLING.** Continue doing the "be a tree" exercise. Play Follow the Lure to increase your dog's focus on you. Anticipate when she is about to pull ahead and, before she can pull, lure in another direction. For Follow the Lure, see page 153.

▶ **WALKING EXERCISE: CHANGING DIRECTION.** Intentionally change directions often as you walk, luring your dog, and helping her to follow your changes. Weave around obstacles. See page 103.

▶ **WALKING EXERCISE: INFORMAL HEELING.** Have your dog generally walk at your side. Mark "good heel," praise and reward her randomly (slot machine technique) while continuing to walk. Practice quick starts and stops. Use tethering. Reminder: This is not a perfect heel, but one to keep your dog walking alongside you with moments to sniff, pee, and be a dog. See Week Three, page 113.

▶ **INFORMAL HEELING: REAL-WORLD WALKS WITH DISTRACTIONS.** When you are confident of your dog's ability to focus on you while facing mild distractions, go to a dog park or another place where there are increased distractions *and* a way to make a quick and safe exit if things don't go well. Do not force your dog to do something she isn't quite ready for. *New skill*.

Skill 4: Down

▶ **LURING.** Start with your dog in a *sit* in front of you. Lure by holding a treat between your fingertips, palm facing down, and sliding the treat slowly toward your dog's chest. Keeping your dog's attention on the treat, draw your hand down. When your dog touches down, mark "good down," praise, and treat. Use hand signal only, no verbal cues. See Week Two, page 96.

▶ **PUPPY PUSHUPS.** Cue your dog with your hand signal to *sit*, then *down*, then *sit* again. Mark each response (say "good" after every *sit* or *down*), and lavish the praise and reward with the food treat only after the full rep (one rep = *sit*, *down*, *sit*). As she becomes fluent, add complexity starting with an extra down at the end and building toward an extra Puppy Pushup before you give the reward. When your dog learns more cues and dog tricks, include them in the Puppy Pushups routine. See Week Three, page 106.

▸ **ADDING THE VERBAL CUE.** Lure your dog into the *down* and add the verbal cue as she starts to respond. Remember that you are establishing a link between the hand signal and the verbal cue, so that your dog understands that this behavior also has a name. See Week Four, page 121.

▸ **INCORPORATING THE VERBAL CUE WITH PUPPY PUSHUPS.** When introducing all verbal cues the process is straightforward: After your dog understands your hand signal fluently, you are able to tag on a name. Once you have established the link between the visual and verbal cues, your dog will respond to both. Since your dog already knows how to do Puppy Pushups, tag on the verbal cues "sit" and "down" along with the visual hand signals. See Week Four, page 121.

▸ **DOWN AND SIT AT A DISTANCE.** Add distance one foot at a time, mixing random verbal and hand cues for *sit* and *down*. Initially, reward with treats at each small increase of distance (go to your dog and treat her for each success), and then begin to withdraw treats. Also combine this with longer *stay* exercises (see below). *New skill.*

Skill 5: Stay

▸ **COOKIE SIT AND TAKE IT.** This exercise prepares your dog to learn to stay by having him sit quickly and look to you for help instead of going after a cookie without your permission. Wrap about half of your dog's leash around your hand to shorten the tether enough that your other hand can comfortably reach his nose when he pulls forward during this exercise. With your dog sitting at your side and your hand that holds his leash "glued" to your hip, touch a treat to his nose (with your other hand) and let him sniff it. Next, toss the treat a few feet in front of him and stand still as he tries to get the treat (but cannot reach it because you're holding the leash short). When your dog looks back at you, mark it (say "good"), then cue him to sit with your hand signal, mark once more when he sits (say "good" again), and then immediately direct him to take the treat (point to it and say "take it") as you quickly unwrap the leash from your hand. See Week Three, page 107.

▶ **COOKIE SIT-STAYS.** Similar to *cookie sit*, but now add waiting time before releasing your dog to take the cookie. See Week Three, page 107.

▶ **STAY: THE CONVENTIONAL CUE.** As your dog sits in front of you, slide your outstretched palm gently toward his face as if stopping traffic, and say "stay." Keep your hand in position while you intermittently give treats for staying. Mark "good stay," praise, and reward him with another treat that you have in your other hand. The goal is to teach your dog that the longer he remains in the *sit-stay*, the more treats he will get. The better he stays, the fewer treats he will *need* because he now understands what he is being rewarded for. At first, keep the *stays* short and sweet, then build up his staying power slowly and successfully. As your dog builds up his *stay* power beyond 30 seconds, insert another cue to *stay* in the middle of that *stay* time (and reward for success) so he understands that longer *stays* get more rewards. See Week Three, page 109.

Skill 6: Standing Pose

▶ **LURING.** While your dog sits at your side, hold a treat in your fingertips and slowly lure her forward. As she moves to a standing pose to sniff the treat, mark it (say "good"), praise, and let her have the treat. As she gains success, practice this behavior starting with her sitting at your other side. Repeat the sequence to ultimate success as she learns to *pose* and remain steady while waiting for the treat to come to her. See Week Four, page 121.

▶ **THE VISUAL CUE.** Use the same setup as with the hand signal luring into a *pose*, but this time only pretend to hold a lure in your fingertips. When your dog follows your pretend lure, mark (say "good"), then praise and give her a treat with your other hand. See Week Four, page 122.

▶ **ADDING VERBAL CUES.** Once your dog is fluent with the *pose* cue starting on either side of you, add the verbal name "pose" once she is fully standing. See Week Four, page 123.

▶ **POSE FROM DOWN POSITION.** Once your dog is fluent with *posing* from the *sit* position on either side of you, and you have successfully named the verbal *pose* cue, start at the *down* position and use both the hand signal and verbal cue until she becomes fluent. See Week Four, page 123.

▶ **CUE COMBINATIONS: ADDING POSE TO PUPPY PUSHUPS.** Once your dog is fluent with the *sit-down-sit-down* Puppy Pushup combination, and she *poses* fluently from both a *sit* and a *down*, mix the three cues—*sit*, *down*, *pose*—and randomize the pattern. See Week Four, page 133.

Skill 7: Settle Down

▶ **SETTLE DOWN.** While he's in a *down* position, silently reward your dog as if you're a human vending machine with six to eight treats, one at a time. As he relaxes and settles, mark ("good settle"), feed the remaining treats (if any), then count to five silently and slowly, mark (say "good"), praise, reward, and *release* him. The reward for a well-performed *settle* is the happy release, lavish praise, and petting for a job well done, possibly leaving him eager to try it again. Don't end the *settle* behavior with another treat or he may link the last treat to your *release* cue and may subsequently think he should jump ahead of you and release himself before you do. See Week Four, page 131.

▶ **SETTLE WITH REWARD.** Once your dog has acquired the above *settle*, eliminate the human vending machine and give him a visual hand signal, such as an open hand over his head, as you verbally cue the word "settle." After about five to eight seconds, mark, praise, and reward, but do not release him. Jackpot initially to let him know that he is getting it. Once he gets it, increase the total time that you have him settle, with mark-praise-reward feedback every 8 to 10 seconds. Once he can settle fluently for 30 seconds, introduce the slot machine technique (withdraw treats randomly), with the ultimate goal of phasing out the treats completely, as you would with all successfully learned behaviors. For longer *settles*, you can reward with a stuffed Kong for a minute or two, and then take it away using the *off and take it* trade technique. Phase out the treats (withdraw them using the slot machine technique) once he has become fluent. See Week Four, page 131.

▶ **REAL-LIFE SETTLE.** When your dog is with you in a public place—while standing in line at the bank or at a friend's home—practice *settle*. Mark, praise, and reward (jackpot initially). *New skill.*

Skill 8: Release

▶ **RELEASE: VERBAL CUE.** During all supervised play periods, drop your dog's leash—assuming that you're indoors or in a fenced-off area so that he can't run completely away—and say "release" with a happy voice. See Week Two, page 98.

Skill 9: Off and Take It Trades

▶ **TAKE IT: COOKIE SIT-STAYS (REVIEW).** The *off and take it* trade builds on the *cookie sit-stay* behavior, so please review that skill so that your dog is fluent before you progress to the next stage. Remember to make it fun so that she will want to play this "game" some more. See the *cookie sit-stay* review in this chapter on page 142, and the detailed lesson in Week Three, page 106.

▶ **TAKE IT EXERCISE.** Put one treat in your fingertips at dog's nose level, pivot just your hand—don't move your arm—and say "take it." Mark (say "good"), and repeat immediately. See below for the *off* part of this trade. See Week Three, page 111.

▶ **OFF AND TAKE IT TRADE, PHASE 1.** Do three *take it* exercises one after another, and then on the fourth do *not* say "take it." When your dog tries to take the treat, say "off" suddenly and loudly enough to be slightly shocking. Typically, the dog will back away and look up at you, trying to understand what you want. As soon as she moves even the slightest little bit away from your hand, mark (say "good") and give her the treat, praising her lavishly in the happiest tone of voice you can muster up. Once she seems to understand the "off" and "take it" directions, increase the delay between *off* and *take it*. See Week Three, page 111.

▶ **OFF AND TAKE IT TRADE, PHASE 2.** Pair *off* cue with *take it* at your dog's food bowl to diminish food guarding. Use a stuffed Kong reward or other item that she values as much as or more than her food bowl. See Week Four, page 123.

Skill 10: Boundary Training

▶ **INTERIOR DOORS, PART ONE.** *Sit* and *stay* at doorway while on the leash. Mark your dog's good *stay*, praise, and reward. Open the door; if he starts to get up, close the door and re-cue him to *sit* and *stay*. Open the door again very slowly. If he stays for a moment, mark for the good *stay*, open the door and lead him through it. Require your dog to *sit-stay* a bit longer on each subsequent rep before opening the door all the way and leading your dog through. This phase is complete when you can open the door all the way without your dog moving. See Week Four, page 127.

▶ **INTERIOR DOORS, PART TWO.** Once the previous skill has been acquired, walk through the open doorway as your dog continues to *sit-stay*. After a moment, lure your dog to "come here" and then have him follow you through the door. Mark, praise him, and give him a treat. See Week Four, page 128.

▶ **FRONT DOOR.** At the closed front door, hold the leash as in *cookie sit-stay* (leash hand "glued" to your hip), have a partner ring or knock, and keep the leash glued to your hip as the dog barks and jumps. Remain silent until your dog focuses on you, then mark it and lure him as you *recall* with "come here." Tell your partner to ring again. When your dog stays and focuses on you, slowly open door. Close the door again if he tries to jump on the visitor. If dog remains sitting, then jackpot. See Week Four, page 129.

▶ **VISITOR.** Allow a visitor to enter; he shouldn't approach your dog if there is any hint that the dog may get excited, fearful, or protective. If the dog remains calm, the visitor may approach. See Week Four, page 130.

▶ **FURNITURE AND ROOMS.** Plan ahead and use baby gates and x-pens to keep areas off-limits. Use *off* cue only when you catch your dog as he takes his first step or two onto or into the off-limits space. See Week Four, page 130.

▶ **CLIMBING STAIRS.** Use baby gates and x-pens to keep your dog off the stairs while he's uncrated. Use a short leash and keep him near you and against the wall as you walk stairs with him at your side, neither ahead of nor behind you. See Week Four, page 126.

Congratulations! You and your dog have done it. You have created a spirited bond. You are a team. It might be a good idea to bookmark this Quick Guide and take a few moments to flip back through the pages of the Fundamentals Training Program as you review each cue. You could probably turn to just about any page at random and recall a specific breakthrough, challenge, or story that makes you laugh . . . or just shake your head because what once seemed impossible is now becoming ordinary. If your dog could high-five right now, this would be the time to do it. The good news is that the chapters ahead will actually teach her the High Five and other tricks, along with full-fledged canine good citizenship. As you'll see, continuing your training will strengthen your dog's bond with your family, keep her focused on figuring out how to earn more rewards, and give her less time to figure out how to be destructive. You've done the hardest work; now you will want to maintain your dog's good behaviors with consistent practice.

THE
NEXT STEPS

Training Games and Activities

AS I'M SURE you learned the moment you brought your new dog home, these creatures *love* to play. The more we make learning fun for them (and for ourselves), the more our dogs want to learn.

At the end of each chapter of your Fundamentals Program, I have listed activities that I think may help with that week's lessons, but I encourage you to experiment with any games you think may interest your dog and match her skill level. Some activities will start as favorites and then fade into the background as other games capture her interest even more. Keep an open mind and try as many of them as you can. You'll come up with ideas for modifying them as your dog (and you) gets more skilled.

You'll also invent your own games, especially if you involve your children in training. (Turn to page 158 if you're looking for ideas to involve kids in these

Consult this chapter to find more information on all the training games and activities I've discussed throughout the rest of the book. I cover relationship development activities, skill training games, exercises for reinforcing behavior and safety, and socialization opportunities. Also in this chapter are suggestions for including your children in the training of your dog, plus fun ideas for dog parties.

HOMEWORK TIPS

◆ **FOLLOW THE GROUND RULES.** Have fun. Be patient. Remember that every interaction—every walk, meal, lovefest—is a learning opportunity, and that dogs learn better in short bursts.

◆ **USE THE TRAINING LOG.** Be disciplined about using your log even if it feels like busywork or a waste of time. Lost yours? Download a free logging form from my website (lovethatdogbook.com).

games and activities.) Share your own games with me at my website (lovethatdogbook.com) and I'll post some of them with your name.

Whatever game or activity you choose, always remember to help your dog learn and clearly understand the rules of the game by marking her behavior and praising and rewarding her when she is successful.

The activities included here are designed to give your dog practice in four specific areas:

▶ Relationship development

▶ Skill training

▶ Behavior and safety

▶ Socialization opportunities

Relationship Development Activities

THESE SIMPLE GAMES ARE intended to enforce the bond between you and your dog. The goal of each is to get your dog to focus his attention more intensely on you.

1. **WHICH HAND?** This is a simple guessing game. Start by letting your dog see you put a treat in one hand. Close both hands and put them behind your back. Then bring them both out in front of your dog and say "which hand?" Open the hand that your dog first sniffs or touches; if it holds the treat, he gets to eat it while you gleefully praise him. If he guesses wrong, open the other hand for him to see it for a moment before you shut both hands. Then try another round. This game can be used to warm up a dog for training; once your dog understands the rules, use it if he starts to lose focus.

2. **FIND ME.** This game is also known as Hide-and-Seek for Dogs. Your dog is ready to play this game once she can *sit-stay* for 60 seconds and can hold her *stay* for about 10

seconds when you leave the room. Start teaching the game by standing in plain sight in the next room while your dog holds her perfect *stay.* Then call her name and say "find me." When your dog finds you, mark that ("good find me"), praise her lavishly as you touch her collar, and reward her. Start the next round from the spot at which your dog just found you. Build up to harder-to-find hiding places and move to outdoor fenced-in locations.

Variation for beginners: If your dog can't yet *sit-stay* on her own for 60 seconds, you can use a training partner to keep her sitting while you hide. When you call out "find me," your partner releases your dog and (if necessary) lures her in your general direction.

3. **THE NAME GAME.** Some games and activities can be simple, and this is one of them. The goal is to help your dog love hearing his name. Say your dog's name when you hand-feed him, when you quietly pet him, and at random moments during training. As your training comes to include exercises with greater distractions, test your dog's Name Game attention with random calls of his name when you're at home and in separate rooms, adding the cue "come here" once the dog knows his name.

4. **EYE-CONTACT EXERCISE.** Ask for eye contact at random moments. For example, immediately after you have rewarded your dog for demonstrating a skill, touch another treat lure to her nose to establish her interest, then bring the treat to your eyes and, if her attention remains steady, mark, praise, and reward. If you have established an eye-contact verbal cue, such as "ready," "look," or "watch me," use it in these exercises. More advanced eye-contact exercises are to ask for eye contact using the verbal cue at random moments during a walk and when there are competing distractions.

5. **CATCH YOUR DOG DOING SOMETHING YOU LIKE.** At least once every day, acknowledge a moment when your dog offers a good behavior without being asked. It can be eye contact, a smile, an offered *sit,* improved walking by your side, remaining attentive for a relatively long time, and so forth. I believe that the more you acknowledge your dog's volunteered efforts, the harder he will try to offer even more. For more on this, see page 112.

Variation: Select a "bonus behavior of the day": Whenever your dog volunteers it, he gets an extra jackpot (excited praise and extra treats). This variation helps you become more focused on your dog; when you play this game, you will probably also notice other behaviors that he volunteers on his own.

Skill Training Games

SOME OF THESE SKILL TRAINING GAMES are used to test behaviors and cues that your dog already understands; others will teach new skills and tricks. Or try adapting them to practice a variety of cues simultaneously.

1. COME AND GO. Your dog will need to have acquired some degree of *recall* to play this game, and you'll need a partner who is also armed with treats. Start by asking your dog to sit at your partner's side while you stand about 10 feet away. Have your partner crouch, point to you, and say "go!" An instant later you will crouch, open your arms, and say your dog's name as you recall her enthusiastically. For example, I would call my dog by saying "Brieo, come here!" When your dog comes to you, cue her to *sit* in front of you, mark ("good sit"), praise her, touch her collar, and give her a treat. Then tell her to sit at your side, crouch, and point to your partner and say "go!" It's now your partner's turn to crouch with open arms and recall her enthusiastically. Back and forth, take turns recalling your dog, cueing her to sit for a treat. In addition to reinforcing skills, Come and Go socializes her to take cues from a trusted partner.

Variations: 1) Increase the distance; 2) have your dog perform a different cue or behavior (one that she already knows) on each lap, such as a *down*, Puppy Pushup, or some other trick; 3) combine Come and Go with Find Me by recalling your dog to and from a different room than your partner is in; 4) play with more than one partner at a time and randomize which person your dog will go to next.

2. **FOLLOW THE LURE.** This is a fun and easy game that builds your dog's positive reinforcement history. Touch a treat to his nose and slowly move it away so that he follows the treat. After about three seconds, praise him and, as you touch his collar, give him the treat. Take out another treat and do the exercise for four seconds, then five seconds, then six, and so forth. Lure him around you in a circle, through your legs, take a step or two forward, reverse directions. As he realizes how this game is played, start luring a bit faster. You are not aiming to trick him or to cause him to fail but rather to build up his skill at following your lures.

3. **FIND IT.** Similar to the game Find Me, this game (also called Find the Treasure) teaches your dog to find an object. Your dog is ready to play this game once she can *sit-stay* for enough time for you to get out of the room, hide an object, and return (at least 10 seconds). Start with a toy that your dog is interested in, and let her sniff the toy. Then cue a *sit-stay* and hide the object in the next room; place it in plain sight on the first trial, and on subsequent trials build up to more difficult hiding spots. As you progress with this game beyond the Fundamentals Training Program, add naming the object, which teaches your dog to distinguish certain objects.

4. **TETHERING.** With your dog tethered to your belt, mark, praise, and reward him for focusing on you and for heeling, especially as you speed up, slow down, and make abrupt turns. You can also add other cues to these brief tethering exercises. (See page 80 for a more detailed introduction to this leash-walking exercise.)

5. **SUPERVISED PLAY WITH RECALL AND RELEASE.** It's important that your dog have free play opportunities to bring variety to her training program. You have been directing the training lessons; she needs to have some time not to be directed. It is wonderful to witness two similar-size, well-socialized dogs square off in a play bow and wrestle. If both dogs are able to share toys, you can introduce a tug toy (see "Tug" below) as a trading game.

To make supervised play also a learning opportunity, *recall* both dogs after a minute (or two minutes if both of them are playing particularly well), then mark, praise, and reward for the successful recall. As soon as your dog can sit, lure her to you and cue *sit*, mark, praise, and reward. Do not have your dog learn a cue during the *recall*, so if she recalls successfully but does not sit yet, praise her for the "come here." Make this *recall* brief and *release* her back to play, ideally at the same time as your partner releases his dog to begin another round of play.

6. **TUG.** Playing tug with a rope toy or other tug toy can be tricky. On one hand, you want your dog to try to "own" the toy as he tries to tug it away from you; on the other hand, it is important for safety that your dog understand that this is a game that you control. To teach him to tug by your rules means that you need to teach it as a trading game, rather than a game about "owning" the object. As you've already learned, trading activities are an important step toward making sure your dog doesn't guard toys and food. Every trade needs to be for something he values at least as much as what he currently has. For many dogs, a reliable way to make the toy trade valuable is to offer a treat along with it.

The first time you give your dog the tug toy, have another toy and a good treat ready to help him trade away the tug toy immediately, using the *off and take it* trade protocols from Weeks Three and Four. Be prepared to cue *off* somewhat more forcefully than usual on the first couple of trials, and make sure that the trade is a valuable one from your dog's perspective.

The Play Bow is an invitation to play.

Trade back to the tug toy right away, so that your dog learns that giving up the tug does not always mean that playtime is over. The more rigorous you are with controlling these early tug trades, the better your dog will become at *off and take it* trades.

7. RETRIEVE. While some dogs simply don't enjoy retrieving, others are practically addicted to it. If your dog falls in the latter camp, you can use retrieving objects (a ball, a flying disc, or a toy that has been designed for retrieving) as lures.

Teaching a dog to retrieve starts with getting her excited about having the toy that has been reserved especially for this game. Most puppies will get excited about the special toy, while it is not uncommon to teach an older dog to fetch by using a special toy or ball that holds a treat that she will get to eat when she picks it up. Actually, you need two toys that you take out only for retrieving. Make sure your dog is excited about this toy before you toss it close enough that she will remain focused on it and will be able to focus back to you when you *recall* her. Try the verbal cue "fetch" as you toss the toy, although she will undoubtedly be more focused on the visual than on what you have to say.

The moment your dog picks up the prize, mark it ("good fetch"). After she enjoys her prize for a few moments, recall her with "come here" as you wave an identical toy to entice her. If your dog brings the first toy, you're in luck, so praise her profusely as you get her to drop it by showing her the other one and treating her when she does drop it. At the same time, toss the identical toy a few feet away and cue "fetch." If she returns without the first toy, then toss the second one the moment she reaches you and run to the first one. When she gets the second toy, *recall* her as you lure her toward you with the first one—sometimes a dog will carry one toy to the other one if they are fairly close together. Getting your dog to drop the retrieved first toy usually makes for a good *recall* skill as well as a good *off and take it* trade.

Another way to build your dog's interest in fetching is to keep her in *cookie sit-stay* (keep the leash "glued" to your hip after you toss the toy) for an extra moment until she focuses on you. This technique works best if your dog has already mastered the *cookie sit-stay* lesson. For more on retrieving, see Chapter Ten's dog tricks detailed breakdown on page 177.

Behavior and Safety

YOU CAN TURN BASIC behavior and safety training into games, which will make learning these very essential skills more fun and engaging.

1. HAND-FEEDING (see Chapter Three for hand-feeding protocol). While you're practicing the hand-feeding protocol, you can also play some of the games described in this section. Play Find Me by feeding a portion of your dog's meal each time she finds you, and take her food bowl with you when you hide again. Play Come and Go with a partner with whom you have already conditioned your dog to accept hand-feeding. You can even play a rally game (see page 257) by feeding your dog a portion of her meal at each station.

2. BITE INHIBITION, HANDLING, AND GENTLING (see Chapter Three and the Fundamentals Training Program Week One for more detail). Randomly, throughout the day, pet your puppy as a handling and gentling exercise; this may require rewards if he is uncomfortable with being touched. Play Pass the Puppy and Peekaboo, count his toes, handle his feet, pretend to clip his nails. Explore your dog's mouth, massage his gums, count his teeth—and remember to say "ouch" to help him learn his bite inhibition.

3. CRATE TRAINING (see Chapter Three for additional detail). When you play Find It, include your dog's crate as a hiding place. Play games and do training exercises right around the crate. In general, make your dog's crate her sanctuary and also a familiar place that is not isolated from the rest of her real-life experience.

4. LEASH WALKING (see walking exercises throughout the training program). Think of every walk as a training opportunity that is also a game: Pause to practice a couple of cues that your dog already knows, and then continue walking. Be sure to mark, praise, and reward his correct behaviors. Your dog's success during those random training moments during a walk will give him a sense of accomplishment along with variety and fun.

Socialization Opportunities

A WELL-SOCIALIZED DOG IS ONE that gets along calmly and confidently with other dogs and other people without being fearful, aggressive, or too exuberant. The sooner you make socialization a regular part of your schedule, the sooner you both will be able to reap the rewards: more opportunities for fun, filled with new experiences and people.

1. VISITS. Make a plan to visit public places as often as you feel that your dog is ready. Go to the vet just to say hi, and if you plan on using a groomer, do the same: just a friendly visit to say hi . . . and get a treat and some petting. Find stores and outdoor public places that a dog is allowed to visit.

2. WALK TRAINING: GREET YOUR NEIGHBOR. It's likely you'll meet other people walking their dogs when you walk yours. As you approach another person with a dog—assuming that you feel comfortable and safe—call out hello as you stop and cue your dog to *sit* and *stay*. If the neighbor continues to advance, ask her in a friendly voice to pause because you and your dog are training right now. Generally, the neighbor will gladly comply. If both of you have time for a brief chat, speak to each other at a slight distance, then advance a few paces and pause again. Try to keep your dog in a *sit-stay*, regardless of what the other dog is doing; however, as always, it is best to avoid problems rather than try to cure them once they happen. As your dog learns greater impulse control, you will be able to greet some neighbors with a handshake while your respective dogs are sitting.

3. DOG PARK VISIT (see page 225 for more on dog park visits). When you first go to a dog park, try to go at off-peak hours so you and your dog can acclimate, do some training, and get comfortable. Make sure to practice *recalling* and *releasing* your dog, so that she gets conditioned to *recalls* equaling a reward far more often than the end of playtime. Your ability to recall your dog reliably also means that in the event of a dog fight, you will be better able to get your dog out of the melee. In fact, with experience, you will notice certain combinations and body postures that are signs that a fight is about to erupt, and you can recall your dog in anticipation.

4. **SUPERVISED FREE PLAY.** Try to organize playdates at the dog park during off-peak times. Use periodic recalls and encourage your play partner to do the same, before releasing your dog back to play. This will help your dog understand that a *recall* does not mean the end of playtime.

Kids and Dogs

YOUR GOAL IS TO HELP your dog enjoy kids, not merely tolerate them. If you don't have kids of your own (and assuming that your dog has been checked out by your vet or a qualified trainer and does not have a fear of or an aggression toward kids), I want you to beg, borrow, or steal someone else's . . . well, stealing may be going a bit far. Make sure to involve the child's parent to help you monitor safety while the child learns the proper way to interact with your dog. By the way, it is probably more comfortable and safer for a child to give your dog a treat from a flat palm than from closed fingertips.

Almost all the games described in this chapter can involve kids, depending on each child's maturity, self-control, confidence, and coordination. Don't force children to do something they're not ready to do, even if you have made special arrangements to have a child come and play with your dog. Some kids get freaked out if a dog licks their hand; they are content to merely pet a dog or watch from a distance—which is fine because just having a child around will provide a mild distraction for your dog. Many children love the games Which Hand, Come and Go, and Find Me. To help build your dog's trust and comfort with children, involve them in hand-feeding if both the kid and dog are ready to do that. Supervise all interactions very carefully.

Kids will also invent some wonderful games. My kids have invented many that make me smile just thinking about them:

▶ **CASH REGISTER.** Fill a toy cash register with dog treats. When the dog sits, shakes paws, or does some other cue, the child pushes the cash register key and gets a treat for the dog. Sometimes the game includes dressing up the very patient dog in loose clothing and parading like at a fashion show.

▶ **TEA PARTY.** The child-size table is set for high tea, complete with plastic cups and folded napkins. The dog gets a setting at the table with his own tiny bowl and a bib napkin draped on his chest. Somehow, my children often wound up eating part of a dog biscuit, while my dog got the peanut butter sandwich. Although it's harmless, I don't recommend integrating this into your version of the game.

▶ **FIRST COMMUNION.** The kids adapted the Beg trick (see page 184) to pray together with the dog. One kid blesses everyone and doles out crackers and dog biscuits to the parishioners.

Dog Parties

THE MORE ELABORATE kids' games and activities include dog parties. If you have guests at a dog party, make sure beforehand that your dog enjoys being around each of those guests. The same goes for guest dogs: Make sure that any dog that is invited already gets along with every other dog and person. Dog parties should be relatively brief and have structured quiet time. If the party is at a park, be careful about other possible guarding issues. My cowriter Larry's animalwow.com website always features wonderful kid-appropriate dog party ideas. Here are a few of my favorites:

▶ **WELCOME HOME PARTY.** This quiet party happens at least a week or two after you first bring home your new best friend. Depending on how your dog is adjusting to having new people around, you may be able to have a couple of guests hand-feed or pet him. Your kids can take some "ownership" for the new family dog's enjoyment by giving tours of the dog's new setup, by making decorations, and by leading a quiet game.

▶ **BIRTHDAY PARTY.** Your dog has two birthday anniversaries: the day she was born and the day she came home with you. Show off the tricks and cues your dog can do. Play some of the games in this section. Loosely wrap a present with some smelly treats in newspaper for your dog to shred open.

▶ **DOG TRAINING SCHOOL GRADUATION.** Proudly show off your dog's new skills and tricks that you learned in this Fundamentals Training Program. By now, your dog's socialization will be stronger, so you may want to have at least part of the celebration in public. If other dogs are involved, you may want to include a fun dog show where everyone shows off what his or her dog can do.

Clicker Training and Dog Tricks

AFTER MY CANINE STUDENTS complete the five-week fundamentals course, I begin the next, more advanced phase of instruction with trick training. I like to combine teaching dog tricks with what is called clicker training, because the clicker can dramatically speed up learning tricks. And a dog who knows tricks is a challenged and spirited dog. The opposite—a bored unengaged dog—is more likely to become destructive or dispirited or both. It's not so unlike how our children behave in school when they're bored, or when the work becomes much too easy for them. When that happens—when, say, gifted children must sit through eight hours of lessons

The clicker is a useful tool for training your dog to do tricks above and beyond the standard *sit* and *down*. Introduce your dog to the clicker while hand-feeding her, and then you can move on to more complicated tricks such as the Paw Shake, the Rollover, the Paw Wave, the High Five, the Fist Bump, and Ringing the Bell. Clickers are also helpful for teaching your dog to fetch, beg, and clean up her toys. But be sure to take time to look back and celebrate how far you both have come since your dog first arrived at your home.

that they already understand and are not challenged by in any way—they may become restless, distracted, and frustrated. They may look for things to occupy their minds; often, those things include disruptive behaviors.

The same goes for our dogs. When they feel consistently challenged in positive ways, they are far less likely to get into trouble. The five-week fundamentals course required you to invest a lot of time with your dog: time during which you were focused almost exclusively on her, when you challenged her a lot, praised her often, and provided her with many treats. Now that we've completed that phase, it's unrealistic to think that your dog won't want the same level of attention and interaction. She will. Tricks are a great way to provide that positive attention, and clicker training makes learning tricks easier and more successful. Once you and your dog understand the basics of clicker training, it will probably take the two of you about one week to learn each trick if you practice for five minutes about five times each day. If you don't have that much time, then it may take a little longer. In all cases, maintain the real-life rewards system of having your dog sit before "earning" anything.

Tricks are also fun. Let us not forget that one of the reasons that we own dogs is because they bring our families joy. Countless times, I've had the pleasure of watching my students experience the amusement and pride that comes with showing off their dog's ability to shake hands, roll over, or fetch the newspaper. And it's equally fun for our dogs, who are hardwired to play.

"Click" Marks the Spot

IN THE FUNDAMENTALS TRAINING PROGRAM, you learned to mark your dog's success at following your lures and cues by saying a marker word such as "good." As we embark on this next phase of training, I am going to introduce you to a different method of cueing and rewarding your dog called clicker training. In clicker training, we replace the marker word such as "good" with a *click* sound from a handheld clicker.

The clicker has advantages over voice marking. For example, the clicker makes a clearer and more distinct noise than our voices, which can fluctuate in tone and volume. While your voice may be affected by the weather or the kind of day you're having, the clicker makes a consistent sound that your dog will come to associate with treats. The result? Less confusion, as well as easier work, for the dog. And the precision of the clicker means you can mark the *exact* moment your dog has performed a particular behavior, such as lifting a paw to start a handshake. A clicker is like a single snapshot; your voice, on the other hand, is like a long-exposure photo. That ability to mark behavior precisely also means the clicker is a wonderful tool for acknowledging any behavior that your dog offers naturally. I'll show you how to use the clicker to "free shape" your dog's natural quirks into delightful tricks.

Karen Pryor, the godmother of clicker training, was among those who first popularized the technique to train marine mammals. In the 1960s, Karen's husband, who was preparing to open Sea Life Park in Oahu, Hawaii, asked her to help train the park's dolphins. A mom raising young children, she had previously studied zoology and behavioral biology. The dolphin training that Karen and other trainers developed was so effective and efficient that the clicker technique eventually became common throughout marine mammal parks around the world. However, it took Karen many years to introduce clicker techniques into the dog world, in part because old-school aversive training seemed to do the job well enough.

Today, the clicker plays an important role in training dogs using positive reinforcement. To understand why, imagine this simple example: When you taught your dog to sit, you first lured his nose up, causing his back legs to fold. When his rump touched down, you *marked* it by saying "good," then you praised him, and rewarded him with a treat. In clicker training, instead of saying "good" to mark a desired behavior, you click the clicker once to mark the precise moment your dog's rump touches the floor. After the click, you praise and treat as before.

CLICKERS

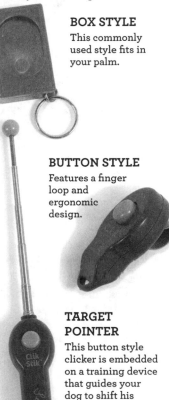

While clickers have evolved since having been introduced more than a hundred years ago as a children's "cricket" toy, they all make that distinctive click sound to mark the precise moment when your dog does what you have requested.

BOX STYLE
This commonly used style fits in your palm.

BUTTON STYLE
Features a finger loop and ergonomic design.

TARGET POINTER
This button style clicker is embedded on a training device that guides your dog to shift his head, paw, or body to a specific posture or target.

Believe me, it works! But one word of caution: When you train using the clicker, limit the length of each training session to five minutes. As you learned in the fundamentals program, dogs learn better in short sessions several times each day than in one long session. If your dog seems to have interest and focus left over at the end of the session, that's great—it probably means he will be more interested when you begin the next session. It is also typical to finish a training session before you and your dog have fully shaped the new behavior into a new cue. When that is the case, start the next session by reviewing a few steps so that your dog builds up a habit of success and locks in the learning from the previous session.

Introducing the Clicker with Hand-Feeding

YOUR FIRST JOB IS to teach your dog the value of the click. Let's begin that lesson by once again hand-feeding all your dog's meals over the next four days. In general, I find that hand-feeding is a good exercise to reintroduce whenever my dogs (or other dogs that I am boarding and training) are

CLICKER AND HAND-FEEDING ON A CHAIR

Teach your dog the reward meaning of the click sound by hand-feeding all meals for about four days before you begin training tricks or cues with the clicker. You may wish to tether your dog to help her focus on you.

GET YOUR DOG'S FOCUS

When she is looking at you, click and then feed her a small handful of her meal. Hold the clicker where your dog won't be distracted by looking at it.

CLICK THROUGH THE ENTIRE MEAL

Continue clicking and treating for your dog's entire meal. Make sure to get her focus before each click.

CLICKER AND HAND-FEEDING ON THE FLOOR

If you have a smaller dog or puppy, it may work better to sit on the floor while doing the hand-feeding exercise. Follow the same steps that I've demonstrated for hand-feeding while sitting on a chair.

FOCUS BEFORE YOU START
Don't click until your dog is focused on you or her food (and not on the clicker).

SILENCE ONCE YOU START
By keeping other sounds to a minimum, the distinct sound of the clicker is easier for your dog to focus on.

learning a new, difficult skill, or when I sense that they are beginning to lose focus.

STEP ONE. Sit on the floor or on a chair and have your dog sit in front of you. With his food bowl in your lap or at your side, hold the clicker where your dog can't focus on it. (Your dog should hear the sound but not focus on the clicker.) As soon as you click, hand-feed a bite of food. When your dog finishes the bite of food, pause for a moment and click again. Let your dog see you reach immediately into the bowl for his next handful. Pause once more before clicking again. Repeat these steps about five times to help your dog begin to make the connection between the click and the food. Most dogs pick this up fairly fast and enjoy this new game.

STEP TWO. This time, pause a second longer for the click; continue to feed immediately after the click. On each of the next five handfuls, lengthen the intervening pause by one additional second. Then, on the next five

> **TRAINING TIP**
>
> **"** The sound of the clicker may alarm or frighten some dogs. If that's the case, muffle the clicker by wrapping it with a couple of heavy socks. Peel off layers of socks as she seems more comfortable. If she still seems frightened, try adding more socks so that the click is barely audible. Help demystify the clicker for your timid dog by allowing her to sniff the clicker (but do not force her to do so), and let her watch you put the clicker in your hand and wrap it with socks. **"**

handfuls, randomize the length of pauses between clicks from one to 10 seconds. Keep giving the food immediately after the click.

STEP THREE. Your dog's happy, animated body language will let you know he is getting the connection between the click and the food. Once he figures that out, try adding a slight delay after the click before giving him each handful of food. Watch your dog to see if he is looking at the food after the click; this means he understands that a treat will follow each sound of the clicker. It also means he is having fun learning what, to him, is another new game.

For subsequent meals, go through step one more quickly, saving more of the meal for steps two and three. Within a few days, your dog should be making a clear connection between the click and the food. Remember to hand-feed him at different locations to help him generalize the connection between the click and the treat.

The Paw Shake

LET'S PRACTICE clicking on a brand-new skill, rather than on one your dog has already learned, which will also bring us to our first trick: the Paw Shake. As a reminder: I recommend teaching a new trick in a quiet room where there are no distractions.

First, with your dog sitting in front of you, let her see you place a treat in the palm of your hand and then close your hand around the treat. Hold that closed hand at the level of her chin, then move it up slightly. As her nose follows the treat going up, her body will try to stretch up to get it, meaning she may move her paws or even slightly lift one. Be sure to watch her paw movements and be ready to click! If she moves one of her paws even a little bit, click and treat her. It's okay if her head stretches up to try getting the treat, because her paw will move, too—even if ever so slightly—and that's the moment when you click and treat. If she doesn't move her paw after five seconds, reset to a different spot (for example, turn around) and signal her to do a cue that she already knows, such as a *down*. When she performs the cue, click and open your hand for her to get the treat. You're helping her understand that the click is her marker for good behavior—and most important to her, a signal that she has earned a treat.

If she succeeds, do it again: Whenever she moves her paw, click and open your hand for her to eat the treat. If she fails, ignore it this time: no click, no treat, just start over, no harm done. She will come to understand the clicker game. She will also understand that she needs to figure out what she did that earned that last successful click and treat. She will try again, so be patient.

Let's say she's now beginning to move her paw a little toward your hand. Mark the slight paw movement with a click and reward her with the treat every time. Within five minutes she will catch on that you're waiting and watching for her to move her paw. When that moment happens, it will seem like a light in her brain has switched on and is getting brighter—she's catching on. Now she's moving her paw a little more deliberately each time, so, little by little, delay the click (and treat) until she moves her paw ever more deliberately. This may take a number of sessions, so be patient.

Now you will put your open, empty hand in her view. Since she is already moving her paw, challenge her by delaying the click (and treat) until she raises her paw slightly higher, coming closer and closer to touching your hand. When she finally touches your hand with her paw, click and treat her with a jackpot. The correct way to jackpot with the

PAW SHAKE

If your dog doesn't offer this trick naturally, you can *shape* his shake from an initial slight paw movement to a fully raised Paw Shake. I discuss shaping techniques starting on page 168.

STAGE ONE

Offer your hand. If your dog moves his paw at all, then click and treat. Gradually condition him to offer his paw by using shaping techniques.

STAGE TWO

Use your outstretched hand as your dog's balance bar as you lure him to raise his paw in order to sniff the treat. Click and treat when his paw raises off the ground, even if just an inch at first. Then shape his paw higher.

POLISH THE TRICK

Once your dog offers the Paw Shake consistently, delay clicking and treating until he shows more polished form.

TRAINING CONCEPT: SHAPING

As you taught your dog the Paw Shake, you were shaping his behavior—in other words, gradually conditioning him to do what you want. Many dogs offer a paw shake naturally, which often makes this a great early trick. Look for those behaviors that *your* dog does naturally, because those will be the easiest to shape and put on cue.

Later in this chapter, I'll show you some free-shaping techniques that are designed to discover and encourage your dog's natural behaviors.

You've been shaping your dog's behavior throughout the Fundamentals Training Program. For example, think back to when you first taught your dog *recall*. At first, you rewarded him for a recall of just a step or two. Then you rewarded him for recalling from many steps away. You eventually shaped his full recall across a room, eventually adding a *sit*, until you reached a fluent full recall in many different locations. Little by little, your dog's behavior was being shaped as he came to understand that he was to come to you whenever you recalled him, from whatever distance, regardless of the distractions.

There are two types of shaping techniques we'll discuss as you learn clicker training: directed shaping and free shaping. I recommend that you and your dog learn both techniques, as each one has advantages in specific situations to expand your dog's learning abilities.

clicker is to click only once, give her the extra treats in your open palm, and praise the heck out of her again! Pay attention to petting her around her collar, which reminds her that touching her collar is a good thing.

When your dog paws at your hand a few times in a row, it means that she is making the connection between the Paw Shake, the click, and the treat, so taper the jackpots back to a single treat. Teaching each trick becomes a game of waiting, watching, and clicking to mark the right behavior when it is offered. If she offers a different behavior, ignore it. You must stay focused on just a single behavior at a time when teaching a new trick.

Once your dog understands what you want and is touching your hand confidently, it is time to name that behavior anything you want. Most people like to say "shake," so let's go with adding that word as your verbal cue, while you also continue to cue with the visual hand signal.

Now that the behavior is named and she understands what you want, you can raise the bar—perhaps clicking only when she touches your hand right away. If she's too slow, don't click. Instead, just ignore it and request another shake. When you want more from your dog, it can cause a bit of frustration, but in a good way, because during a phase of mild frustration the dog will work harder to get to the next level you've set. She wants to hear the click and get the treat.

Once your dog becomes quick and completely fluent with the Paw Shake, it's time to raise the stakes again: Try giving the verbal cue without the hand gesture. (The first time she shakes successfully with only your verbal cue, that's worth a jackpot.) Next, interchange reps of verbal-only and visual-only cues, then pair verbal and visual cues together again, then separate and interchange them again. Continue to click and treat for each success. Once your dog achieves fluency with the verbal-only and visual-only cues, start withdrawing the treats slot-machine style.

Congratulations! Your dog has mastered her first dog trick, and you have successfully learned to shape a behavior.

Directed Shaping

YOU USED DIRECTED SHAPING when you taught your dog the Paw Shake. You directed her when you held the lure slightly above her head so she would stretch up to try and get it. When she moved her paw, you clicked that behavior and gave her a treat. As you raised the criteria by delaying the click until she lifted her paw higher and higher, you continued to direct her behavior, shaping it to touch your hand. After she first touched your hand, you continued to use directed shaping to refine her movement and reduce her response time.

Targeting: Rollover

WHEN YOU USED DIRECTED shaping to teach your dog the Paw Shake, your hand became a target for your dog to touch. If you choose to enrich your dog training experience with dog tricks, you will want to teach your dog the generalized skill of target touching your hand with his nose. Once your dog has learned that your hand is a target, you will be able to direct him to touch it whenever and wherever you hold it out and say the word "target" or "touch." To transform your hand into a target, hold a treat in your fingertips or your open hand (use your thumb to hold the treat in place). When he fluently touches your hand target, it's

THE ROLLOVER

Start with your dog in a *down*. You'll lure her to roll over in the opposite direction from the way that her hips are tucked.

LURE ACROSS

As your dog's nose follows the lure across her shoulders, click and treat.

ONTO HER BACK

When your dog is able to roll straight up onto her back, that's worth a jackpot!

FLOP AND ROLL UP

Use gravity as you lure your dog to flop to the other side for another jackpot. Polish the trick by shaping the roll up, full circle into the *down* again.

time to name it ("touch" or "target") by using the visual hand target and verbal cue together. After a few days of fluency, try alternating verbal-only and visual-only cues, also using a few reps of verbal and visual cues together. Once your dog has learned that your hand is the target that he is supposed to touch, it's time to start using it to teach a specific trick.

Let's use target touching to teach your dog to roll over. The Rollover is a fun trick to show off, and it also helps build your dog's trust that he's safe when you put him on his back. Not only will an audience appreciate that, but so will your vet and groomer. If your dog has hip problems, the Rollover may not be a healthy trick; instead, try luring him onto his side. Even if your dog has healthy hips and back, it's best to teach the Rollover on a somewhat soft surface such as a carpet or the lawn.

To teach the Rollover, start by cueing your dog to lie down. Then put a treat in your fingertips and lure from his nose across the back of his shoulder area. As his nose follows the lure, his chin will slide across his shoulders and face the side that his body will follow and flop over to. Click and treat at the point when his nose and head follow the lure, even if it's just a little. Rep by rep, inch by inch, lure farther and farther across his shoulders, and treat each time he catches up to touch your slow-moving hand with his nose while he starts rolling onto his back. When your dog gets to this halfway point (he's fully on his back), that's worth a jackpot. After the halfway point, keep luring him to flop over to his other side.

Once he has flopped over, continue to lure him to that final upright *down* position. Getting there earns him another jackpot. When he starts to gain coordination for the full motion, speed up his movement by luring a little faster, but not so fast that he can't keep up to touch your hand. Click and treat each landmark success.

Next, shorten the sweeping motion of the lure into a hand cue. Start the luring motion with your palm facing up, and when your dog gets to the halfway point (he's up on his back), flip your luring hand over so that it's now palm down as you sweep down the other side of his body and your dog flops to follow. Continue clicking and treating as your dog masters this step. As he becomes fluent with your luring motion, add the verbal cue "roll over." Begin to experiment with giving only a verbal cue once he is fluent with the hand lure and the new verbal cue together. When your dog follows only the verbal cue, that's worth a jackpot.

Removing the Target to Teach Paw Wave, High Five, Fist Bump

LET'S RETURN TO THE PAW SHAKE. Since you don't want your hand target to be part of the finished trick, the next step is to remove the target. Let's do that by teaching your dog to raise her paw in the air as if she were waving. This trick is a variation on the Paw Shake, as you'll teach her to wave using a similar movement, but you will want her to raise her paw higher and not touch the target.

First, you'll transform the Paw Shake into a High Five or Fist Bump by raising the target (your hand) higher and higher. With each success, remember to click and treat as you have done with previous tricks and behaviors. Make sure to generalize your dog's understanding by offering your hand a little to the left, to the right, higher, and lower. Typically, a dog picks up this "game" of touching your moving hand quite quickly. But anytime your dog doesn't get it, just back up to the step where she was last successful and restart by breaking down the next sequence. Rotate your hand so that your palm faces your dog and you have a High Five for her to touch. Close your hand and you'll teach her the Fist Bump. Now you have taught your dog three tricks in one: Paw Shake, High Five, and Fist Bump.

To shape the Paw Shake into the Wave, offer your dog the signal to shake by moving your hand in toward her. As she tries to

HAND TARGETING

One common training technique for tricks is to teach your dog to touch your hand with his nose or paw. Touching your hand is not the finished trick, but just a breakdown step. We call this technique *targeting*, and you will eventually train your dog to target when you hold out your hand and say the verbal cue "target" or "touch."

PALM TARGETING

Teach your dog to target your open palm with either his paw or nose. Shape your dog's movements by moving your hand slowly and clicking later into his target touch.

FIST TARGETING

Some advanced trick trainers distinguish between requesting nose touches and paw touches by using a fist target for one and a palm target for the other, as well as distinct verbal cues for each.

touch your hand, move it a little higher. Click and treat on her upward motion before her paw actually touches your hand. On subsequent reps, raise your hand a little higher for your dog to earn the click and treat. As she becomes fluent with the upward motion, try shaping her movement to follow your hand in a pattern of up, down, then up again in a wave (and of course, click and treat for each success) until she becomes fluent with following that pattern. If she's not catching on, break it down: Just go up and down until she's fluent.

When your dog has become fluent with that step, it's time to wave from a short distance. On this next trial, as she follows up, down, up and is about to touch your hand, move your hand away as you click, then treat her. Even though she didn't touch your hand target, she did follow your hand gestures and was waving, which gets a click and a reward. Little by little, withdraw your hand a bit farther. Mix in some low Paw Shakes to create a guessing game—where will your hand appear next? Your dog will probably like this added challenge as long as she continues to win most of the time.

Add the verbal cue—at the same time you're giving the hand signal—when your dog achieves fluency. Typical verbal cues for the Wave are "wave" and "hi." Once she's fluent with that step, try alternating verbal-only and visual-only cues. If that doesn't come naturally for your dog, go back to the point where she was successful and try again (click and treat), reestablishing fluency before advancing to the next step. Eventually you'll be able to stand a few paces away, flash your dog a Wave hand signal or verbal cue, and have her Wave in return. Cute!

As your dog learns this trick, you will also remove the target (your hand). Removing the target and replacing it with a hand signal and/or verbal cue is an important finishing step in teaching dog tricks.

More Targeting Techniques: Target Object and Target Stick

IF YOU AND YOUR DOG enjoy learning more advanced tricks, you can continue to challenge his learning and precision by using a couple of training aids that professional trainers use: the target object and the target stick. A target is like a substitute for a lure: When your dog touches the target upon your cue, he knows that he will be clicked and rewarded. You have already used your hand as a target when you taught your dog Paw Shake and Rollover: When he touched your hand, he earned a click and treat. Now your dog will learn that he'll be clicked and rewarded when he touches a target object or special pointer.

Let's start with the target object. I recommend using a soft plastic lid from a large yogurt container, a Frisbee (which is larger and easier for the dog to see), or a soccer cone (which he can see at a distance).

OBJECT TARGETING

Similar to hand targeting, you can teach your dog to touch a target object with her nose or paw. Here are two common target objects.

DISC TARGET

As your dog becomes fluent with disc targeting, you can decrease the size of the flat disc. Start with a Frisbee and advance to smaller and smaller discs, such as soft plastic food container lids.

CONE TARGET

Train your dog to go to a certain spot by using a cone target that she can see at a distance. Once your dog learns to touch the cone fluently, gradually increase its distance as you cue her to "touch" or "target."

TARGET STICK: THE SPIN

Also called a *target pointer* (see close-up photo on page 163), it is useful in teaching "movement tricks," such as shaping a spin. Before you begin using the pointer to teach a trick, train your dog to associate touching the stick's tip as a target that earns a click and reward (see facing page).

① HEAD TURN
Movement starts with a head turn. Reward even the slightest head movement at first.

② FRONT PAWS MOVE
When your dog's front paws move, that means she's beginning to follow the pointer. It's worth a jackpot!

③ BACK PAWS MOVE
Jackpot again when her whole body moves. It's more challenging to direct a dog to move away from you than toward you.

④ SECOND HALF
Click first the head turn, then the front paws, and finally the back paws.

⑤ JACKPOT!
Once your dog has mastered one complete spin, add a second spin and move the target stick faster to add speed.

The first step is to get your dog curious about the target. Toss it on the floor near him; if he looks at it, click and treat. Shape your dog's curiosity about the target object by clicking and rewarding as he moves closer to it. Reward your biggest jackpot when he touches the target for the first time with either his nose or his paw. (You'll see later that some cues require a nose touch, such as when he's learning to walk through a dog door flap; other tricks, such as ringing a bell to get you to open the door for him to go potty, work better with a paw touch.)

Once your dog fully understands that he gets rewarded when he touches the target, have him sit before you, and then cue him by pointing to the target and also by naming the behavior (I recommend "touch" or simply "target"), then click and reward when he does. Make sure to use good timing: Click precisely at the moment he touches the target. After each successful trial, move the target a bit farther away or to the side. Once he becomes more fluent with touching the target, have him *sit-stay* until you say "touch" or "target" as you point to the disc. Your dog will probably understand the verbal cue right away if you hold his *sit-stay* until you see his focus shift to the target. Then cue him verbally as you point to the target. In subsequent reps, withdraw your pointing gesture and just use the verbal cue.

You will use a similar technique to train your dog to touch the pointer end of your target stick. A target stick is typically one to three feet long and can be a dowel, ruler, yardstick, or a telescoping pointer (see page 163) made especially for clicker training. It should have a soft rubber pointer or padded tip for safety; also, the padded tip helps your dog distinguish what he's supposed to touch. Although I'm going to teach you to use the target stick, I urge you to exercise caution with it, especially around children, for safety reasons. The average family is better off using an object or hand for targeting.

To start training your dog to touch the target stick, hold the stick an inch from the tip, then click and treat when he looks at it. Move the stick a little closer to your dog and begin shaping his behavior toward touching the tip with his nose. Once he's done this, repeat until he can do it again easily. As he gets better at touching the target stick, hold it farther down the shaft. Place it high, low, and on your shoe. Once your dog gets the basic idea that he gets clicked and rewarded when he touches only the tip of the target stick, you can start moving it to shape his movement. Move the stick slowly between your legs, around your body, and so forth. As you move, you'll see that having your dog follow the pointer end will move him in a pattern, such as walking around you or spinning in circles. Begin withdrawing rewards to shape his movement to become smoother and swifter. You can use the same verbal cue that you used with the disc target: "target" or "touch."

Removing the Target to Teach Ring the Bell

THE FINAL STEP IS to replace the target (disc, stick, or hand) with a hand signal and/or verbal cue. Let's practice this by teaching your dog to ring a bell to let you know that she needs to go outside to potty.

Hang a cowbell or other large bell on the door you use to let her outside, and place it low enough that she can sniff it or bat it with her paw. Start to shape her understanding of the bell's meaning by ringing it yourself the moment before you open the door to take her outside to potty. Bend down to ring it—you want her to see you. Repeat this step over the course of a week before teaching your dog to ring the bell, so that she can get used to the sound and begin to associate it with going outside. If she's timid about the bell, you might want to dampen the sound by wrapping the bell's clapper in cotton.

The dog does not have to be in any particular position; standing near the bell is sufficient. You can use any kind of target (object, stick, or hand) to attract her to touch the bell. If you use your hand, for example, put it in front of the bell and have her target touch your hand hard enough to ring the bell. It's okay to cheat a bit—that is, if she hits your hand too lightly, you can move it back into the bell.

Once your dog has reached fluency with ringing the bell, begin the process of opening the door and taking her outside on each rep. If you are training her at times when she doesn't need to go potty, be sure to take her outside and over to the potty spot on each rep anyhow, and then bring her right back inside to begin another rep. Do that all in one silent action without cueing her to go potty. Remember to use the door training skills that your dog learned in the Fundamentals Training Program: She doesn't get to bolt outside ahead of you. Rather, she must wait until you cue her to go outside. My experience is that over the course of a month or two, your dog will learn to ask you to go potty by ringing the bell on her own.

Although ringing the bell is a very useful trick, be aware that your dog may train you to come running by ringing the bell. My Flat-Coated Retriever, Merit, would ring that bell anytime he wanted to go out and be with the children in the yard or take a swim in the pool at midnight. Ringing the bell is no different than when a dog learns to bark at the door when he wants to go outside; it's not always about needing to use the outdoor potty. He trained us well, so we had to remove the bell for a while.

Fetch/Bring It Here

RETRIEVING (FETCHING) IS USEFUL in real life when you want your dog to go get her Kong or ball from nearby, if you drop your keys on the floor and you can't bend over to get them, or if you want her to pick up her toys and put them in her toy basket. (And who wouldn't want that?) Retrieving is also useful in helping redirect your dog's attention when you anticipate that she may be about to have a behavior problem; I'll talk more about that in Chapter Eleven. You may also want to review Chapter Nine's fundamentals about retrieving.

To train your dog to fetch, start with him on leash and teach him the last part first: Let him take a retrieving toy such as a Kong or knotted rope toy to hold in his mouth by saying "take it." As he opens his mouth, click and give him the toy, then reward him with lots of praise as he holds the toy proudly in his mouth. After a few seconds, say "off" and offer your open hands underneath the toy. When he drops the toy, click, praise, and reward. You're using the cookie trade (or toy trade or *off and take it* trade) and *bring it here* techniques that you learned in the fundamentals course. (To review those techniques, see page 144.) If he has trouble with the previous steps but already knows how to *take it*, you can help him by breaking down those trade behaviors.

Once your dog can take the retrieving toy into his mouth and hold it reliably when you say "take it," it's time to move to the next step: Get into the *cookie sit* position ("glue" your hand to your hip with half the length of your dog's leash wrapped around that hand; see page 106 to review). However, do not ask your dog to sit. You want him to *stand (pose)* as you move the toy in front of his nose (using the empty hand) and toss it about three feet in front of him (or as far as needed to get to it when he does). If he stays, wait

SHAPING BY BACK CHAINING

When you teach your dog to fetch, you use a behavior training technique called *back chaining*. Break down the whole *retrieve* behavior into parts and then link each part of the trick together. You *back chain* them by starting with the last part and working your way in reverse order to the beginning. For example, we use back chaining in the song "The Twelve Days of Christmas." We sing the last part first ("a partridge in a pear tree"), and repeat it over and over as we build backward day by day to the first and final part ("twelve drummers drumming"). When I sing that song, I relax at "five golden rings" on each verse, knowing that I can easily remember the upcoming five back-chained parts. But sometimes I forget how many geese are a-laying or pipers are piping. That's what it's like for your dog when she learns a complex cue, trick, or routine: She looks forward to the doggy equivalent of those five golden rings, confident from that point that she can take it back to the ever-familiar end.

As you teach tricks to your dog, help her learn a complex behavior by breaking it down into parts, which you'll then back chain as you shape them back together in reverse order.

a second and then direct him to the toy by saying "take it." Run with him to get it. The moment he puts his mouth on the toy, click and reward with verbal and physical praise, but don't give him a treat. Instead, hold the treat on his nose. As soon as he sniffs the treat, he will drop the toy into your open hand. Click again and reward him with the treat for dropping the toy. When he can reliably run with you the three feet to pick up the retrieving toy when you say "take it" and then give it to you when you say "off," it's time to add a little more distance: On the next rep, toss the toy a foot farther away and run the exercise the same as before.

When your dog becomes fluent at four feet, don't add any more distance; he is now ready to learn the next step: bringing the toy back to you. In the starting position, toss the toy four feet away, wait a second, then say "take it," run with him, and now allow him to reach the toy before you get there. As soon as he picks it up and turns to bring it back to you (as he did in previous reps), encourage him by saying "bring it here." Stay where you are as you encourage him to bring the toy to you and drop it in your open hand when you say "off." Don't expect your dog to carry the toy all the way to you just yet, so make sure to be close enough that he just needs to carry it a foot or two before dropping it into your open hand. This is the *basic retrieve.*

Once your dog becomes fluent in these basic retrieving skills, you may increase distance by adding one foot at a time.

If necessary, attach him to a 20-foot leash or a long rope tied securely to the leash handle. Run the exercise exactly as before: Start with your dog standing at your side, toss the toy, wait a second, say "take it" and run with him on the leash to take it, and then run back to do the "off" (he drops the toy into your hand). This procedure helps shape his understanding of the long retrieving route. The maximum distance I recommend right now is 20 feet, and it will probably take you and your dog many months—maybe even a year—before he retrieves toys reliably at this great distance.

A few tips for teaching your dog to retrieve: Remember to jackpot the milestone moments. It is more effective and fun to make this a brief exercise at various times rather than something done at one long training session. Finally, your dog's maturity and impulse control strongly influence how much he can handle without failure. It's much more important for him to pick up and hold the toy when you say "take it," and drop it when you say "off," than to be able to respond at great distances.

Free Shaping

SOMETIMES YOUR DOG WILL DO SOMETHING completely on his own, without your direction or prompting, that you want to reward. That's free shaping, and it improves your dog's problem-solving abilities, gets him interested in offering new behaviors (since those are the ones he gets rewarded for), and helps spirit his personality.

Did you ever play the children's game "hot and cold"? In one variation of the game, your friend would think of one object in the room and you would move around the room to figure out which object your friend was thinking of. When you were far away from the object your friend would say "cold." When you got closer to it your friend would say "warm." When you were right next to the object your friend would say "hot." Free shaping works the same way, but rather than using the words *cold*, *warm*, and *hot*, you will click and treat for any behavior that your dog offers that is "warm" (close to what you want), click and jackpot when he is "hot," and not click when he is "cold." There are no prompts, cues, or messages to tell your dog what you want or how to do it. Free shaping is purely a trial-and-error waiting game.

Let's say that you want to use free shaping to teach your dog to lie down on his brand new mat. You may already be thinking that instead of free shaping, you could simply lure him onto the mat or you could place a target on the mat and direct him to touch the target, then cue him into a *down* or a *settle*. For this exercise, though, instead of using the other tools you already have in your toolbox, let's use free shaping to teach him to lie on the mat. The mat is next to where you are standing, and because your dog sees you with the clicker and the treats, he knows that it's time for fun, so he sits in front of you without being asked. You tell him "good sit," but don't click or treat. He waits patiently, but nothing happens. You wait, your dog waits.

If he doesn't realize that he is supposed to do anything other than just stay still, you can give him a hint by tossing a treat on the mat, then click and jackpot him as soon as he steps onto the mat. Then let him play with a toy before resuming the lesson, or end the session and go for a walk together, depending on his focus and eagerness to continue this game. (Time frames for free-shaping exercises will average 5 to 15 minutes, depending on your dog's experience and curiosity level. Always make sure to end the game on a happy note with his achieving success on the last trial, even if it's by giving an easy jackpot on his new mat.)

In any case, if your dog moves just a little bit, click and treat. He repeats the move and earns another click. He does it a third time, but this time there's no click—you're waiting for him to move toward the mat or even look at the mat. Your dog yawns—a sign that he's getting bored or anxious—and you click that. Now he's puzzled. He's not sure what he's getting clicked for, so he starts offering behaviors randomly. That is a key moment in free shaping. When he turns his head toward the mat, he gets clicked (and treated). He repeats that move, another click. He does it again, a third click. He does it a fourth time, but no click. He turns his head toward the mat again—this time more strongly to make sure you see him move—and this time you reward him with a click and a small jackpot. He repeats that strong move, another click (not a jackpot this time, just one treat). He does it again strongly, another click. And again, click. He moves strongly again, but this time there's no click. So he moves even more strongly and wins a click and a small jackpot.

Now your dog's moves toward the mat become more self-assured. After another minute of trial and error, he touches the mat for the first time and gets a jackpot (after the click, of course). So he touches the mat again with more certainty and gets another jackpot. He stands on the mat—another jackpot. So he continues standing on the mat, but nothing happens. He experiments with a couple of movements and dips his head toward the mat, a click. He dips his head again, another click. He touches the mat with his nose and wins a small jackpot. He repeats the nose touch—a click and one treat (but not a jackpot). He touches his nose to the mat more strongly—click and a couple of treats.

Finally, your dog lies down on the mat and wins a big jackpot, and lots of praise and petting. Then you cue him to sit next to the mat, and as he does so, right away you mark it verbally (say "good" but no click), and you wait. He waits, too. Then he turns and lies down on his mat, and you jackpot him again (and give more praise and petting). You repeat the sequence of having him sit next to the mat again, after which he lies down on the mat. You can now name the behavior ("on your mat" or whatever you choose) as he lies down. On subsequent reps, continue this pattern of saying the name as he initiates the *down*. On each rep, have him sit in a slightly different spot before he goes to the mat, and also reposition the mat slightly—this will help your dog generalize the behavior as you put it on verbal cue ("on your mat"). Once your dog is fluent with those steps, say the verbal cue ("on your mat") before he goes to the mat and jackpot him when he does. Continue reinforcing the verbal cue, and once he becomes fluent, mix in some other cues that he already knows and move the mat around the room.

Congratulations! By depending purely on your dog to offer behavior, you have free shaped a new cue. In addition, you helped him gain confidence in creative problem-solving as he figured out how to get the most clicks and treats.

Free Shaping and the 101 Box

ONE OF MY FAVORITE free shaping exercises to discover a dog's natural behaviors is 101 Things to Do with a Box. Prepare for this exercise by trimming the flaps of a large box so that they are half their previous length. Lay the box on the floor near your dog, tipping it on its side carefully so you don't startle her. When she looks at it, click and treat. If she steps toward it,

101 THINGS TO DO WITH A BOX

One way to better understand your dog is by observing her learning about something—say a cardboard box—totally on her own. Does she first use her nose or her paw to explore the box? When you free shape with the 101 Box, click your dog for *any* new behavior she volunteers, praise and treat lavishly.

another click and treat. If your dog looks at the box again—or exhibits any behavior in relation to the box (sniffing, nosing, etc.)—click and treat. It's pretty simple.

If your dog doesn't seem to be getting it, move away and toss a treat into the box to hint at how you want to shape her behavior. If she takes the treat or even moves toward it, click and treat with a jackpot, and end the session. Always make sure to end the 101 Box game on a happy note by running one last successful trial, then put the box away for now and give her a toy to play with or go out for a walk.

At some point in one of these sessions, your dog will get it: Anything she does with that silly box will earn her a click and a treat. You will probably see the moment when your dog gets it because she will suddenly offer a whole flurry of behaviors: pawing the box, stepping on it, bumping her nose against it, smelling it, flipping a flap, chewing on it, dragging it across the floor, climbing inside, putting her paws on top. When that happens, you'll be clicking and treating as fast as you can.

Once she gets it, start withdrawing treats for behaviors she's already shown. Instead, click and treat only for new behaviors she offers; this indicates that she is testing the box. If she has already moved the box slightly, then click and treat only when she moves it a little more. If she has already put her foot into the box, wait to click until she paws the bottom of the box. When shaping new behaviors, always look for opportunities to raise the bar. What's wonderful about the 101 Box is that there is no particular result that you're looking for; rather, you're simply looking for any new behaviors. Because you've changed the game and are now clicking and treating only for new behaviors, your dog may become a bit frustrated, but that will encourage her to experiment, be creative, and solve problems. Frustration in low doses is okay; it's part of the learning process we all go through.

Some dogs may be shy or scared of the box at first. If this is the case, don't force the situation. Just toss a treat in the box. Toss another treat, and another. If they are treats that your dog already values, she will know that they're in the box. If your dog looks at the treats, click and treat her, and then toss another. Toss a treat near the box. Leave the box on the floor as you shift to another exercise, such as luring her around you and through your legs— maybe she'll forget about her fear of the box as she goes near it. At the end of the exercise, if she hasn't eaten her jackpot of treats that have been accumulating in the box, pick them up and put them away as you put away the box. Try again another time and don't fret; some dogs take a long time to warm up to this strange, bountiful box.

Your log of those freely shaped behaviors—yes, you should still be keeping a training log—may give you insights into your dog's natural patterns. Does she first use her nose or her paw to explore the box? The next time you bring it out, does she repeat patterns or try something new? What does she do if you set down the box with the opening facing upward? You'll probably become as curious about your dog's natural behaviors as she is about the box. Having those insights may help you identify other tricks, toys, and activities that she might enjoy. You may even enjoy making up your own original tricks based on some of your dog's unique behaviors with the 101 Box.

More Dog Tricks

NOW THAT YOU AND YOUR DOG ARE FAMILIAR with clicker training and target touching, let's use that system to learn a few more basic tricks. You may discover that your dog really enjoys tricks training. I love it when my students make up their own tricks, often by observing what their dogs offer naturally and by free shaping. Study your training log. Be aware of how your dog progresses during these lessons so you can choose to focus your efforts on tricks that he is most likely to succeed at. Pick one trick to learn at a time; to keep your dog interested, always be prepared to switch to a game, activity, or other training exercise that he already knows. Once you and he master one trick, add another from the list. Students in my fundamentals classes can usually teach their dogs a new trick in about a week.

Sit Pretty (Beg)

WHILE THE SIT PRETTY can be a good exercise for strengthening your dog's back and core muscles, don't use this trick with dogs that have back or hip problems, or dogs with long backs (such as Dachshunds and Basset Hounds), because it can put too much stress on the back.

For this trick, I recommend using a treat lure, although a target stick can also be effective. Start with your dog in a *sit*, and begin *shaping* the Sit Pretty by holding a lure an inch above her

SIT PRETTY (BEG)

Once your dog has mastered sitting for real-life rewards, you may want to teach him to sit in an extra-special way in order to earn extra-special privileges or objects. The Sit Pretty (also called Beg) challenges your dog's sitting skills.

LURE UP
Start your dog in a *sit,* and then lure straight above his head. When he looks up, that's a click and treat.

BALANCE ASSIST
Once you lure high enough so that your dog begins lifting one paw to sniff the treat, help him learn to balance by crouching and offering your forearm.

BOTH PAWS UP
Next, when your dog becomes more confident and balanced, lure a bit higher so that he needs to lift both paws onto your forearm. To polish the trick, you'll eventually remove your forearm.

head. As she lifts her head to the lure, click and allow her to eat the treat. Next, hold the lure an inch or so higher. On the next rep, hold the lure about three inches above her head.

You are, of course, *shaping* your dog to crane her neck higher and higher to get the treat. Eventually, she will need to lift her paws to eat the lure. Watch her front paws closely; when she lifts a paw, that's a jackpot. Once she lifts a paw three times in a row, start raising the lure a bit higher still. Keep going up inch by inch, and when she lifts both paws for the first time, that's a big jackpot. Now try to get her to lift both paws consistently.

When she is consistent with lifting both paws, make sure to insert your forearm so she has a place to put her paws to help her balance. Make that the new baseline for clicking and earning rewards. Eventually, try luring with an empty hand. When she lifts both paws and rests them on your forearm, that's worth a jackpot—click and treat her with your other hand. Continue the empty-handed luring until your dog seems to have gotten it and becomes fluent.

The next step is to name the trick. The most common verbal cues for this trick are "beg," "prayers," or "sit pretty." Or you can name it something totally silly like Peekaboo and modify it by luring your dog's head downward so her nose and eyes are covered and under your arm. When you first add the verbal cue, say it at the same time you use your hand signal. After a few more reps, try a quick rhythm: On the first and second reps, use both the verbal cue and hand signal. Then, on the third rep, use only the verbal cue. If your dog Sits Pretty on just the verbal cue, that's worth a jackpot. Make sure to mark (say "good beg"), praise, and reward on every successful rep. Mix reps of verbal-only with verbal-plus-visual until your dog seems fluent with the trick on both the visual cue alone (your forearm crosses in front of your dog) and the verbal cue alone. The final step is to phase out treats slowly by using slot machine techniques.

SIT PRETTY. This is what the polished trick looks like.

Cookie Nose

IN THIS TRICK, YOUR DOG BALANCES a dog treat on his nose. On cue, he lets the treat slide off his nose and catches it before it hits the floor. Some dogs will even flip the treat up in the air and

THE COOKIE NOSE TRICK

Balance a biscuit on your dog's nose and teach her to flip it up and catch it in her mouth. The trick teaches impulse control, and it's a real crowd pleaser.

THE BALANCE

Before training your dog to flip the biscuit, practice balancing it on her nose. At first you may use your hands to help your dog keep her head still.

THE FLIP

When you cue "take it" your dog may tip her nose to slide the biscuit off. Some trainers *shape* the flip by placing a hand under the dog's muzzle.

THE CATCH

Improve your dog's catching skill by not allowing her to eat any biscuit that hits the floor.

catch it on its way down. A word of warning: Do not do this trick if your dog still has a food guarding problem; that might be flirting with danger. Also, if you have a flat-faced dog, like a pug or bulldog, it will probably be too difficult to balance a treat on his nose, so I suggest that you skip this trick.

Start by cueing your dog to *sit-stay*. Hold a treat to his nose in much the same way as you learned with the *cookie sit-stay* in the Fundamentals Training Program. If he does not flinch, then click and say "take it" as you bring the treat to his mouth by moving toward your dog to give him the treat rather than allowing him to move forward to take it. This way, you are rewarding your dog for staying still.

If your dog tries to get the treat before you tell him to take it, then say "off." If he responds to your *off* signal, then after a moment say "take it," and allow him to take the treat from your fingertips (after you have moved your hand with the treat toward him). If your dog doesn't respond to your *off* right away, take away the treat and practice a different cue that he'll be successful at before you try the Cookie Nose trick again.

When your dog is able to continue sitting still while you hold the treat on his nose, hold the treat a moment longer before you say "take it." Little by little, increase the amount of time before you say "take it." When he can remain sitting still for 10 seconds while you hold the treat on his nose, it's time to add the next step.

Balance the treat on his nose. Let go of the treat, but do not remove your hand until you're ready to say "take it." Let him take the treat. On the next rep, slowly move your hand an inch away from your dog's nose before you say "take it," and then two inches, and then three, and so forth. Don't allow him to eat the treat off the floor if he misses the catch—that will shift his focus to the floor, where he got the last treat, rather than on you and your directional cues. As you'll see, not only does this trick help your dog practice impulse control, it's also a real crowd pleaser.

Back Up

YOU'LL FIND *BACK UP* to be a useful cue, such as when your dog sits too close to you at the dinner table, or you're in a tight parking lot and you need to open your car door for her to jump up onto the backseat. The *back up* can also be useful during a heeling exercise: If she starts to move ahead of you, say "back up" and she will literally take a step back closer to you as you continue to walk forward.

Start with your dog standing in front of you and take one step toward her. If she backs up, click and treat. Take another step, and if she backs up again, give another click and treat. Continue backing up one step at a time, clicking and treating with each step. As you get closer to a wall or obstacle, lure your dog forward to restart the sequence, backing up one or two steps at a time until she is fluent and confident. Next, add the verbal cue ("back up") and simultaneous hand signal: Turn one hand palm down and gently flick your wrist toward your dog. Practice that one-step and two-step backup using verbal and visual cues together. Once that is fluent, add a third step, and then a fourth. Continue to use the *back up* in a variety of hallways and spaces around your home so she will generalize this behavior to other places.

If your dog doesn't back up easily, use this "chute" technique. Start the *back up* in a hallway or along a wall or fence. Create a narrow chute by placing a row of chairs parallel to the wall. If your dog is smaller and might try to sneak out under the chairs, simply drape a sheet over them. Make the chute narrow enough that she can't turn around in it. Your first step is to stand one step into the chute and cue her to come forward to you—mark verbally (say "good"), but do not click or treat. Then walk toward your dog so that she backs up that one step out of the chute, and when she does so, click and treat. The reason you first cue your dog into the chute and then back her out of it, rather than start by trying to get her to back into the chute, is that it takes advantage of your dog's natural desire to get out of a confined area, rather than force her to go against her natural aversion to being backed up into a confined chute. Repeat that a few times so she becomes fluent with backing up that one step.

When your dog is fluent with that first step into the chute, you can add a verbal cue (say "back up") and simultaneous hand signal: Turn your hands palm down and gently flick your wrists toward your dog. Practice that one-step backup out of the chute using verbal and visual cues together. Once that skill is fluent, stand two steps into the chute and practice until that is fluent. These first steps may seem too easy for some dogs, but I'd like you to do them anyhow: This is an exercise that builds trust— your dog learns that she'll be safe when you're backing her up, that you're not putting her into a dangerous situation that she's unable to see.

This method makes backing up simple and rewarding for most dogs. If it's still too hard for yours, move on to a cue she already knows, and come back to this one another day (even if you're tempted to try to muscle her through it because you went to some effort to make the chute). For these first couple of steps, it's most important that your dog develop trust in you.

Once she is fluent and seems confident with these first two steps, then you can add another step. Start by standing three steps into the chute, cue her to come forward into the chute, mark it verbally when she reaches you, then immediately start to back her out, stepping toward her and using visual and verbal cues together. It will probably take a number of training sessions for your dog to feel comfortable backing up all the way out of the chute without turning around or looking behind her. Take it slowly. If she resists, change to another exercise that she's already successful at, such as doing a set of Puppy Pushups right there, and then lure her forward to you, until you're both out of the chute and ready for another activity. Return to the chute at another training session.

Move the chute to various places around your home so that your dog will generalize the *back up*. Eventually the chute will no longer be needed, so take it down one piece at a time, to help her gain fluency with each modification that you make, before taking down the next piece. Continue to use the *back up* in a variety of hallways and spaces. Eventually, she will generalize this behavior to all places without the chute.

Once your dog is fluent on the *back up*, you might have fun creating a dance step with her: back and forth, back and forth. You might even want to choreograph a dance routine: Keep your back to your dog as she follows you, then turn around and face her so that she backs up. (If dancing with your dog interests you, see the introduction to canine freestyle dancing in Appendix 2.)

Bow

YOU'VE PROBABLY NOTICED YOUR dog bowing to another dog as an invitation to play. You can train your dog to bow, which is a fun trick to cue at the end of a performance, especially if it's made directly from a Sit Pretty or a Wave. To begin shaping his Bow on cue, start with him standing. Lure him toward a down by pulling a treat from his chest to the floor, and click just as his front legs start to bend. (Click at the start of the leg bend to help your dog distinguish this from going all the way down as you have previously taught him.)

If dogs are well socialized, playing together is second nature.

Once your dog has acquired the distinction between the full *down* and this front-leg bend, you can shape the bend down farther while his rump remains up in the air. It's okay to put your arm under his belly next to his back legs to keep his rump up, or you can use his leash as a sling under his belly to hold his back legs up while his front legs bend down. Jackpot him as he touches down the first time. Using the leash in this manner can be tricky; be sure that you know your dog well and that he is comfortable with the leash underneath his belly.

I generally find that it's best to introduce a modified hand signal before withdrawing the sling or arm assist. A distinctive hand signal is to slide an arm down in an arc toward the floor and continue the gentle arc up toward your dog. Once your dog bows fluently to your arcing arm signal, you should be able to completely withdraw the sling or arm assist from under his belly.

When he becomes fluent in bowing without the assist, add the verbal cue ("bow") at the end of each successful rep. After you have done about five successful reps that way, it's time to try a verbal-only cue without the hand signal. To begin, try a quick rhythm: First say the cue and immediately follow with the hand signal, repeat that on the next rep, and on the third rep say the cue as you start the hand signal and click (and stop your hand signal) as he bows. From that point, mix trials of verbal-visual, verbal-only, and visual-only cues.

Here's a polishing tip: To get a deeper Bow, glide your hand closer to your dog's chest before arcing up. As you arc up, ideally your dog will stay in the Bow position as he tilts only his head up to follow your arcing signal.

Circle Me

IN ADDITION TO BEING A FUN TRICK, Circle Me is useful in getting your dog positioned at your heel to begin walking and for general behavior control.

Let's teach Circle Me with a lure. Start with your dog sitting in front of you. Drop your leash if you are at home in a quiet environment that won't distract him, or tether the leash to your belt loop (giving him enough room to circle around you without pulling on it). You should be able to lure him around your right side fairly easily, especially if you've been playing Follow the Lure (see page 153). Click and treat as he moves even with your right hip; that's his first jackpot. Next, continue to shape his movement so that he circles all the way behind you; that's his second jackpot.

When he is behind your back, you'll pass the treat from your right hand to your left hand, and continue to lure him toward your left hip; that's his third jackpot. Finally, lure him to sit at your left side; that's your dog's fourth jackpot. Continue to practice this full circle until he is fluent with circling around you and sitting on your left.

Next, hold a few lures in your left hand and lure with your (empty) right hand. As your dog circles behind you, hold your left hand behind your back to lure him to *sit* at your left side for a jackpot. On subsequent reps, position the left hand closer and closer to the ending position at your left hip. Eventually, you will be able to hold a lure at your left hip while your empty right hand motions your dog to circle all the way around you. When he can circle you fluently, add the verbal cue "circle me." I recommend that you continue to use the hand signal even after you have named the cue for your dog.

CIRCLE ME

Use this skill to reposition your dog to begin walking at your heel. The trick also teaches your dog to pay attention to cues from both of your hands.

1 START THE LURE
Hold the treat in your right hand and lure your dog toward your right side.

2

AROUND YOUR HIP
When your dog can pass your right hip, that's worth a treat—and a jackpot.

3 SHIFT THE LURE
Behind your back, shift the lure to your left hand's fingertips. It's best to practice the shift without your dog present so that you don't fumble during training.

4 TOWARD YOUR HEEL
Move your left hand smoothly as you lure toward your left heel.

5 LURE TO A SIT
You'll see that a *sit* is just about to happen. That's the finish. When your dog becomes fluent, start the trick without a treat in your right hand.

TOY CLEANUP

This complex trick combines retrieving skills with the *off and take it* cue. Try training your dog to enjoy cleaning up her toys by using back chaining (see page 173), and teach the last part of the trick first.

TAKE IT & DROP IT

① Start by having your dog pick up a toy from the box (say "take it") and then drop it back into the box (say "off").

PRACTICE RETRIEVING

② Place a toy near the box, then have your dog fetch and drop it in the box. Use the fetch/retrieve technique taught in this chapter (see page 177).

③

ADD TOYS AND DISTANCE

Once your dog fluently puts one toy in the box, add a second toy. Eventually, you'll add more toys and distance.

Toy Cleanup

AFTER YOUR DOG masters the retrieving skills she learned earlier in this chapter, you can teach her to clean up after herself.

Put a toy on the floor and kneel about three feet away from it. Point to the toy and say "take it." When she does so, that's a click and reward.

She may only look at the toy at first. If that's the case, break down the behavior so that you can shape it into a *take it*. Start by clicking and treating when she merely looks at the toy, then wait to click until she gets closer to it, and then even closer, until she finally touches it for a jackpot. Next, she must pick up the toy for another jackpot. Using the Fetch/Retrieve techniques, teach your dog to bring the toy to you; that's another jackpot. I recommend sitting with the empty toy basket in front of you. If you place your hands over the basket, you may be able to get her to drop the toy in the basket when you say "off." If she does, that's a jackpot.

If dropping the toy into the basket seems difficult for your dog, I recommend teaching that part of the trick separately, and then back chain the rest of the trick onto it. Start to teach the basket part of the trick by having her take the toy out of the basket and immediately clicking and treating when she does so. Then have her drop the toy into the basket by saying "off," then click and offer her another treat. On subsequent reps, have her hold the toy for a few more seconds before you click and treat, and have her drop the toy into the basket again. The next step is to place the basket with the toy a step or two away from your dog, and then signal her to take it, hold it, and drop it into the basket. When that part of the trick seems fluent, try back chaining the rest of the trick: Have her pick up the toy again and drop it in the basket. You will probably need patience and additional breakdown steps to keep your dog motivated.

Once she has mastered picking up one toy and putting it in the basket, add a second toy, and then a third. See how many objects you can actually get her to put in the basket. I think you'll find that once she is fluently putting in three toys, she'll progress to a fourth and fifth fairly easily. When you're teaching this trick, make sure to put the toys and the basket in slightly different spots on each rep to help your dog to generalize this behavior.

The next step is to add a visual signal, like patting the basket, and a verbal cue. I use "clean up" and point to a toy while I am near the basket. Finally, move farther and farther away from the basket as you cue your dog. How far you move away is determined by her success rate. If she is learning this behavior fairly well, you can move a short distance away from the basket. Keep it simple, brief, and fun!

A Glance Back to the Beginning

AT THE END OF MY TRICKS training program, I enjoy asking my students to take turns talking briefly about the time they first brought their dogs home. Can you remember what your dog was like when you first saw him? What were you like? Do you still have the list of goals on your fridge? How have you progressed?

Now that you've learned the fundamentals and have continued to challenge your dog with new skills and tricks, it is a good time to revisit the goals you first set for yourself and your dog.

What are you hoping for in the future? What additional skills or tricks would you like your dog to work toward? As I'm sure you're witnessing, the skills that your dog is mastering are not just helpful around the home, but they also make it possible for your dog to have a wider range of real-life experiences. How wonderful it is to be able to take your confident and spirited dog into public places.

As you move forward, keep your dog's training sharp by adding new skills, tricks, and socialization opportunities.

CHAPTER 11

Behavior Problems

DESPITE THE NUMBER of hours you spend training, even the best-behaved dog may, at some time in his life, develop bad habits—from chewing or soiling the house to exhibiting aggression. Behavior problems are not a reason to panic or, worse, to give up on a dog. The truth of the matter is that most problems are not the fault of the dog, they are a result of human error. Even though we mean well, we sometimes make mistakes that cause our dogs to misbehave. For example, many dogs are relinquished to shelters and rescue organizations for being destructive or going potty in the home too many times. But both of these behaviors are preventable, and are often a result of our lack of attention to our dog's natural needs or our failure to set appropriate boundaries. When we're impatient with our dog's mistakes, we might aggravate his misbehavior by exiling him to the

I hope that with patient practice and careful training, you and your dog will have a happy and healthy relationship with very few problems. Still, behavior issues sometimes arise, and this chapter is designed to help you deal with them. First I'll detail some of the main causes of behavioral problems, including both health and environmental triggers. Then, with tools like redirecting, substitution trades, and counterconditioning, you'll be able to help your dog get over any training or socialization problems he may have developed. You'll also find some more detailed information about what type of training collar might be best for your dog.

basement, garage, or laundry room, or simply by ceasing to spend the time required to train him, and he's left on his own, having to raise himself.

When a dog needs more attention, he'll do anything to get it, even if that something is bad. Dogs are social animals that want to belong to a pack, and they may rather be scolded than ignored, because to a dog, any attention (even if it's negative or punishing) is better than none at all. This can cause a destructive cycle. The more we scold him, the more he'll engage in the behavior that brings about a scolding. We promote this destructive cycle when we unwittingly reinforce our dog's bad behavior and encourage him to do it some more. Too many times, this cycle will reach a breaking point, where we decide the growing problem is just too much to handle, and end up giving up on the dog . . . and on ourselves. If you have done that, trust me, there's no reason to feel any shame about it. You will make mistakes. The key is to learn from them.

> **When a dog needs more attention, he'll do anything to get it.**

The first thing to understand is that a dog doesn't know that he is misbehaving. All he knows is that he's acting like he's supposed to: like a dog. Later, we'll discuss how to use specific tools to prevent and stop certain behaviors. But let me first outline a few common mistakes we all make with our dogs, all of which can, and should, be avoided.

One of the most common training errors we commit is to punish a dog *after* he's committed the offense—even if it's just minutes after, it makes things worse, not better. Say, for example, you come home to find your sofa pillow shredded, and your dog sleeping calmly on his mat, with pillow fuzz all over his beard. While you are, I imagine, understandably upset, he's just thrilled to see you and doesn't even remember the shredding. Therefore, if you scold him by yelling at him and rubbing his nose in the evidence, it's unlikely that he'll make the connection or remember the reprimand the next time he has an impulse to shred. Instead, he is more apt to learn that whenever you come home to find him lying calmly on his mat, he's going to get scolded. This conduct just confuses our beloved dogs and, I believe, weakens our bond with them. The best way to stop an unwanted behavior is to catch your dog in the act and redirect him to a different activity.

Dogs desire consistency, and they don't understand how to behave if we suddenly change the rules. For example, when we first get a puppy, it's common to let the little bundle of fur climb and jump all over us. After all, we're trying to bond with him, and frankly, we love the feeling of being close to him. But when he eventually grows bigger and his climbing stops being a novelty, we change the rules: no more jumping, no more climbing, no more pawing, no more cute begging. If you change the rules on your dog, it's not fair to expect him to understand immediately either that things have changed or why he is being punished when he continues to follow the old rules. From the dog's perspective, your behavior seems arbitrary and mean. It's we who have been inconsistent, not the dog.

We also unintentionally cause or reinforce our dog's bad behavior by teaching him that what we say isn't important. As we discussed in Chapter Five (see page 95), behaviorists call this learned irrelevance. We need to remember to pay attention to our verbal cues, consistently offering them only once and in the same tone of voice. The same goes for visual cues: Offer a hand signal only once, and with precisely the same gesture as last time.

Learned irrelevance can also come about if we give too much praise. It's like eating too much candy. The first piece is delicious and we savor it, but the tenth piece . . . not so much. So it is with praising our dog: If we constantly praise or reward every little tiny thing he does, each instance of praise seems less valuable. Over time, our well-meaning attempts to provide positive reinforcement can start to backfire, as our dog learns that there is no special consequence to obeying a cue; whatever he does will be rewarded. And the same goes for punishment. If we reprimand or scold our dog too harshly or frequently, he will learn to tune it out or, worse, will give up and lose his spirit. Always be sure that what you say to him is important and has consequences.

Why Do Dogs' Behaviors Suddenly Change?

PEOPLE OFTEN CALL, their voices steeped with worry, to ask me why their typically obedient and well-behaved dog has suddenly developed a bad habit. While there is never a simple or sure answer to this question, it's good to look first for some common triggers that can cause a dog to lose focus. Think of yourself: A sudden back spasm or chronic toothache distracts you in the middle of cooking, and you burn the dinner. Hearing that certain song on the car radio triggers a memory of prom night all those years ago, you lose focus . . . and the highway turnoff. Some triggers we love, while others make us into absolute monsters. The same goes for dogs: Some triggers can suddenly turn our sweet dogs into hellhounds. We need to learn what our dog's triggers are, anticipate them, and replace the undesirable behaviors with desirable ones.

Health Triggers

MY IRISH WATER SPANIEL, Aisley, was the perfect puppy. She learned quickly and was well socialized. But when Aisley was nine months old she had a small seizure, after which she would snap at imaginary flies, get up in the middle of the night and twirl, and hide behind a chair as if she was trying to get away from the flies. Aisley also became increasingly aggressive toward other dogs and started displaying fearful behaviors toward strangers and my children. It was sudden and scary. A sudden behavior change for no apparent reason may mean your dog has a health issue that he can't communicate to you. His hip pain might make him snap at any dog that gets near his hindquarters. If he has a toothache, he may respond aggressively if you try to touch his face.

Therefore, my first word of advice to anyone whose dog suddenly develops a behavior change is to take her to a vet and determine whether there are underlying health issues. Also call the shelter or breeder where you got your dog, and discuss what you are experiencing.

Environmental Triggers

A DOG'S ENVIRONMENT IS CONSTANTLY CHANGING. Maybe your child's friend accidentally hurt him when your back was turned, and now when there's a sleepover, that child triggers your dog to hide or growl. Certain people or other animals trigger your dog's aggression or fearful behavior for what seems like no reason. Or the reason may seem obvious: Ever since the neighbor's tomcat bloodied your dog's nose, he barks and cowers behind you when any cat is around. The vacuum cleaner's monstrous rumble triggers her to start barking the moment she sees you take it out of the closet. That vacuum cleaner and other strange moving objects such as shopping carts, skateboards, and wheelchairs may trigger your dog's impulse to escape or try to run them down to tear them apart.

Tools to Address Behavior Problems

HE SAYING GOES that when the only tool you have is a hammer, everything looks like a nail. A good trainer's toolbox is chock-full of implements so that we can be sure to have at least one workable solution ready to use. It takes knowledge to know which tool to use in a given situation, and practice in how to use it well, so don't get frustrated if modifying your dog's bad behavior takes time and tests your patience. Just be consistent, firm, and loving—and, most of all, keep using positive reinforcement techniques—and I promise that you'll see a difference.

Redirecting

HAVE LEARNED THAT when your dog is engaging in bad behavior, it's always more effective to refocus him—a training technique we refer to as *redirecting*—than it is to punish him.

Boz, the rescue Border Collie that I'm currently fostering and training, got very anxious and excited whenever he heard either a soda can being opened or the sound of my printer working. He'd start whimpering, growling, and rushing around until he found something to destroy, such as my appointment book or bedspread.

Once I recognized this pattern, I knew that the best way to stop it was to redirect him: Direct him to something else before I opened a can. I began by tossing Boz his favorite ball and cueing him to take it. Once he had the ball in his mouth, I'd pop the can, and before he could react, I'd tell him to bring me the ball (using the Retrieve trick that is detailed on page 177). I'd hold the can as if it were no big deal, request a *sit* from him, and ask him to drop

REDIRECTING

I f you catch your dog in the act of going near contraband or an off-limits area (such as a garbage pail), redirect her attention to something positive, such as a special toy. (The other recommended way to lessen this kind of unwanted behavior is to keep your home dogproofed.)

1

REACT EARLY

As soon as you see your dog wander, get that special object. Over time, you'll learn to anticipate your dog's moves and be ready more quickly.

2

REDIRECT HER ATTENTION

Get your dog to focus on the high-value object and away from the unwanted behavior.

3

REDIRECT HER ACTION

Engage her fully with the rewarding activity and praise.

the ball in my hand. Then I'd throw it for him to retrieve. I did this over and over again, several times a day for a while, and now when Boz sees me with a soda can in my hand, he automatically brings me his ball 80 percent of the time, knowing that he will be praised and rewarded. I have redirected Boz's barking and frantic behavior with a behavior that is far more rewarding for him: holding a ball in his mouth to bite on, retrieving, bringing it back to me, and starting the game over. I'm still working on him. . . .

Redirecting is a useful technique for modifying many unwanted behaviors, and the key to it is good timing. For example, I need to make sure that Boz's ball is available *before* I get a soda can from the fridge. If it isn't visible and ready, and I wait until he is already barking at the can to find it, he will be very distracted and anxious, and it will be far more difficult to redirect him to get it. I need to time the redirection to occur before he begins barking.

Substitution Trades

ANOTHER USEFUL TECHNIQUE IS the *substitution* trade. Dogs love making trades for something of equal or greater value. Remember my dog Merit's story? He stole the chicken carcass off the kitchen counter (where it should not have been left unattended), and brought it to me knowing that he would probably get an excellent trade, and he did: a stuffed Kong and tons of praise!

The key to making a substitution trade is to have the alternative ready at all times; you never know when you'll need it. I always have a stuffed Kong ready in the fridge or freezer. If your dog has a toy she particularly loves, make sure that it's in a place you can get to quickly. I recommend that you begin practicing substitution trades regularly along with the *off and take it* trades in the Fundamentals Training Program.

Counterconditioning, Desensitizing, Habituation

WHEN BOZ SEES ME get a soda can, he's currently learning to redirect his own focus and get his ball. Since Boz's impulse is to behave destructively when he hears that soda can open, I am *counterconditioning* his reactions. Counterconditioning is the process of teaching a dog to do something that goes against his natural impulses. Merit dropped the chicken rather than give in to his impulse to eat it because I had counterconditioned him continually from eight weeks of age to know the value of making a substitution trade.

Desensitizing is a key component of counterconditionings, so much so that behaviorists often refer to them together with the acronym DSCC: desensitizing and counterconditioning.

In the Fundamentals Training Program, you learned to desensitize your dog to the sound of the doorbell by completely ignoring the sound when your partner rang it. You probably needed a whole lot of patience while your dog barked his brains out when the bell rang, but eventually he became accustomed to this sound—you had desensitized him to it. In other words, you taught him that the doorbell meant nothing at all, and reacting to it brought no reward. You modeled desensitized behavior for your dog by ignoring the doorbell yourself.

Sometimes, a dog needs to be counterconditioned gradually to deal with fears that may seem irrational to us. In my class there was once a Border Collie, Pip, that was fearful of the classroom's slippery linoleum floor. For Pip, touching the slick floor was like walking on ice, so she couldn't concentrate and couldn't learn. Pip was so fearful in the classroom that she wouldn't let me touch her. I suggested that Pip's owners bring a carpet to class. We rolled out the carpet every week for Pip to train on. She was comfortable on the carpet; she started to learn. Between classes, Pip's owners did homework with her on the carpet in different environments. Then they started generalizing with Pip, moving off the carpet and onto other nonslick surfaces. Back in the classroom, we reduced the size of Pip's carpet each week, but we always started training with her at exactly the same spot on the carpet. By week four, we were able to move the smaller carpet toward another area of the classroom. By the end of week five, Pip was training without the carpet, totally focused on her owners and the current lesson, not on the environment. She also allowed me to touch her body and her collar, hand her food, and cue her to sit. Pip became desensitized to the linoleum floor because we worked at a pace that made sense for her.

Also related to desensitization is the concept of *habituation.* An example of habituation is when next-door neighbors renovate their home. At first, the construction noise is distracting and we may find it challenging to focus, but after a while the noise fades into the background and we are no longer distracted. Sometimes we become so habituated that it actually seems too quiet when the sounds stop. The joke goes that the aristocrat from the big city couldn't sleep at his quiet country villa until he instructed his servants to carry garbage cans up to his bedroom and bang on them until he fell asleep. We can become habituated to the strangest things, and so can our dogs.

I habituated my Giant Schnauzer, Saxon, to the vacuum cleaner . . . very slowly. At first, I moved him out of the room whenever I turned on the vacuum cleaner (I have a lot of dog hair in my home). Then, I left the vacuum cleaner out in the living room in plain sight. Over time, Saxon came to see it as part of our decor—just another piece of furniture. Once he became habituated and stopped reacting to the vacuum's sound and movements, I took it one step further: I wanted to help him actually enjoy the vacuum cleaner. I dropped treats around it; I fed his meals around it; we trained next to it. Saxon made such a positive association with that machine that he followed it around as if it somehow fed him treats, and I had to tell him to move out of the way so I could vacuum the floors.

Solving Specific Behavior Problems

IT'S HELPFUL to sort behavior problems into two main categories: *training problems* and *social problems*. While there is some overlap between the two, you will find that when you identify the category, it will be easier to select an effective remedy. In general, training problems are solved by using tools that refocus or diminish behaviors, such as desensitization and counterconditioning (DSCC) techniques, whereas social problems also require us to help our dog play well with others.

Training Problems

EACH OF THE PROBLEMS in this section comes about when a dog's training fundamentals have begun to break down. This happens. Even after you and your dog complete the Fundamentals Training Program, and your dog seems to be well trained, it's important to keep up the training—doing homework exercises or learning new tricks—or problems may arise. The good news is that most of these problems can be fixed by recommitting to the fundamentals and by using DSCC tools to diminish problem behaviors by replacing them with desirable ones.

HOUSE SOILING

SOMETIMES A FULLY HOUSE-TRAINED DOG will start going potty inside the home. Before you address house soiling as a behavior problem, consult your veterinarian to rule out a possible health issue. If your dog develops a house-soiling problem, please remain committed to solving this manageable behavior problem with the spirit of learning and fun, and not with the threat of punishment. Unfortunately, house soiling is one of the most common reasons dogs are relinquished to shelters. Not necessary! All you need is patience and commitment. I have heard a long list of reasons my clients believe that their dogs have regressed when it comes to potty training: anxiety, not getting enough attention, new pets, new family members, a family member's stress, illness or departure, the urine smell in the carpeting from a previous dog or cat, a new cleaning product, new furniture, reupholstered furniture, rearranging the old furniture, or just a phase that the dog is maturing through. I respect all reasons; I look to all of them for possible clues that may have triggered a dog's changed behavior. Whatever the cause, the first step (after a vet checkup) is to retrain your dog beginning from step one: Show her the potty spot, walk the same route to get there, reteach her potty signals and cues, and restart the same positive reinforcement potty-training methods you used when you first welcomed her into your family. Take her out to potty as if she were a puppy again. Go as often as possible: when you wake up, before you go to work, after meals, as soon as you come home, before and after any excitement, before going to sleep. Dogproof your home again, put up the x-pens and baby gates, close the doors, and make sure that everyone in the family is on board with this retraining plan.

Starting over also means reestablishing your dog's routine. That includes restarting crate training and the hand-feeding protocol. Reread this book's sections on potty training, crate training, and the hand-feeding protocol, and resume the assignments related to those lessons. As you start over, think back and make a list of changes in the environment to help you determine what may be causing your dog to regress. You may discover environmental changes; if so, you'll need to desensitize and countercondition your dog to adapt—on her own timetable. You may need to look at the rewards you are providing and determine whether you need to change them. Maybe you need to change *how* you give the rewards by making them seem as valuable and exciting as you did when your dog was a puppy.

Part of your detective work means being honest with what I believe to be the most important factor: your own consistency and behavior. Perhaps somewhere along the line you took it for granted that your dog was fully trained, and you therefore stopped praising and rewarding her too soon. Maybe you inadvertently encouraged your dog's house soiling by giving her too much negative attention or consoling pity when you first noticed an accident. If so, try to remain calm and matter-of-fact as you redirect your dog's focus, clean up the mess, and give her appropriate positive attention. You may need to give her more consistent interaction and supervision. You may need to modify your own schedule, provide more positive socialization opportunities, attend group training classes, or bring in caretakers to help you.

CHEWING

ALONG WITH HOUSE SOILING, chewing is the second most common reason that owners give up their dogs. Some dog owners will put up with chewing and not do anything about it for a while. Maybe they aren't sure of how to deal with it, or maybe they think that their dogs will stop on their own. Eventually, they become so frustrated over the destruction that they give up their dog. It pains me to see this happen because, in my experience, chewing happens when we do not give our dog enough valuable activity or attention. We end up punishing the dog for our mistake.

If your dog is a "chewer," your first question is this: "Is he bored?" Oftentimes a dog chews when there's nothing else for him to do. Is your dog getting enough exercise? Have you continued to put enough time into maintaining his training? In other words, is he getting enough positive interaction and stimulating challenge?

Chewing is a lot more tempting for dogs when their environment isn't dogproofed. Help your dog to be successful by gating off areas that are too tempting. Put away all contraband, use non-staining bitter spray on tempting areas, and reread this book's section on dogproofing your home for more specifics. When your dog is out of his crate, supervise him. Make sure that you are continuing to help him love his crate, and that he doesn't view it as a place of exile. Chewing does not go away on its own; the problem requires your active participation in redirecting your dog's focus toward positive and engaging experiences. If you permit chewing (or other unwanted behaviors) to continue, you will be providing an unhealthy environment for your dog in which happy energy will diminish.

LEASH PULLING

THE BEST WAY TO CORRECT LEASH PULLING is to have a zero tolerance policy. The more a dog is allowed to pull during

(continued on page 208)

CORRECTIVE COLLARS AND PROPER HARNESSING

I support the careful use of a few specific training collars that are used only while walking a dog on leash. I recommend the Gentle Leader head halter, the no-pull body harness, and the Martingale collar (also referred to as a Greyhound collar). Please keep in mind that the improper use of any training collar can hurt your dog, so follow the manufacturer's instructions and consider getting assistance from a knowledgeable trainer. For safety, take off any training collar when your dog plays with another dog or goes to the dog park.

As I've discussed earlier, I am against using choke chains and prong collars, which I find inhumane and ineffective. At best, these devices punish a dog for doing something wrong, without leading the dog toward the correct behavior. At worst, they can hurt a dog and suppress dangerous aggression. Suppressing a behavior can create a pressure-cooker effect: The aggressive impulse is still in the dog, and who the heck knows when the pressure will blow and the dog may become dangerous? If you've previously trained your dog this way, remember that it's never too late to cross over as I did; my dogs' retired choke chains now decorate the inside of my parrots' cages, attached to parrot toys.

The Gentle Leader head halter is an effective training tool for proper leash walking. The leash attaches to the halter

RECOMMENDED TRAINING COLLARS AND HARNESSES

I f you use a training collar or harness for walking your dog, he still always wears his "uniform": a flat buckle collar that displays his dog tags.

GENTLE LEADER
Like a horse halter, it helps you lead your dog by his chin. Learn to use it safely.

BODY HARNESS
Use only a harness which a leash clips to at the chest, in order to lead your dog more effectively.

MARTINGALE
Also called Greyhound collars, they are especially effective for dogs with narrow heads (like Greyhounds) and can be used with most breeds.

under the dog's chin, so that when the dog pulls, she automatically turns back toward you. Be careful using a head halter; if the dog pulls too hard, she could flip around, twist her neck, and hurt herself.

Most dogs need to become accustomed to wearing a head halter before learning to walk while wearing one. Proceed very slowly; use lots of praise and treats. Start teaching your dog to like her head halter by giving her treats as you touch the halter to her head. Little by little, lure her to put her head inside the halter as you give her treats and jackpots, and take the halter away at the end of each rep. Before you snap the halter onto her face for the first time, loosen it all the way, and feed her treats while she focuses on you. Try some Puppy Pushups to take her mind off the halter. On subsequent reps, you'll see where you need to adjust the halter; make those adjustments when you take the device off her head. Once you get to the point that she allows you to buckle the halter, buckle it for only a moment at first while you treat her. On subsequent reps, add time and practice some training behaviors that she already knows. Before you try a walk, have her wear the head halter while she eats a few of her meals (supervised, of course). Continue to condition your dog to accept this strange device very slowly and for short periods of time.

When it's time to start walking, you may, as a safety precaution, use a second leash that is attached to her regular flat-buckle collar so that if she pulls too hard, you can give a little slack on the leash that's attached to the halter so that she doesn't hurt her neck. Ideally, when she pulls, she'll feel just enough pressure around her head so that she'll turn toward you. As she does, mark the behavior, praise her, and lure or guide her to walk with you in the opposite direction.

Many people mistake a head halter for a muzzle and may think that your dog will bite. If people ask you why your dog is wearing a muzzle, I suggest that you take a moment to educate them in a friendly way that it's a training device and not a muzzle, and demonstrate how it works, which turns it into a socialization experience for your dog. Most people appreciate knowing this information, and you will help spread the word about positive reinforcement training.

Be aware that short-snouted dogs (technically known as brachycephalic)—such as Bulldogs, Boxers, Pugs, and Boston Terriers—can slip out of most types of head halters because they have flat muzzles. It's not impossible to use a head halter on a flat-faced dog, but you should take precaution by attaching a second leash to her flat-buckle collar so that your dog doesn't run loose if she slips out.

I also support the use of certain body harnesses that connect to the leash at the dog's chest (rather than above the dog's spine), as long as you follow the manufacturer's instructions. Similar to the head halter, a body harness that has a leash attachment at the chest will cause a pulling dog to turn back toward you.

The Martingale, or Greyhound collar, is a nonslip collar for dogs with narrow heads, like Greyhounds, Whippets, Ibizan Hounds, and other slender sighthounds (dogs that hunt by sight rather than by scent) on which a regular flat-buckle collar would slip off. The Martingale hangs fairly loosely around the dog's neck until the dog pulls, which tightens the collar without strangling. While wearing a Martingale, she should also continue to wear the flat-buckle collar to which her tags are attached.

Even if you use a training collar or harness, continue to develop your dog's excellent leash walking skills through attention, treats, and positive reinforcement. Your goal is to have a well-behaved dog that walks nicely on a loose leash and is focused on you.

(continued from page 205)

walks, the more he will get into the habit of thinking he's in control of the walk, making it increasingly difficult for you to get back your control over his walking behavior. If your dog starts to pull, stop and do the "be a tree" exercise you learned in the Fundamentals Training Program (see page 81). Resume walking only after you have his full attention, and then lead him in a new direction. And if you're having pulling issues, it is better to go out for brief walks several times a day rather than a few long ones.

Review and incorporate the other leash walking exercises from the Fundamentals Training Program, including Follow the Lure and tethering. I also recommend doing some focusing exercises during the walks, such as a sudden stop followed by a quick cue to something, like a Puppy Pushup, with which your dog is already fluent. If you notice that some areas are too tempting or distracting, avoid those places until your dog has built up a history of success while on leash. After all, dogs see, smell, and hear things that we cannot, so be aware of this when leash walking. On some walks, try a give-and-take approach: Take control and keep your dog close to your heel for certain parts of the walk, then reward him with a looser leash to allow a round of sniffing and pee marking.

You may wish to consider a training collar (see box on page 206), but don't use one as a substitute for proper on-leash walk training. If a dog pulls too hard, he could injure his neck and trachea, so be aware that any coughing or choking may require you to stop the walk immediately and get professional help. If you have a dog walker who takes him out for midday exercise while you are at work, keep in mind that many professional walkers take several dogs at a time, so leash pulling can escalate. If you can afford a private dog walker, you may wish to consider that option.

DIGGING

MOST DOGS LIKE TO DIG; it's in their genes. Dogs can smell, hear, and sense creatures in the ground, so they will dig to find them. Digging engages all of a dog's senses: sight, hearing, touch, smell, and taste. If you don't want your flowers or plants dug up, you may have to fence them off. While that may not be the garden aesthetic you were hoping for, it might be better than a garden full of uprooted plants and potholes.

For persistent diggers, 1 recommend a compromise—what about allowing your dog to dig in certain areas? One of my favorite ways to make digging fun and acceptable is to buy or build a children's sandbox, fill it with sand, and hide a few newspaper-wrapped surprises in it. The dog gets to dig around for the packages, pull them up, tear them open, and eat the treat or play with the toy. To keep the sandbox in good shape, put a waterproof cover over it when it is not in use.

When you don't want your dog to dig, supervise her and redirect her behavior to a fun game before she gets too engrossed in the excavation. Get to know her behavior when she is about to dig (such as light pawing or jumping at the ground after she has sniffed the area) and redirect her to an activity that you can be actively involved in together.

JUMPING

IN CHAPTER ONE, I told you about the Australian Shepherd, Wallaby, and his annoying jumping habit, which we turned into a fun trick. We thwarted his bad jumping by rewarding him only for good jumping (which happened when we asked him to jump).

Problem jumping usually happens because we have changed our dog's rules. We unintentionally encouraged him to jump by allowing him to jump on us as a puppy. We didn't set boundaries from day one, and now we are trying to change the rules. To him, our rule change seems arbitrary.

So what do you do if your dog suddenly starts jumping or, as is more common, you decide you no longer want him to jump? In order to be effective, you may need to change a few of your own behaviors, too. One solution to the jumping problem is to ignore it. For example, when you enter your home, help your dog relax by acting calmly. As he jumps, ignore him while you go about your business for a few minutes. Once he quiets down, praise him for his calm behavior. Show him that jumping gets him nothing, whereas being calm earns him attention and praise.

Alternatively, as you enter, have a special chew toy in your hand and request your dog to sit. Your dog gets the toy only when he sits. Even though he wants to jump, he likely wants the toy even more. Over time, you will have successfully redirected your dog to sit whenever you enter your home. I keep extra chew toys and treats in my car in preparation for entering my house.

Another training technique is to ask a partner to hold your dog on a six-foot leash. Walk up to greet the dog. If he jumps, abruptly turn around and walk about six feet away from him, then count off 10 seconds and have your partner cue him to *sit*. Then try again. Repeat the procedure until your dog can sit still. When he succeeds, mark it, give him a treat from your pocket, and give him attention unless he starts to jump again. After a few failures, dogs tend to sit more quickly; if they see you turn abruptly, they may even sit right down. If your dog just stands quietly instead of sitting, reward this behavior. As you observe him starting to make the connection between getting your attention and his not jumping, decrease the amount of time that you stay turned away from him. Eventually you will decrease the time to one second, and after that the jumping will cease for a brief while. Continue to practice this to keep his jumping impulses under control.

If your dog jumps and tries to get your attention while you're trying to talk with someone, you have what I call an opportunistic jumper. The person you're talking with may give your dog mixed messages by rewarding him with affection when he jumps and then pushing him away. To manage opportunistic jumping, stand on your dog's leash while you continue to hold the leash handle, giving him just enough free tether to sit, stand, or lie down, but not enough to jump. You also need to teach others that your dog is not allowed to jump. If the person is willing, request that she stand still while you move back a couple steps and then cue your dog to *sit*. Then try to walk toward the person again. If your dog doesn't jump, mark and praise that; if he does, have your friend turn away while you stand on the leash as described above. This exercise helps a dog generalize his calm behavior.

ANKLE BITING

MANY DOGS—ESPECIALLY SMALL DOGS, young puppies, and herding dogs—love to chase moving objects such as our ankles, trouser bottoms, and fuzzy slippers. If your dog bites your ankles, stop moving and wait for her to let go (or at least pause), then *redirect* her to sit. Now that you have your dog's attention, mark it with some calm praise and redirect her again toward a new activity such as a game or a stuffed Kong. If you're concerned that it seems like you're rewarding your dog for ankle biting, redirect her to perform a brief series of exercises, like Puppy Pushups or Follow the Lure. Mark the behavior, praise her, and reward her. Whatever the redirected activity, make sure that you reward her, since her ankle biting may be her way of communicating that she needs to feel rewarded and noticed. Make sure to give your dog healthy attention.

You may also try deterring an ankle biter by spraying your ankles with bitter apple spray in advance. Make sure to test it for staining. Be aware that bitter apple spray doesn't change a dog's behavior overnight. You may need to do this for a whole month, while also practicing redirecting exercises.

BARKING

WHEN YOUR DOG BARKS, you may be unintentionally rewarding him by your efforts to make him stop. Do you pet him and coo in a soothing voice that there's nothing to worry about? Or do you call out for him to stop it right now? Either way, you are teaching your dog that when he barks, he gets your attention.

Instead of trying to tell your dog what you *don't* want, you'll be more effective if you redirect your dog toward what you *do* want him to do. When he starts barking, redirect him to perform cues he's mastered, including Puppy Pushups and eye-contact exercises. Make sure that you're giving him this kind of attention at other times, so that you don't accidentally encourage him to bark in order to get your attention.

> Barking can be a sign that your dog is anxious or fearful.

Many dogs bark when they are bored, excited, fearful, or experience a change in the environment like the sound of a car outside or a barking dog in your neighbor's yard. These distractions engage a dog, and they feel exciting or scary enough to cause him to respond. You can, therefore, reduce your dog's barking by regularly challenging and stimulating him with ongoing training exercises. As I'm sure you've noticed, dogs tend to bark less during training because they are focused on you and the task you have requested. They are so intent on figuring out how to earn that reward, they don't even remember to bark.

Some breeds are particularly vocal, prone to bark at every little thing they experience. If you have a yappy dog that barks to get attention, you may want to risk teaching him to bark and then *shush* on cue. The concept is similar to how we taught Wallaby, the jumping Australian Shepherd, to jump only on cue. Let's say your intensely vocal dog—we'll call him Placido—is barking right now. Walk up to Placido and quietly tell him "shush" as you put a treat on his nose. Hold it there for 10 seconds while you continue saying "shush" with your soothing voice. Then mark the behavior ("good shush") and let him eat his reward. After about 10 seconds of quiet, ask Placido to bark ("Placido, bark" or "Placido, sing"). If he barks, then mark it ("good bark") and hold another treat on his nose while saying "shush," and reward him as you did the first time. If Placido didn't bark when you asked, you can still put another treat on his nose, say "shush," and reward him after 10 seconds (if he remains quiet). If Placido starts barking during the *shush* cue, then withdraw the treat and redirect him to perform a few skills that he already knows fluently. Over time, you will have success with the *shush* cue, followed by redirection to a skills performance. Eventually, Placido will also learn to bark only on cue because that's the only time his solos are rewarded.

Barking can also be a sign that your dog is anxious or fearful, especially if he often barks—and also lunges—at other dogs, people, or inanimate objects. If this is the case, try to keep him calm and supported when he encounters things that spark his barking. For example, if, during a walk, you see a dog approaching that always triggers your dog to bark, try *redirecting* your dog's attention by requesting a *sit* as he maintains eye contact with you, and reward and praise him during his success. Once the dog has passed by, reward and praise your dog once more, and quickly move on. If, however, your dog has already started barking at the trigger dog before you can deal with the problem, your task is more challenging. In this case, try to lure your dog to a neutral spot as you *redirect* his focus to a treat, and then to you, as you cue him to *sit*. Do your best to keep his focus as the other dog passes. It's far easier to redirect your dog *before* he has been triggered, so sharpen your awareness and reaction time on walks.

During these walks, you can begin to move a little closer to the triggering distraction once your dog has become fluent with the exercise in which he sits and focuses on you. Watch his body language. Be content with just one single step closer to the trigger on each subsequent encounter as you set your dog up for long-term success, rather than risk a short-term experiment gone awry. Eventually, you will be able to have your dog sit as the trigger pauses, too, and perhaps the two can meet. If, on the other hand, the experiment does go awry and your dog goes crazy (or the other dog gets excited or starts barking and lunging), then immediately lure your dog away and try to ask the other handler nicely to move on. Make a mental note that you need to back up a few training steps so that your dog gets it right, and progress more slowly after that.

I highly recommend using a training partner to practice well-socialized approaches, including the Greet Your Neighbor exercise and other socialization activities in Chapter Nine.

NOISE PHOBIAS

IT'S NOT UNUSUAL FOR A DOG TO BE STARTLED by a loud or sudden noise—the alarm clock, the garage door opening, the television being turned on—but some dogs go absolutely crazy with excitement or fear when they hear such noises. Most noise triggers can be handled by *desensitizing*; oftentimes, *counterconditioning* should follow. With Boz, I started to desensitize him by first redirecting his focus onto the ball as I opened the soda can. Subsequently, I counterconditioned him to get his ball when he saw me hold the unopened soda can.

To desensitize your dog to a noise trigger, begin to regularly introduce the sound at a low volume and from some distance away. Once your dog becomes more accustomed to the noise, and exhibits less anxiety around it, slowly begin to bring her closer to the source. You may also want to introduce a counterconditioning behavior, such as offering a toy that she already values, *just prior* to the noise being made. If she gets anxious, proceed more slowly, starting by taking a break from this exercise.

One interesting thing about sound sensitivity that I have learned over the years is that dogs that live with hair in their eyes tend to be more reactive to sound because they can't see enough of what is going on around them. Consider trimming the

EATING PROBLEMS

Overfeeding our dogs is not a sign of how much we love them. Dogs that carry extra weight are at greater risk for orthopedic problems, heart disease, stroke, and cancer. Sometimes we overfeed because we feel that we're not giving our dogs enough attention, but food is not a worthy substitute for that. If your dog has a weight problem, you should first check with your vet or a veterinary nutritionist to help you determine whether there is a health or diet issue at cause.

Managing your dog's everyday food environment is key to keeping him healthy. Keep food out of jumping and counter-surfing height. If you have kids, don't let them feed the dog from the dinner table or walk away and leave their plates, which can tempt a dog. Be aware of your dog's daily lifestyle, including calorie intake and exercise. If he begins to grow overweight during training, keep in mind that training treats are part of his daily food portion, so account for the extra calories in his training treats. Many trainers believe that if your dog is fat, then *you* aren't getting enough exercise.

Eating too fast can be a cause of trouble, most severely resulting in gastric torsion (also called bloat): twisting of the stomach that causes severe bloating very quickly. Gastric torsion is often life-threatening and must be dealt with as a medical emergency. I believe in erring on the side of caution: Slow down a dog's eating rate, refrain from vigorous exercise an hour before and after feeding, and feed smaller meals more than once a day. Veterinarians continue to debate the causes of gastric torsion. Some believe that a little water should be added to processed kibble in order to release gases and slow down the bloat; the verdict is still out. Besides the risk of gastric torsion, if your dog eats too fast you may sympathetically offer him more food than is healthy for him.

To slow down a dog's food intake, put a large obstacle in the bowl, such as a big rock or large steel ball that cannot be swallowed. Wash the obstacle just as you wash your dog's bowl and make sure it's not made of lead or coated with sealer or paint. For my dogs and guest dogs that eat too fast, a Kong once again comes to the rescue: I put some of the meal into the Kong and then place it in the bowl along with the rest of the dog's food. In addition to helping a dog eat more slowly, the stuffed Kong also provides an engaging challenge as the dog figures out how to work the food out of the Kong.

hair from your dog's eyes (if appropriate for his breed), so that he can see where the sounds are coming from. Clear vision will also enable your dog to focus on you with greater eye contact and attention.

Socialization Problems

I BELIEVE THAT A WELL-SOCIALIZED PUPPY is a puppy that has been positively exposed to many dogs, kids, grown-ups, and environments that he may encounter again in his life. As long as we don't flood a dog with more than he is ready to handle, we can never oversocialize him. In my experience, many dog owners don't socialize their dogs comprehensively enough throughout their dogs' lives.

Ideally, learning proper social manners should begin before a puppy reaches four months of age. After four months, problems in socialization begin to grow, including an inability to understand other dogs' body language and behavioral feedback, like playing too rough and biting too hard, or a fear of people and other dogs that can trigger shyness or bullying. Dogs that have socialization problems tend to get fewer opportunities to socialize, and so their manners deteriorate even further. Unless socialization problems are corrected, a dog may eventually pose a serious safety risk.

My Ibizan Hound, Brieo, started life very well socialized. He accompanied me to my puppy training classes, where he had a seemingly endless supply of supervised play opportunities. However, as Brieo neared age two, he started to get pushy with some of the student puppies. I paid close attention to Brieo's "teen-age period," and eventually realized that he was ready to socialize with more mature dogs. I decided to move him out of the puppy class and up to the next level; I saw an instant change. Now at age seven, Brieo has excellent social manners. He helps me babysit boarding guest dogs, entertaining them with excellent play skills, and loves playing with young puppies too.

For a dog that has developed serious socialization problems, positive reinforcement methods offer the best guarantee of lasting rehabilitation. In Chapter One I told you about the Vicktory Dogs, the 22 pit bulls that Best Friends Animal Society in Kanab, Utah, rescued from pro football player Michael Vick's illegal dog-fighting operation (see page 10). Although other experts determined that the dogs were beyond redemption and that the most humane act would be to euthanize them, Best Friends' Dogtown training manager, John Garcia, and certified pet dog trainer Ann Allums took in the dogs. Garcia and Allums rehabilitated these "death row dogs" using only positive reinforcement methods. Today, some of the Vicktory Dogs are fully rehabilitated, Canine Good Citizen–certified, and placed happily in new homes. (See Appendix 1 for information on the Canine Good Citizen certificate.)

Garcia and Allums treat each behavior problem as a puzzle that needs to be figured out. "We take it slow and treat every dog as an individual, just like humans," Garcia says. One particularly aggressive dog, Meryl, needed to learn that people could approach her in friendship rather than to get her to fight. Allums says that "within five minutes we found most of her triggers. It took one day to build basic trust with Meryl." She adds that if they had used punishment aversion methods, "Meryl would have lashed out and gotten worse."

Garcia's and Allums' first step to building positive relationships was to get the Vicktory Dogs comfortable enough to hand-feed them, and then feed them in different locations to desensitize food aggression. The dogs began to think of their trainers as "great big goodie jars," says Garcia. Best Friends trainers reinforced the few things that each dog was doing right, introduced them slowly to other dogs and people to socialize them, and brought them into new situations (such as riding in a car) only when they were ready. Garcia and Allums have also given the dogs plenty of mental stimulation with stuffed Kongs and other interactive toys, cue training, and target training.

FOOD GUARDING AND RESOURCE GUARDING

IF A DOG GUARDS HIS FOOD OR TOYS, that may be a warning that he could, at some point, become dangerous—and even vicious—without warning. It may happen, for example, that a dog used to guarding his food is peacefully gnawing on a favorite toy when a child arrives to pet him. The dog may suddenly become protective of his toy and lash out at the child.

When I train a dog that might be a food guarder, I watch his body language around the food bowl; if he drops his shoulder and head deeper into the bowl as I walk by, that's often a sign that he could be (or become) a guarder. In that case, I toss food around the bowl. Little by little I move closer, observing whether he's getting less sensitive to my presence.

If you fear that your dog has begun guarding his food, immediately resume the hand-feeding protocol discussed in Chapter Three. Remember to hand-feed your dog in different areas of your home and use different bowls, so that he doesn't perceive that he "owns" either his supper spot or bowl—all spots, bowls, and food belong to you and you are sharing them with your dog. When you feel it's time to transition away from hand-feeding, return to putting portions of the food in your dog's bowl so that he can clearly see that you are keeping the rest of it. Review the hand-feeding protocol to prepare your dog to accept food from other people and to be fed in the presence of other dogs and people.

If you are afraid to hand-feed your dog, you may want to bring in a professional to help you. One technique that I like to use with dogs that are too fearful or aggressive to be hand-fed is to have the dog watch me measure his total daily food ration and put it in a big bowl. I want him to understand that I am the giver of all good things, that I control the food bowl. Next, I let him see me put a handful into the dinner bowl and place the bowl on the floor— ideally, once he is sitting (if he is already fluent with that cue). After he eats that handful, it's very likely that he will look at me, at which point I say, "Good. You want some more?" Then I drop a few treats or kibble on the floor away from the bowl; as he goes for the treats I pick up the bowl, put more food in it, and set it down again. This is a quick and effective way to communicate that I'm in charge of the food. I may repeat that step until I'm confident that I can move closer to the bowl when he's eating. At that point I'll drop in a treat (such as a piece of cheese) while he's eating. We want the dog to understand that when hands reach into the food bowl we are giving more food and not taking it away, which helps relax anxiety and raises his confidence level to have us around him while he's eating. Once I'm confident that he's calm and accepts that I control the food, he's ready to begin hand-feeding.

As for other resources that could be guarded, such as a Kong treat, I don't ever let a dog chew uninterrupted for more than five minutes. That Kong belongs to me and is on loan to my dog in exchange for his polite behavior, starting with a *sit* to earn it. One sign that a dog may be a toy guarder is that he carries the toy away to a remote area of the home to chew it.

When taking a chew toy away from a dog, always make a trade for another treat or toy. That way he understands that you provide a variety of valuable resources. When I trade for a special toy such as a stuffed Kong, I often offer a nice piece of hamburger. Practice the *off and take it* trades and cookie trades that you learned earlier, and make frequent trades with your dog so that he experiences getting something back after he lets you take something else away. The more experience he has with trades, the more comfortable he will be chewing toys around you (and around other people as you include them safely in this training).

AGGRESSION TOWARD PEOPLE

I F YOU HAVE A DOG THAT IS AGGRESSIVE toward people, you may want to use a qualified trainer or behaviorist to help identify her triggers and attempt to desensitize and redirect them.

When I evaluate an aggressive dog, I always involve a veterinarian to assess and diagnose any possible health or injury issue that may be causing the dog to behave in a way that most people would refer to as "aggressive." That word gets thrown around a lot when describing a dog's behavior and is often, in my experience, misused. Not all dogs that growl, guard, bite ankles, or bark a lot are aggressive. I'm very careful about using this word because too often, once that label is placed on the dog, it may seal her fate. There are few places that will rehome a dog that has been labeled aggressive.

A dog is typically called aggressive when she initiates dangerous behavior toward people—often arising from lack of human contact, incomplete socialization of the dog during the first four months, or the lingering effects of past trauma. In each of those cases, the dog doesn't know whom to trust and is not truly aggressive, but is acting out of fear.

The first step in dealing with aggression is to identify the dog's triggers. At the same time, the dog needs to trust someone. I approach this scenario with caution and in the most positive way possible. I read the dog's body language very carefully and make sure that she can read mine. I work patiently at a pace that is comfortable for that particular dog, always looking to increase her bonds to me.

In this exercise, you and your training partner will use food to help desensitize your dog. Make sure that she is hungry when you start this work. If you are able to put a leash on her safely, attach a long leash (6 to 12 feet) to your dog's collar, and rather than you or your partner holding it right away, let her drag it on the floor. Letting your dog drag the leash now will help her feel less trapped or frustrated later when you hold it, tether it to your belt loop, or step on the handle to stop her forward movement to a place that you don't want her to go. Anticipate the dog's moves by looking calmly for body language that says she is fearful or uncomfortable. A short list of such body signals includes hair standing on end, hunched shoulders, lowered head, cowering, hiding, and removing herself from the company of people or other dogs.

Begin by taking your dog to a calm environment. If the dog is comfortable with you but shows aggressive or fearful posture toward your partner, you have identified a trigger. As you and your partner chat pleasantly, have him toss a little kibble about halfway to your dog, and allow your dog to get it. Continue the calm chat with your partner as he tosses a little more kibble; the dog will get the kibble only when she feels comfortable and safe. There is no force and no timetable. The treats help your dog understand that no one will harm her, and furthermore that people are generally good. Carefully work the treats closer and closer to your partner.

As your dog becomes more comfortable with your partner, you will eventually be able to have him hand-feed her and work with her in training, games, and walks. In time, these kinds of introductions to more people will become more comfortable for your dog, which will help her confidence rise. It's difficult to put a time frame on how long it will take for your dog to progress to each level of success. That will depend on the severity of her problem and how committed you are to helping her. It may take three months of consistently rehearsing these exercises or it may take a full year.

If your dog has mild fear aggression around the veterinarian or groomer, take brief desensitization trips there just to go inside, give your dog a treat, and then leave. If they have a moment to greet her and give a treat, it will help.

AGGRESSION TOWARD DOGS

SOME DOGS CAN BE DELIGHTFUL AND GENTLE with people but behave shyly or aggressively toward other dogs. As in dealing with aggression or fearful behavior toward people, you may want a qualified professional to help identify and desensitize your dog's triggers. Try to learn your dog's history with other dogs and ask your vet to rule out health issues.

In this case, you will need patient canine partners to help desensitize and socialize your dog. My canine partner is Brieo. When I take on a new behavioral case or agree to foster a dog that has been labeled aggressive, I first evaluate the dog (which may take a week or two, including time for bonding). Nine times out of 10 I find that the dog would like to play with Brieo but doesn't know how. The so-called aggressive dog's attempts to play are harsh, mouthy, pushy, and overwhelming. The dog doesn't understand or acknowledge Brieo's body language—Brieo's way of conveying his boundaries.

For this assessment and desensitization training, I sometimes put a band muzzle on the problem dog. This prevents him from opening his mouth wide enough to bite hard, but allows him to drink, eat, pant, and play. If you use a muzzle, understand that it requires very close supervision and an extreme amount of knowledge and care. For example, never use a muzzle to prevent a dog from chewing furniture. Also, never muzzle a dog if another dog might take advantage of the situation. Fortunately, Brieo is naturally good-natured, well-trained, and socialized so he won't take advantage.

One behavior that is often labeled aggressive is mounting. While mounting is undesirable and very annoying, it is not automatically "aggressive" per se. Mounting is a natural canine behavior and often occurs during acceptable play experiences. That said, when your dog tries to mount another dog, you should redirect your dog. Sometimes mounting can trigger a fight. Use your cue word "off" to stop your dog from mounting. Within a small group of well-socialized dogs, sometimes you and the other handler may use your combined judgment to allow the dog that is being mounted to turn around and growl or even snap at the mounting dog. For well-socialized dogs, that warning should be sufficient to communicate that that particular dog is off-limits. Watch the mounting dog's body language; if he squares up behind another dog and creeps forward, that's a sign that he's getting ready to mount and the perfect opportunity to cue "off." Both owners should redirect their dogs away from each other and practice some cues before resuming play.

> Decrease aggression by first learning your dog's triggers.

An unacceptable aggressive behavior is fence fighting among neighbor dogs, as it can lead an otherwise sociable dog to behave aggressively. If they are not stopped and managed, both dogs may learn that fence fighting is acceptable, and it can become a bad habit that escalates to more aggressive lunging, digging to get under the fence, and even climbing over it, which can lead to a serious dog fight. The longer you allow fence fighting to continue unchecked, the worse it can get. If possible, try talking to your neighbors to see if they are willing to find a safe way to try socializing and desensitizing the dogs to each other. Sometimes neighbors cooperate to make sure that when one dog is outside, the other dog is inside. Sometimes noncooperation on fence fighting dogs can escalate to human fence fighting, so it's worth a shot to talk things over calmly and try to come up with a plan that works for both of you.

Dog parks, while wonderful public spaces for off-leash socialization, can also become laboratories for aggression, fear, and improper play. In Chapter Twelve, I'll give you tips on making the dog park experience as successful as possible. That said, not all dogs are dog park material, and it is possible that your dog will not be able to enjoy that environment, especially once he matures or becomes less playful with other dogs as he ages and gets crotchety.

SEPARATION ANXIETY AND SHADOWING

SINCE DOGS ARE PACK ANIMALS, they typically desire to be part of a group. Therefore, for some dogs, being alone can lead to anxiety and fear. In my opinion, some common causes of separation anxiety are incomplete crate training, allowing your dog to shadow you all around your home, and never teaching him that being alone at times is healthy. If your dog has separation anxiety, immediately restart the crate training protocol that is detailed in Chapter Three. Successful crate training almost always *habituates* a dog to being alone, so that she enjoys the safety and comfort of her den. Here are a few crate training reminders:

▶ Slowly increase the time you keep your dog in the crate and the amount of time you leave her alone while she's in it.

▶ If your dog barks while she's in the crate, wait until she stops barking before you return to her, and don't make a big deal when you leave home or return.

▶ If you work at home (as I often do), do not let your dog shadow you around the house, to the bathroom, and so forth. Use the crate training protocol even when you are at home.

In general, if you're working with your dog to overcome separation anxiety or shadowing, slowly habituate your dog to her crate and leave her for short durations as you go from one room to another, then reappear before she gets anxious.

FEAR OF NEW SITUATIONS

IF YOUR DOG HAS A PATTERN OF FEARFUL BEHAVIOR in new situations, continue to socialize him, but do it slowly. Before you put him in new situations, reinforce his sense of well-being in those environments where he already seems comfortable, and don't force him into situations that make him uncomfortable. For example, if your dog is fearful when riding in the car, don't force him to go out with you whenever you'd like his company. Instead, introduce him to the car a step at a time, similar to the way you may have introduced him to his crate. Before getting him inside the car, take him around the parked car, feed and praise him, and then walk away with him. Another time, with the car door already open, let your dog sniff inside and eat a few treats, but don't try to lure him in just yet. You may then toss a few treats inside the car the next time; maybe he'll go in, but if not, don't force it.

The technique of forcing a dog to do something he doesn't want to do—which is, in essence, asking him to face his fears all at once—is called *flooding*. The thinking behind flooding is a belief that the sooner an irrational fear is exposed as "meaningless," that there is nothing that the dog needs to worry about, the sooner he will get over that fear. This technique is advocated by some trainers, but is one to which I am strongly opposed. In my professional judgment, forcing a dog to face fears you want to eliminate before he is ready would be like sticking me in a roomful of snakes and telling me that I just need to get over it.

I used to be terribly afraid of snakes. Even today, snakes are among my least favorite things to encounter in the wild. But some years ago, my family got a pet snake. It was not my idea. My son, Blaise, had just returned from visiting his cousin who had one. Blaise thought a snake would be the perfect pet for him. I needed to get comfortable with the whole idea . . . in my own time (preferably years). I began by reading about snakes and found that the more I learned about them, the more curious I became. So I watched videos about snakes, researched snakes on the Internet, located breeders who specialized in snakes, and talked to snake owners. I'm fortunate to live not too far from the National Zoo in Washington, D.C., which has a good collection of snakes. I planted myself safely behind the thick plate glass in the Reptile Discovery Center and stood there as long as I could, watching the tree snakes, water snakes, cobras, pythons, boa constrictors, and anacondas.

When it got to be too much for me—it didn't take long—I could get out of there quickly (and find refuge in the Gorilla Grove).

What I was doing—or at least trying to do—was to face my fears by desensitizing myself gradually. When the time came to bring home a baby ball python, I was ready and actually fairly comfortable with the idea. I even helped feed our snake and put her in the travel terrarium to transport her to the veterinarian for regular checkups.

Now, I know for a fact that if someone had said, "Dawn, your fear of snakes is irrational. Here, I'm going to lock you in a room with 10 nonpoisonous snakes and when you come out alive, you'll see how silly you're being," I would have either died of a heart attack or been imprisoned for murder.

We can't expect anything different from our dogs. It's far better—and, if you ask me, far more loving—to desensitize dogs

A NOTE ON MAGIC POTIONS—THERE AREN'T ANY

I know that we'd all like easy solutions to cure our dogs' behavior problems. But the fact is, there aren't any. The only real solution is consistent attention, commitment, and hard work. Over the 20 years that I have been training, I have seen an increase in the prescription of medicines that are supposed to cure certain canine behavioral issues such as anxiety. However, if the dog owner doesn't also change his or her own behavior along with the dog's environment and routine, the medicine won't be effective.

Some people use electronic training collars as if they were magic tools, but I always urge them to think again. These collars administer an adjustable penalty tingle/shock (ranging from mild to strong) via a handheld remote control. When used effectively, they can shape a dog's behavior similar to the way clicker training works. However, these collars must be used with great care, and I've worked with far too many dogs that have been repeatedly, and painfully, shocked by improperly used collars.

I was once adamantly against electronic fencing, which can give a dog a mild shock if he wanders beyond a perimeter barrier; however, I know there may be no other reasonable alternative in a neighborhood that prohibits the building of actual fences. If you must use electronic fencing, please use it only as a short-term confinement—maybe while you're gardening or cleaning your yard and want your dog with you. And it's certainly appropriate to use it during outdoor supervised play or training sessions. That said, I don't think it's right to put your dog outside for the day while you go to work or run errands, leaving him contained only by the electronic fence. Chasing a squirrel or deer may seem so exciting to a dog that he decides it's worth more than the electrical shock. But once he has crossed that boundary, he may not return for fear of being shocked again.

than it is to flood them and risk causing them emotional stress or, worse, to become more fearful or aggressive. Some examples of flooding include forcing a dog to go to a dog park, dragging a dog into a swimming pool to teach him to swim, surrounding a dog with kids because he is afraid of them, or (as discussed earlier) forcing a dog to walk on a slippery floor that he fears.

If you're considering using a professional to help with your dog's behavior problems, stay away from anyone who wants to use flooding techniques. I feel that strongly about it.

HIDING

IF YOUR DOG IS HIDING AT HOME, that may mean she's not getting enough downtime away from people, especially playful children. Don't let your kids initiate contact with your dog when she is hiding. Be aware of potential family dynamics or behaviors, such as a family member unintentionally disturbing the dog while you have your back turned for a moment, or perhaps incomplete socialization with a family member who is away from home a lot. In the latter case, slowly introduce your dog to that family member and use food treats to help make positive associations. Also, make sure to check if your dog has any health issues or injuries; dogs often hide their weaknesses, maybe because they fear being hurt again or being cut off from the pack.

You probably know from your own life that bad habits are hard to break. Even when we have stopped a bad habit, it can return, were we to give up our continued effort. Our dogs' behavior problems can also flare up again, and when they do, we must recommit and address the problem, regardless of the time and effort it requires.

The alternative to correcting our dogs' behavior problems is to ignore them until they become so serious and destructive that we give up on the dogs. Correcting behavior problems by using positive reinforcement gives us the blessing of a rich life together with our beloved best friends. When we cherish our dogs as living, breathing creatures of God that see, hear, and feel pleasure and pain in ways similar to our own, we develop greater respect for other humans and for ourselves. How glorious to be inspired by a creature that shares so little of our language but so much of our heart.

Your Dog in the World

DOG TRAINING NEVER ENDS; it just gets easier. Socializing always needs a tune-up. And you still need to treat everyday experiences as training opportunities. If you keep your eyes open, you'll see that "teaching moments" happen every day.

Once you and your dog have gotten in plenty of practice, you'll be ready to leave the house knowing that you can count on each other to be the perfect companion. Prepare for dog park excursions and long family road trips by consulting this chapter—but not before studying up on water safety, also detailed here. You'll find guidance on choosing the right veterinarian, day care, dog walker, pet sitter, groomer, and other caregivers. Finally, if you still feel like you and your dog could use some extra help, I've provided some advice on finding a professional who will train your dog through positive reinforcement.

Dog Parks

YOUR DOG NEEDS TO be socialized off leash as well as on leash. Even dogs that like the comfort of knowing you're in control of the leash may experience frustration at the limitations the leash places on them. It's like a child in a toy store: The child wants to touch the toys. If the parent holds her back too much, she may act out. Your dog can respond similarly. Supervised off-leash time is important to keeping him from becoming frustrated, and it is a great technique to help spirit your dog.

For many dogs, an off-leash visit to a dog park can be the highlight of the day. Unfortunately, that visit can be fraught with challenges. The frequent occurrence of dog bites, dog fights, and poop on our shoes has given some dog parks a bad rap.

Dog park etiquette is essential. Translation? Use good manners and common sense. Here are some tips:

▶ Remove any harness, special collar, or clothing except for the flat-buckle collar that holds your dog's ID tags. He could get tangled in his or another dog's fashion statement. Obey leash laws; keep your dog on leash until you have entered the play area, and keep his leash with you.

▶ Dog parks are not for small children. Accidents can happen quickly, especially when exuberant dogs are happily chasing and wrestling.

Don't attempt off-leash play unless the area is fenced in.

▶ Scoop the poop. A poopy park is a health hazard, and not cleaning up after your dog is discourteous. Carry at least one bag at all times, or use the park's waste disposal tools.

▶ Volunteer to help keep your dog park clean and safe; consider making a donation for cleanup tools, toys, even play structures and fence repair. Many parks have volunteer cleanup activities and etiquette presentations, with an increasing number of them sponsored by local pet shops and pet product makers. I support this good trend.

▶ Make sure your dog has good *recall:* Practice *recall* each and every time you visit the dog park. (Remind yourself of the technique by checking out the Recall Quick Guide in the Fundamentals Training Program on page 138.) Your dog needs to learn that your cue to *come here* usually does not signal the end of playtime, and that he'll often be able to return immediately to playing with his buddies. When I see owners chasing

Playing with other dogs is an important part of socialization.

their dogs when it's time to leave the dog park, I know they must have inadvertently taught them that *come here* always means the end of playtime.

▶ Use *recalls* as segues to other training cues that your dog already excels at. This will strengthen his ability to follow your instructions consistently, even in the midst of distractions. Make these training moments extremely brief at first; your dog needs and wants free play without too many instructions.

▶ Never leave your dog alone or unsupervised at a dog park. Even when you're socializing with other owners, make sure that you know exactly what he is doing.

▶ Don't let him rush at a dog that is entering the play area. It may intimidate the dog that is about to join the playgroup.

▶ Know when your dog has had enough and leave the park on a happy note. Like children, dogs can get grouchy when they're tired or overheated.

▶ Be honest about your dog's socialization abilities. A dog park is not appropriate for dogs that are aggressive, unsocialized, or have a history of fighting, biting, or uncontrollable barking. If your dog has any of these issues, resolve them before your first trip to the dog park, and do not use the park as a way to desensitize your dog's behavioral shortcomings.

▶ Your dog may not get along with all other dogs, just as humans don't get along with all humans. Try to anticipate his or another dog's aggressive or uncomfortable body language, and remove your dog from the potentially dangerous situation before a fight starts.

▶ If a fight breaks out, take responsibility for controlling your dog and removing him from the fight right away. Do your best to keep a calm voice so that you don't add to the chaos. Many fights escalate into a melee or bully pack for no apparent reason. The more you practice successful *recalls*, the greater the likelihood that your dog will recall to you when a fight breaks out.

▶ Fights can break out over guarding toys or food. Therefore, it's best not to show your treats. I am very careful and sneaky when I give my dog a quick treat for good behavior, such as a *recall.* If you take a toy, figure that you have donated it to the park; but don't take it at all if you're not sure your dog can and will share it with any other dog.

▶ Apologize quickly if your dog makes a mistake, even if you feel embarrassed, defensive, have an explanation, or want to blame another dog or human. Mistakes are inevitable; learn from them. But don't expect others to apologize to you, even if you apologize to them when it's clearly a no-fault situation.

▶ Avoid disciplining another dog. It's best to focus on removing your dog from the situation if a dog is overly aggressive with yours. If you need to request another owner to control her dog better, be polite and kind. For example, if you need to ask that someone's dog not terrorize yours when you're trying to enter the park, try also to say something nice about her lovely dog.

Road Trips

WHEN MY THREE KIDS WERE YOUNG, my family would spend one month every summer driving from Virginia to Palm Beach, Florida, to visit my mother. We'd go to the beach every day, visit play parks, and spend hours at the animal safari experience. I loved exposing my children to life in Florida, where I grew up. The van would be packed with us humans, plus three dogs—Jock, the Border Collie; Merit, the Flat-Coated Retriever; and Saxon, the Giant Schnauzer—and two parrots, Maude and Jules. We were a traveling circus.

At the halfway point, we usually stayed in the same motel—it was called South of the Border—because it welcomed our trained menagerie. We'd rent the honeymoon suite so the gang could enjoy the Jacuzzi bathtub together. The kids would hold treats underwater, and the dogs would dive to get them. If we went out to dinner or to the swimming pool, the pets stayed in the room. I turned on the TV set and air-conditioning to drown out hallway noise that might agitate them. Fortunately, the dogs and birds kept fairly quiet, even when I was training them by exiting the motel room and returning with rewards and praise for quiet *settles.* I built up longer and longer periods of being out of the

WHISTLE RECALL

The whistle is especially useful at a dog park or in a wilderness location where your dog is off leash. But make sure that your dog is fluent with the voice *recall* ("come here") before you attempt a *whistle recall*. If you can whistle with your mouth, make sure that you can make a consistent, loud sound. Otherwise, I highly recommend using a loud mechanical whistle for recall; an unbreakable metal whistle that can be heard over long distances if your dog happens to run off, get lost, and panic. My cowriter, Larry, often recalls his Golden Retriever, Higgins, with a metal whistle that he has kept on his key chain for more than seven years. For beginners, I recommend using a whistle that you can hear rather than an ultrasonic dog whistle that takes a bit of getting used to. (If you want to use an ultrasonic whistle, be sure to follow the directions so you blow it properly. Learn how to test and tune its screw adjustment, and don't blow too hard or you will overpower the tones.)

Start teaching the *whistle recall* by whistling while you stand next to your dog and treating him as if you were a vending machine, so that he associates the sound with the reward.

Then build up *recalls* to a few paces, combining the whistle with the lure, the visual cue, and the verbal "come here"—we're using all the cues and not leaving anything to chance. Little by little, increase the distance and withdraw some of the cues.

Once you have built up to a *whistle recall* distance of about 10 yards, the next step is to use it during supervised play. The other dog may also come to you, but that's okay if it encourages your dog to *recall* successfully. At the beginning, use it at an off-peak time. Build success with that by being sure to reward your dog for coming when recalled, and then releasing him to play again so that he associates the *whistle recall* with a positive reward rather than the end of playtime.

When your dog has excellent *whistle recall*, generalized to all kinds of distracting settings, it's up to you to decide whether he is ready for a wilderness trial. Train your dog to *recall* with the whistle at short distances by playing Come and Go (see page 152) with your hiking partner, gradually increasing the distance between the two of you. Make sure to bring great treats to help motivate great *recalls*.

---

room, until I was eventually able to go out to dinner without having to check on the pets midway through the meal. The dogs got a final walk before settling in for the night, and a first walk the next morning before we loaded ourselves back into the van.

In the van, during those rare moments when all was quiet, I would look in my rearview mirror to see sleeping kids still buckled in and slumped over sleeping dogs that were draped across their laps. Those long drives were punctuated by rest stops, where we unloaded all the animals, stretched our legs, aired the bird cages, and ate quick snacks in the shade.

In Florida, we spent most of our time at the beach. All my dogs loved to swim, but Jock couldn't stand the feel of the sand under his paws and would always turn and head back to the car. Before long, I realized that I couldn't make him love the beach the way I wanted him to, and I had to leave him behind with my mom.

I'm telling you my story in the hope that you'll be able to glean some tips for making car trips with your dog workable and enjoyable. Before you risk a road trip, make sure that she can handle long rides. Start by acclimating her to the car with short trips around town, to shopping centers, a friend's home, the dog park. Spend a Sunday afternoon taking your dog (and your family) out to a picnic area or to a lovely trail for a hike or nature walk.

If your dog has a tendency to get car sick, make sure you have gotten her over it before attempting a long family trip in the car. (Take her on short rides on an empty stomach for starters.) There are remedies and medications that your veterinarian can recommend or prescribe for you. Make sure you test her reaction to the medication before you take off on your family adventure.

Check in advance whether dogs are allowed where you will be going. Locate places to stay and eat that allow dogs. Hotels are most likely to take your dog if she is crate trained. Some cafés provide outside dining with limited space for well-trained dogs. In advance, find out where emergency vet services are. If it's hot where you're going, remember that your dog is wearing a fur coat, so make sure that she will have plenty of shade and opportunities to cool down and rest. If you plan on camping, nighttime can be an adventure. If the weather is cold, protect your dog from hypothermia by taking an extra blanket or sleeping bag for her. Perhaps she could use a sweater to sleep in, too. I recommend tethering her leash while you sleep, so that she isn't apt to go chasing off in pursuit of a midnight sound or smell. You can stake the tether to the ground next to you or even tie her leash to you, as long as you don't choke either of you or make it impossible for either of you to get comfortable.

Consider getting a specialized seat belt to keep your dog safe on long trips.

When I take my dogs hiking, I almost always keep them on leash. I live in deer-hunting country and my Ibizan Hound Brieo looks, runs, and jumps like a deer, so I am extra cautious about letting him go off leash. The longer your dog is conditioned to accept being on the leash, the easier it is to take the leash off and get good *recalls*.

While all dogs are different, I've found that most are generally ready to start going off leash in controlled situations after age five, as long as you have already laid an excellent foundation of training skills that includes a reliable *recall* system. I don't want to put a damper on anyone's dream of having a dog that can be off leash most of the time, but sadly, even the best-trained dogs can make mistakes or be in the wrong place at the wrong time. My Border Collie, Jock, was excellent off leash wherever we went. In 2002, we were attending a Super Bowl party in the countryside and Jock was in heaven retrieving sticks for the guests. When I called him he would turn on a dime to come back to me as fast as he could. Unfortunately, he was hit by a car and died instantly when a driver swayed off the road at high speed and hit him. Jock was 9½ years old and he was within my sight, but the car was going too fast. He never had a chance, and the driver who hit him kept going. So I advise not letting your dog off leash for long periods, and make sure you know where he is at all times.

Trip Checklist

NOTHING IS MORE IMPORTANT for a happy trip than a well-packed bag of doggie supplies. What follows is a basic list of trip necessities; over time, you will learn to customize the list for your dog's particular needs. For example, if she is prone to sticking her nose where she shouldn't, you'll probably want to load up on extra Benadryl—though be sure to check with your vet about dosage first. Once, Jock stuck his nose into a hill of fire ants while we were at a rest stop in Florida. He was not a happy camper. Fortunately, I had an emergency kit in my van for the kids and the dogs and was able to clean Jock's nose, disinfect it, and then give him a Benadryl tablet to reduce the possibility of an allergic reaction. One more example: Sometimes the change in drinking water can make a dog sick or affect his appetite, so you may need to mix home water with the new water.

TRIP CHECKLIST

❑ Trip dog tag with destination phone number and address

❑ Rabies shot certificate or tag

❑ Local phone numbers: emergency vet, poison control, snakebite assistance

❑ Leash

❑ Poop pickup bags

❑ Flashlight with extra batteries

❑ Dog food

❑ Training treats

❑ Clean drinking water from home

❑ Food and water bowls

❑ Lightweight travel bowl for hiking

❑ Blankets/dog bed

❑ X-pen or crate

❑ First-aid kit: includes tweezers, tick remover, snakebite kit, antibiotic cream, hydrogen peroxide, sterile gauze bandages, and tape

❑ Mylar space blanket for treating hypothermia

❑ Medicine if necessary (Remember, some medication needs to be refrigerated; if so, you must make accommodations for that.)

❑ Flea and tick prevention (including heartworm pills in many locales)

❑ Mosquito repellent (on coat, not rubbed into skin) and mosquito-repelling citronella candles

❑ Medicated ear and eye cleaners

❑ Grooming kit: comb, brush, blow dryer (if needed), shampoo, creme rinse

❑ Dog towels

❑ Toys: Kong, balls, safe toys that can't be swallowed

Water Safety

ALTHOUGH SOME BREEDS LOVE to swim, many dogs don't know how and need to be taught. For nearly 20 years I owned a home with a swimming pool, and I've also sailed with my dogs off the coast of Florida and in the Caribbean. So, I had to teach my dogs *and* my kids to swim. Some breeds are at a disadvantage in the water, such as those with long bodies or flat faces, including Dachshunds, Basset Hounds, Pugs, and Boston Terriers. Bulldogs have very short legs compared to their broad bodies and heavy heads, which makes it dangerous for most of them to swim at all.

Other breeds, such as Porties, Poodles, Labradors, and many water retrievers and spaniels, were originally bred for water work and generally take to water quickly. However, never assume that your dog will be a natural in the water, no matter what its breed. Tragically, I know of an owner who threw his water dog puppy into the Potomac River thinking that would "teach" it to swim by instinct, but the dog failed and drowned.

For many dogs, swimming in a pool that has a single exit can be a more fearful experience than swimming in a lake or at a calm beach that has a sloping, visible shore. In all cases, you may want to start out having your dog wear a life jacket; there are some excellent brands made specifically for dogs. If you're teaching her to swim in a pool or off a boat, you may want to invest in a water ramp for dogs.

When using a life jacket, follow the manufacturer's instructions. Get your dog used to wearing it, make adjustments, and practice swimming in shallow water before going out in a boat.

In a pool, start teaching your dog to swim by luring her into the water with a treat, or picking her up and taking her into the water with you. Keep her very close to you at first while you determine how comfortable she is, and remain very near the steps, ladder, or ramp. Help her become familiar with this exit by helping her climb the stairs or ladder. Having another, swim-trained dog along to "demonstrate" swimming can give her confidence and encouragement. If your dog resists, do not force her, as that may increase fear. Help her in the beginning by keeping your hand under her tummy, toward her rear legs. This will help her stay balanced.

In lakes, rivers, and beaches, be aware of strong currents that could overpower your dog or cause her to panic. Be aware of water temperature as well, as water that is too cold can cause dangerous hypothermia. If the shore or beach is hot, your dog's paws may blister, so use caution. If it is a hot day, remember that your dog is wearing a fur coat and could get heatstroke more easily than you, so keep her shaded and cool, and keep plenty of drinking water on hand. Most dogs swallow water as they swim, so use your judgment about letting her swim in stagnant or ocean water. After swimming, rinse her off and dry her, paying careful attention to her ears and eyes, which can easily become infected.

If your dog is confident around water, teach her to go in only with permission. Use boundary training techniques like the ones you learned in the fundamentals program (see the Quick Guide for boundary training on page 145), and *sit-stay*, which serves as your dog's request to you for permission to swim. Having a solid *recall* could save your dog's life, so practice that in and around the water. If your dog is willing, practice retrieving and swimming games and activities by modifying the retrieving techniques I shared with you in Chapters Nine and Ten.

Always supervise your dog around water. Be ready to guide her to safety, and potentially to rescue her if she gets into trouble. To be safest, you should learn basic lifesaving techniques. Consider taking a dog first-aid and CPR course, or at least viewing a related DVD or Internet video.

Breathing resuscitation on a dog is performed mouth-to-nose while sealing off her mouth so that air does not escape. Chest compression, Heimlich, and back slaps are done similarly to the ways they are on humans. Ask your vet for recommendations on these lifesaving subjects.

Veterinarian Visits and Your Dog's Health

TAKING A DOG TO the vet is essential . . . but it is not always a happy moment for the dog. Try to take your dog for a health checkup if you are planning a family vacation, or if you will be leaving him behind with a caretaker for an extended time, in order to get a baseline reading of his health. Help him get used to vet visits by dropping in for quick, periodic "hello" visits (rather than for a medical reason), so that he can get used to going into the office and be less anxious when a medical visit or checkup is required.

Maintaining your dog's health can also affect training. Sight, hearing, orthopedic issues, general health, and energy level will change over time. For example, an older dog with arthritis or hip dysplasia may be unwilling to jump up into the car and may no longer sit easily. Bladder problems can lead to peeing in the house. Watch your dog's behavior; if it changes, you should take him to the vet for a checkup.

Your dog's nutritional needs will also change as he gets older. As I've mentioned, if your dog is getting fat, it usually means that *you* are not getting enough exercise. However, don't just dash off on a hike that your dog may not be ready for—the first thing to do is to visit your vet for a special "old dog checkup" before deciding if it is a matter of lack of exercise, a behavioral issue, or perhaps an underlying health problem. A common myth that mixed breeds and mutts are automatically healthier than purebreds is indeed a mutt myth.

Dental care is important because diseases of the mouth, teeth, or gums can infect the dog's bloodstream and quickly shut down his kidneys, which can be fatal. Use the handling and gentling exercises to inspect your dog's mouth, teeth, and gums. Regularly brush his teeth (see page 65), and give him dental treats now and then.

Grooming

LIKE CHILDREN, DOGS NEED to be bathed regularly, have their hair brushed often, and get their nails clipped. Some dogs also require special grooming to trim their hair, especially in warm weather. To prepare your dog for her first grooming experience, make sure she is comfortable with being handled. Next, run a soft brush or comb lightly over her as you praise and treat her. I hand-feed a dog her entire meal while I groom her for the first time. Pretend to clip her nails, too, before attempting it for the first time, so that she gets used to the look and sound of the clipper. She may never learn to like getting her nails clipped, but it's necessary, and with practice, she'll eventually come to at least tolerate it.

If you groom your dog yourself, keep her hair out of her eyes. While a dog is in training, I prefer to clip the dog's eye hair away, even if the breed standard calls for a shaggy face. If you are really set against clipping the hair around her eyes, at least use hair clips or make a ponytail if she tolerates it. Your dog must be able to see clearly while she trains.

Before you give your dog her first bath (or even turn on the water), hand-feed a meal to her in the bath area. The next day, get plenty of treats on hand, tap into all your patience, and put on some old clothes! While the dog is in the tub or shower, hand-feed some treats before you start to wash her. If you use a tub, take a facecloth, tie it in a knot, wedge a treat in it, and let your dog splash around with the homemade toy. With my Flat-Coated Retriever, I put my bathing suit on and got in the tub with him to help him enjoy being there. If the weather is warm, get a kiddie pool, fill it with water, and let the kids and your dog splash around together—while you supervise carefully. My kids were always feeding treats to the dogs when they were in the kiddie pool together.

If you decide to hire a professional groomer, the groomer may encourage you to bring your dog by for a quick visit just to get some treats and praise before the first grooming session. To find a groomer, begin by asking owners of well-groomed dogs who they use. Find a groomer in your price range who has good rapport with your dog, and who follows instructions and is willing to look at photos of cuts you admire. Some groomers will allow you to stay during the session to make your dog more comfortable. Every groomer I have worked with has allowed me to leave all my puppies for two- to three-hour short grooming sessions, before ever leaving them for the long all-day grooming process.

Hiring Caregivers

OF ALL PETS, DOGS NEED THE MOST ATTENTION while their owners are away. Therefore, you may need to enlist someone to care for your dog while you go on a business trip or vacation or if you work long hours. See the Caregiver's Checklist on page 240.

Dog Walkers and Pet Sitters

DOG WALKERS come to your home, exercise your dog, and return him home safely. Some dog walkers will also give your dog his medication at precise times, feed meals, provide bathing and grooming services, and help with training.

Decide whether you need a professional dog walker who is licensed, bonded, and insured, or whether you will rely on a trusted neighbor or friend. National membership organizations, notably the National Association of Professional Pet Sitters and Pet Sitters International, host certification and continuing education programs, provide insurance and business services to members, and provide online listings for the public to find their members. There are also many online directories of local pet sitters, and some veterinarians' staff members provide pet-sitting services as a side business.

If you're thinking of hiring a professional dog sitter or dog walker, make sure to do a phone interview and check references, ideally for at least three candidates so that you can compare. Discuss business terms: cost, how much time she will spend with your dog and what she does, services included and optional services, list of references, licensing, bonding, and insurance. Keep in mind that additional services you want your dog to have, such as hand-feeding, may cost extra. Does the candidate walk more than one dog at a time? If so, ask how she manages that and what sizes the dogs are. Personally, I would not want my dog walked by a person who walks small and large dogs together. Although most pet sitters are not dog trainers, and you shouldn't have high expectations that your dog will be trained while in their care, ask if she uses positive reinforcement. Also ask what her experience is, if she belongs to professional organizations, what continuing education or training courses she is taking, and what her first-aid training is.

With sitters, if a candidate seems acceptable, references are positive, and her good professional status is confirmed, you will want to interview her in your home. Introduce her to your dog. Does she interact with him professionally, positively, and competently? When you demonstrate cues and protocols, does the candidate try them out effectively? A good candidate will also walk your dog with you during the interview, which will help you see how she works and how your dog responds to her.

Once you have made the selection, have a brief orientation session, ideally at your home. If the dog sitter will be staying overnight in your home, find out how many hours she will actually be there and how many hours your dog will be alone and without supervision or companionship, and discuss the morning and evening routines. Be clear about your house rules, including furniture rules, sleeping arrangements, dog toy rules, protocols for coming and going, safety rules, dogproofing requirements (for instance, is it okay to leave a purse unattended, or keep food on countertops?). If your dog has daily medications that he must have, show the sitter (or walker) how to give the dosage and make sure she understands how to do it. Decide what daily training, activities, and games will be done to keep up your dog's skills. Have her practice hand-feeding your dog to get established. Don't worry about seeming fussy or overprotective—a good pet sitter will appreciate your attention to detail.

After you return from your trip, evaluate the experience with the pet sitter. Some pet sitters have evaluation forms and leave notes for you as part of their service. Your dog may behave differently with the pet sitter than with you; find out what those differences are. Discuss any problem areas.

Doggy Day Care

THE QUESTIONS YOU WOULD ASK a pet sitter should also be asked of a dog day care provider, including costs, service options and programs, staffing, experience, business practices, and insurance. Visit the facility; some are located in commercial districts and others are run by individuals who work from home. Does the facility look and smell clean, seem professionally organized, and have a comfortable temperature? What kind of attention, training, and socialization opportunities are provided? Does it have enough space and crated areas for dogs to be left alone when they need it? Are there separate spaces for puppies, smaller dogs, and older dogs? How long have the operators been in business? Are they willing to offer you the names of clients who are happy with their services? If dogs pee or poop in the common area, is it cleaned up right away? Some facilities have indoor and outdoor services and provide walks. If there is an outdoor part of the facility, make sure that the fence is secure, and that there are covered and shaded areas. Some facilities provide pick-up and drop-off services, and even live webcams for you to check on your dog during the day. Remember to prepare your caregiver's checklist (see page 240) for your day care provider; most facilities also provide their own standardized intake form.

Boarding

I **F YOU PLAN TO GO AWAY** without your dog, you may wish to have a facility board her. Many dog day-care facilities have overnight boarding options, as do some veterinarians. Some individuals (like me!) board a few guest dogs in their home, providing the dogs with a family atmosphere.

Interview these facility operators as you would a dog walker, pet sitter, or day-care operator, and prepare your caregiver's checklist accordingly. In addition, you will want to discuss and evaluate their boarding policies. For example, although many boarding facilities provide their own food (it's simpler for their own logistics), I recommend that you arrange to provide your dog's regular food. In my boarding business, I provide bedding and toys to decrease damage and loss and to minimize guarding. Ask for a tour and check out where the dogs are kenneled or crated. Does the entire facility smell and look clean? Do the dogs seem happy, well-groomed, and healthy? If it's a home, does the home appear to be dogproofed and are countertops clear of temptations to counter surf? Ask how often the dogs receive direct attention and go outside to do their business and play.

Board-and-Train Programs

S **OME TRAINERS WHO BOARD** also offer training programs. I have provided board-and-train programs for 20 years, and am proud of the work that I do, so I'll tell you how I do it to help you evaluate board-and-train providers. I started the program to help keep puppies out of kennels where they would otherwise have received inadequate training and socialization. In my program, a few dogs stay in my home for anywhere from two weeks to six months as though they're my own, and we work on a personalized training program. I have dog crates and x-pens all over my home; some dogs may be tethered to me or crated while I evaluate their behavior, social skills, and training. I do not leave dogs outside. My clients' dogs don't meet the other dogs until I am ready to introduce them, and I make those introductions one dog at a time, usually starting with my Ibizan Hound, Brieo. I also offer a program where dogs shuttle back and forth between the owner and me, so that I do the training and the owner keeps up the homework. If clients' dogs are sufficiently socialized and able to travel well, I take them to my group training classes.

No matter how excellent the board-and-train program, the owner must continue the dog's training or the learning will fall apart. Therefore, I accept only dogs of owners who I am confident will do so. Any trainers who promise that their intervention will permanently train or cure your dog aren't being realistic or accurate. Offering any form of a guarantee to a client is considered unethical and you should look elsewhere.

Caregiver's Checklist

AFTER YOU HAVE CAREFULLY SELECTED the people to whom you are entrusting your cherished, spirited best friend, you'll need to provide them with basic information about your dog's habits and requirements, as well as your contact information. Here is a master checklist for you to adapt to your specific needs.

❑ Vet contact

❑ Emergency vet/animal hospital contact

❑ Vaccination record and other health information

❑ Medicine instructions

❑ Your contact info and schedule

❑ Backup contact (friend, neighbor, family member)

❏ Location of supplies: medicine, first-aid kit, food, treats, leash, poop bags, toys, training toys and supplies, grooming and bathing supplies

❏ Meals (when to feed, ingredients, bowl-washing instructions)

❏ Treat instructions (when to give treats, quantity allowed per day, when to use stuffed Kongs)

❏ Leashing instructions (harness; tighten the collar one notch for walk, loosen after walk)

❏ Walking instructions (which side your dog heels on, cues he knows during walks, routes to travel, cautions about any possible trouble spots)

❏ Socializing instructions (whether dog park visits are okay, and if so, the protocol)

❏ Behavior problems, quirks, habits

❏ Crate or bed instructions

❏ List of cues your dog knows with verbal and hand signals

❏ List of tricks, noting verbal and hand signals

❏ Short list of favorite training games and activities

❏ Training cues and/or tricks that your dog is currently learning

❏ Toys for regular use and special training toys

❏ Brushing protocol and location

❏ Bathing and grooming protocol

Selecting Your Dog's Trainer

IF, AFTER YOU'VE COMPLETED our work together—or your dog is exhibiting behavior issues that seem beyond your control—you decide to hire a professional trainer, I applaud your commitment to your dog. In addition to good instruction and feedback, training lessons will provide another valuable socialization experience for your dog. When choosing a trainer, ask for recommendations from your veterinarian or from owners who have well-behaved dogs.

Naturally, I highly recommend that you choose a trainer who uses positive reinforcement rather than aversive punishment training. Unfortunately, there are a few trainers who say that they teach positive reinforcement but actually don't. You can look at the website of the Association of Pet Dog Trainers to try to locate a positive reinforcement trainer in your area.

In the end, I believe it's best that you visit a class before signing on to any training program. A good trainer will explain the lessons so that they are easy to understand, and interact well with people as well as the dogs. The dogs in the class will seem happy. After the class, talk to the students and get their opinions.

Don't be afraid to interview the trainer (in fact, a good trainer will appreciate that). Ask about his experience. Ask if he uses a positive reinforcement method and how he follows those principles. Ask about choke collars and training protocols. Ask if the trainer is flexible about using unorthodox hand signals, which I believe is a good sign that he will be able to help you adapt to your dog's learning pace and tastes. In short, keep asking questions until you're sure you've found a trainer who is right for you and your dog's particular needs.

O N FRIDAY, OCTOBER 9, 2009, Bo Obama celebrated his first birthday with some special guests that included the Kennedy Porties: Splash, Sunny, and Bo's littermate, Cappy, who was also celebrating his first birthday. The one official photo that the White House released to commemorate that day showed Cappy, with his paws up on the table, quickly gobbling up his brother's doggy birthday cake. (As the First Lady later noted in an interview, Bo didn't seem to mind.)

Friday, October 9, 2009, was notable for another reason, too. That was the day President Obama received notice that he had been awarded the 2009 Nobel Peace Prize. In the White House Rose Garden that day, he began his comments to the media by saying that earlier that morning, Malia had said to him: "Daddy, you won the Nobel Peace Prize, and it is Bo's birthday." And, he continued, Sasha had then joined in: "Plus we have a three-day weekend coming up."

The President was clearly humbled by the Nobel committee's surprise announcement. He mused about his daughters' comments: "It's good to have kids to keep things in perspective." I later heard all about it on the news and I thought, "Yes, Mr. President, it's good to have the perspective that comes from having kids . . . and dogs."

APPENDICES

Appendix 1.
Canine Good Citizen (CGC)
Certificate Test Prep Course

THE CANINE GOOD CITIZEN (CGC) Certificate, administered through the American Kennel Club (AKC), is the gold standard when it comes to evaluating a dog's socialization skills. These tests are managed by official AKC evaluators, many of whom offer CGC training classes. There are many benefits to having a CGC-certified dog, including admission to therapy-dog training and being welcomed at an increasing number of workplaces and rental homes.

The CGC exam is challenging. For each of the 10 test items, your dog needs to have reached learning stage #4: always able to perform fluently in many generalized situations (to review the four learning stages, see page 69). You may praise and encourage her throughout the test, but you can't use food treats or toys to lure, encourage, or reward her. A dog is automatically dismissed if she "growls, snaps, bites, attacks, or attempts to attack a person or another dog" or potties during the test.

This appendix is designed to prepare your dog to achieve the CGC level of obedience, even if you never plan to take the test. I believe it's helpful to assess your dog's obedience skills after you've completed the Fundamentals Training Program and to review them each year. But remember: If you and your dog fail, you are still a good dog owner; you just need to continue your training and, perhaps, allow your dog to mature further.

Test Item #1:
Accept a Friendly Stranger

YOUR DOG WILL PASS THIS TEST if, when in public, you can greet people without his causing a disturbance, nosing in, or being fearful. Will he sit still at your heel and stay until cued while someone greets you? Can he accept not being the center of attention while you speak with someone else? In the presence of strangers, does your dog appear comfortable and not shy, fearful, anxious, or aggressive?

Practice by having your training partner hold a treat while approaching you and your dog. Hold your dog's leash with half of it wrapped around your hand, and keep that hand glued to your hip. Get ready to stand like a tree as you did when you taught your dog the *cookie sit-stay*. If he lunges in excitement, your partner should immediately back up a step and stand still. When your dog refocuses on you, mark that (with a click or a verbal "good") and *recall* him using both a verbal cue and hand signal, and have him *sit*. Now ask your partner to resume approaching you. If your dog lunges again, repeat the process. As your partner gets close enough to give him the treat, your dog may get up again, and if so, have your partner withdraw the treat immediately, back up a step, and give a silent hand signal for *sit*. Work with your partner in advance to get the timing right and to teach the hand signal. When your dog earns his first reward treat from your partner, make sure to mark and praise that moment . . . and reward a jackpot.

To help your dog gain fluency for this behavior, gradually increase the amount of time before you mark and reward his calm *sit*. Next, have a friendly conversation with your partner while your dog continues to sit. During these conversations, praise your dog, starting at about 10 seconds and increasing the interval between praises by a couple of seconds at a time.

Since the goal is for your dog to become fully automatic with this cue, practice with different partners and in different situations. After a minute or so of conversation, start walking together and stop again. Try it at home when a friend comes to your front door. Take your dog to a friend's home. Little by little, withdraw food treats. When your dog can consistently accept the approach of most friendly people, and can sit quietly as you and your friend converse, all without treats, then you are ready to pass this test.

Test Item #2: Sit Politely for Petting

THIS TEST REQUIRES that your dog sit calmly and without fear while a friendly stranger pets her. A dog that sits while being petted has confidence and generally does well in social interactions with people. But some dogs fear being petted, and this shows up as aggression or shyness, different sides of what behaviorists call the fight-or-flight-or-freeze response, all of which are fear-generated impulses. Your dog may have no problem passing this part of the test, because she knows the world as a gentle and loving place. However, many dogs have had harsh experiences early in life or are born innately fearful of even the friendliest person who approaches. If your dog has a serious fear problem, refer to Chapter Eleven on behavior issues, and consider working with a behavior specialist.

If your dog has no serious fear issues, she is ready to learn this skill. Maybe she's exuberant or mouthy, so sitting still while someone touches her can be very challenging. The protocol for teaching your dog to sit politely while being petted is similar to the protocol for Test Item #1: Have your partner approach her as long as the dog is calm. The moment she starts to get up out of her *sit* or starts to mouth or paw, your partner needs to back away.

Start by asking people you know to practice the handling and gentling exercises in Chapter Three (see page 64). Start acclimating your dog to being petted by people whom she already knows: trusted partners and members of your family. Consider setting up a hand-feeding protocol with each of them.

Give your dog plenty of food rewards and soothing praise while she is being petted. Little by little over a span of weeks, withdraw the food rewards (but continue the praise). Always be present and calm during these sessions. It may be helpful for you to direct the other person's touch so that your dog knows that you are right there making everything safe and enjoyable for her.

Of course, in the real world, good safety means using common sense and caution in allowing others, especially children, to pet your dog. Children can easily get overexcited and pet a dog inappropriately. Many children will run right at a dog and want to pet her or play. Make certain that the adult who is responsible for that child approves of the child's touching your dog, and know your dog well enough to be sure that she is okay with being touched by this child. Assuming that you're okay with the situation, instruct the child and the adult to pet your calm dog on the side, not on the head, which can spook her.

Test Item #3:
Appearance and Grooming

WILL YOUR DOG SIT or stand calmly while being groomed? Can an expert, such as a vet, examine him all over? What happens when someone touches his paws, ears, nose, and collar, and looks in his mouth? Does he appear healthy (well-groomed, clean coat and ears, alert, proper weight)?

The first step to having someone else brush and examine your dog is being able to do that for him yourself. Chapter Three's handling and gentling exercises will help get ready for this test. Have various partners brush him gently while you give him treats and lots of calm praise and encouragement. They should examine your dog all over: check his ears, eyes, nose, teeth, collar, feet, shoulders, hips, tail, back, belly region. Have him lie down, sit, and stand for various exams, and note any positions that are more challenging for him to tolerate being touched.

Test Item #4: Walk on a Loose Leash

WILL YOUR DOG WALK on a loose leash while doing each of the Fundamentals Training Program lessons? Does your dog pay attention to you while walking so that when you turn, stop, or speed up, she stays with you?

In this test, you will not be judged for a competition-style walking at heel. But your dog will be required to stay with you as you walk through a course set up with markers or perform a series of turns (left, right, U-turn), stops, and starts.

When you practice the Fundamentals walking exercises, check in with your dog at random moments to keep her focus on you. Incorporate those turns, stops, starts, and changes of pace. Withdraw the treat lures and emphasize giving her well-timed praise to mark her correct loose-leash walking.

Test Item #5: Walk Through a Crowd

WILL YOUR DOG STAY FOCUSED on you as you walk with him past other people, or does he get excited and tug on his leash to check them out? Can he walk through a crowd without showing signs of fight-or-flight-or-freeze fear or anxiety?

Start by walking in familiar places with people who are familiar to your dog. At first, have these people spread out and stand still as you walk through the "crowd." Next, have them bunch a little closer together, and after that have them move around a bit. Little by little, you'll build up your dog's tolerance for distractions.

If treat lures help keep him focused on you, by all means use them while you train, and then phase them out later. Use your voice to keep him focused on you.

If you want to get really fancy with training for this test, weave through the crowd while keeping your dog focused on you, so that during the test a straight path through the crowd will seem simple.

Test Item #6: Sit, Down, and Stay at 20 Feet

WHEN YOU LEAVE YOUR DOG'S SIDE, does she have enough impulse control to continue to sit and stay where you left her? When you're 20 feet away from her, will she listen to you and perform some basic cues?

During the test, the evaluator will clip a 20-foot leash onto your dog's collar or harness. Get your dog comfortable with having her collar handled, and practice by having a partner clip a strange leash or a long lead onto your dog's collar. If you practice this cue in a park, make doubly sure that you have that long lead clipped on.

The Fundamentals Training Program covered this skill thoroughly, though you may not have built up the distance to 20 feet. Practice Puppy Pushups at longer distances, and if your dog responds to you beyond 20 feet, this item will probably seem easy on exam day.

Build her impulse control by putting her in a *sit* or a *down*, and then turn and walk away from her. If necessary, stop after just one step before turning to face and praise your dog. Go back to her to give more praise and a reward. In the next round, add another step before turning around, and keep adding steps. See if you can build up the distance beyond 20 feet, meanwhile phasing out the treats.

As you walk back to your dog, she must stay in place. Practice this part of the test item by stopping if she tries to move as you return. During the test, you are allowed to remind your dog to stay as often as you need to when you walk toward her. Still, I suggest that you build up her distance and duration when you practice, so that a single cue will work. Doing Puppy Pushups, giving praise, and pausing frequently will help keep her focused on what you're asking.

Test Item #7:
Recall (Come When Called)

WHEN YOU *RECALL* YOUR DOG from 10 feet away, does he come to you right away, even when there are mild distractions? During the exam, the evaluator will provide mild distractions, such as petting your dog when you recall him. Practice distractions, such as petting and supervised play with a partner's dog, so that yours understands that coming to you when called needs to be his top priority at any moment. Make sure to reward him for *recalls* during training with a high-value reward (and possibly a high-value activity such as being released back to supervised play), so that he learns the incentive for always coming to you when called. Review the recall section in the Fundamentals Quick Guide (see page 138).

Test Item #8:
Reaction to Another Dog

WHEN YOU GREET SOMEONE who is also walking a dog, does your dog remain focused on you? Is your dog unable to control her impulse to run right up to the other dog, or will she stay at your side while you speak briefly with the other person? Will she cower from or be aggressive toward the other dog, or will she be able to show appropriate and mild interest?

In the test, you and your dog will approach another dog and handler, and then stop when you're close enough to shake hands with the handler and engage in a brief conversation before moving on. During that exchange, your dog needs to stay at your side and show just a mild interest in the other dog, and stay focused on your cues to stop walking, stay, and then start walking again.

To train for this, arrange with your training partner to walk your respective dogs toward each other on cue. How well socialized your dogs already are with each other will help you determine how close you can come to each other. The goal is to walk close enough to shake hands, but that will probably take many trials. If possible, train for this skill with many dogs (because yours will probably perform better with some dogs than with others), until she builds up skill, confidence, and impulse control.

Test Item #9: Reaction to Distractions

HOW WILL YOUR DOG REACT when a startling distraction happens? Will he panic and run away, become aggressive and bark or lunge, or just get startled for a moment and then express appropriately mild curiosity? How does he react not only to sudden or loud noises, but also to visual distractions?

A CGC-socialized dog behaves well around all kinds of distractions that happen within five feet of him. The evaluator will assess your dog's response to sudden loud noises, such as a door slamming or a metal folding chair being dropped on a hard floor. Your dog will be expected to react to these disturbances with nothing more than natural curiosity.

The more distractions your dog is exposed to, the better, as long as you don't make him more fearful. Always be jolly when the noise happens (see "The Jollies" on page 66), and be prepared to move on to something else right away if it doesn't go well. It's helpful to desensitize your dog to these strange noises and visual distractions in short training increments and then move on to another exercise or game before returning for another brief distraction exercise. If he becomes fearful, move onto something else or go back to his last successful trial. Moving ahead too quickly may cause your dog to panic unnecessarily or go potty on the floor (which, unfortunately, means he automatically flunks the CGC test) and make him fearful about things he wasn't fearful about beforehand. Take all the time your dog needs to adjust; his long-term well-being is more important than earning the CGC certificate before he is ready.

For the noise distractions, introduce them at a distance and make sure that your dog can see the action as it is happening. At the start, drop the items only a few inches from the ground and at a farther distance. Over time, build up height to shoulder level and closer ranges.

To desensitize your dog to a visual distraction (such as a stroller, portable lawn sprinkler, or even a plant that sways in the breeze), start with the item on the floor or ground and let your dog sniff it. To build a dog's confidence and comfort level, work with him as he stands near the object but do not introduce him to it. Instead, play with him near the object, or review some training that he already knows. If he shows curiosity on his own, praise and reward him. Much like the way you introduced your dog to his crate or the 101 Things to Do with a Box (page 181), it's helpful to put treats around and even on the object and be very patient as your dog warms up on his own time schedule. Always be upbeat and jolly when you're introducing these objects, but don't push your dog faster than he's ready, because that would be flooding, which I am opposed to and discussed in Chapter Eleven. Instead of flooding, desensitize your dog to the object at a pace that makes him comfortable.

The next step with the visual objects is to experiment by introducing a bit of movement. Get down on his level and touch the object as you act jolly (and confidently move that stroller or touch the lawn sprinkler or swaying plant a little). Little by little, move closer.

Test Item #10: Supervised Separation

WHAT HAPPENS WHEN YOU LEAVE your dog with someone else for a few minutes? Does she continue to be a well-mannered dog, or does she become fearful or agitated? A well-socialized dog is confident and comfortable enough to be away from you without barking or whining.

Train your dog to do this valuable social skill much as you trained her to *sit-stay* for longer and longer times, including when you left the room. Start this lesson with a training partner whom she already knows and likes. Let your partner play with, handle, brush, or train her as you move a little distance away. Keep coming back to praise and treat your dog, and then move a little farther or stay away for a little longer.

Build up your dog's comfort level so that she is at ease with your leaving the room for a moment, and then longer moments, building up her comfort beyond three minutes. Praise and treat when you return, but don't be too effusive. Many dogs perform better on this skill when you treat and praise as you leave, too, but when you leave the room, don't make a big deal about that either. Just be calm when you leave and when you return.

Appendix 2.
Specialized Training

WHEN I WAS IN my early twenties, I got bitten—quite hard, in fact—by the dog show bug. I'll never forget the first show I attended, at an arena in Fairfax, Virginia. I was floored. I loved being around people with so much knowledge about different breeds, and seeing how talented they and the dogs were. Where did these people come from, I wondered. What made them so devoted? How did they become so knowledgeable? And how did they get their dogs so well trained? I began to understand that there was far more to a champion dog than just good genes.

After I had children, I took them along to dog shows on the weekends and eventually my three children, Ebony (our Portie) and I were a common sight at dog shows around the Washington, D.C., area. It wasn't always easy traveling with this entourage. I remember at one show, one of my daughters started to complain, soon after we arrived, that she had to go potty. Our only option was a portable outhouse. So I parked and unloaded the stroller, and, since I had nobody to keep an eye on my kids or Ebony, the five of us pushed our way into the tiny plastic restroom. Inside, as efficiently and cleanly as possible, I was able to get Courtlandt and Blaise, my two older children, to do their business without falling down the hole while I put a fresh diaper on Paige—all while holding Ebony's leash. When I opened the door, we were met by a cheering crowd. "Portie in a Porta-Potty!" someone yelled. Yes, we were a colorful part of the local scene.

Another time, I took my kids to see one of our favorite dogs, Nina, compete in a conformation dog show. Nina was a beautiful Briard that I had trained and boarded often. Nina belonged to the late Helga Meyer Bullock, opera singer and mother of actress Sandra Bullock. My kids knew Nina well. They hand-fed her and loved brushing her lush coat and making a fuss over her. Once when Helga came to the house, she discovered her dog's long coat pinned up in my daughters' brightly colored barrettes. We all laughed as Nina strutted around the house with her show dog "look at me" attitude while sporting her unique coiffure. Anyway, at the dog show, my kids got so excited when Nina finally entered the ring that they couldn't help squealing in delight. Nina got distracted and looked toward the familiar squeals, broke her show dog strut, and lost that dog show. Oops.

While you may never want to show your dog at this level, there are many great activities and extraordinary experiences awaiting you and your best friend. Each of these activities requires specialized training. This appendix will give you ideas about activities and specialized training experiences that are available—many of which you can participate in through a local American Kennel Club affiliate. Some clubs invite all breeds, including mixed-breed dogs. Other AKC clubs specialize in a specific breed. To find out about local AKC club programs that sanction more than 22,000 dog events annually, check the AKC website (akc.org/clubs).

There are also many excellent non-AKC events. Check out the Association of Pet Dog Trainers' website (apdt.org), which lists many specialized training events for the public, especially APDT Rally competitions, which I'll tell you about later in this appendix. The APDT encourages all dogs to participate, including those with physical disabilities.

So, let's get started.

Therapy Dogs

IN THE 1960S, child psychologist Boris Levinson coined the term "pet therapy" after he accidentally discovered that his patients made significant progress when they interacted with his dog, Jingles. Now therapy dogs and their owners volunteer in hospitals, rehab centers, literacy programs, hospices, disaster relief, and trauma and therapeutic environments.

Just touching a dog can lift the spirit.

Although I have long believed in the value of using dogs to help people heal, I didn't truly understand the extent to which this is true until I myself became the recipient of therapy dog service. In April 2006, I was hospitalized after a serious car wreck. While driving along the peaceful, picturesque northern

Virginia country roads, I swerved to avoid a deer herd. My SUV rolled over, skidded off the road, and tumbled into a ditch. At least that's what I was told; I have little recollection. I remember floating in and out of consciousness as my Giant Schnauzer, Saxon, lay across my chest after having climbed from the safety pen, which had popped open. He nuzzled my neck and growled fiercely at anyone who tried to come near me. It was my good luck that a neighbor appeared. I have a vague recollection of her speaking very gently to Saxon, assuring him that he was a good dog and that the police, ambulance, firefighters, and MedEvac helicopter were all there to help me. He trusted her and allowed her to coax him away from protecting me so that they could help me. Bless this woman, who I believe to this day was my guardian angel.

A highly skilled team of doctors were able to save my life. But six weeks later, my recovery took a turn for the worse and I was MedEvac'ed to another hospital when my broken clavicle pierced an artery and I developed a potentially fatal blood clot. After a 12-hour emergency surgery, I began my real recovery.

My time in the hospital was incredibly challenging—not only physically, but psychologically. While I lay in the hospital bed, having to undergo a seemingly endless array of emergency procedures and assessments at all hours (while also battling tremendous pain), I became terrified of dying. I was more convinced each day, as I failed to make progress in healing, that I was getting closer to death. (I was so scared that I wouldn't allow my hospital door to be closed.) I was slowly losing my will to live.

And then it happened. It was an innocent moment, a small gesture that changed my life. A stranger walked into my room holding a little terrier and put him on my tummy. I could barely move, but was able to pet the dog with one arm. Simply by putting an arm around that small dog for that brief visit, I got away from thinking about my pain and fear, and I felt back in touch with life.

I am now so committed to the training of therapy dogs that I have made that part of my business. I work with the dog owner to make sure that the candidate is extremely well socialized and able to stay calm regardless of the setting. I expose the dog to a variety of potential distractions: visual, sound, movement, and smell. I take the dog around to many other people and dogs. I also do my best to make sure that dog owners are prepared to face the emotional challenges of therapeutic settings while handling their dogs.

I'm currently training Ripley, a young German Shepherd, to become a therapy dog at the Walter Reed Army Medical Center. Ripley belongs to William Waybourn, whose Hank (also a German Shepherd) already does therapy work at Walter Reed. William came to me because he believes, as I do, that the only effective way to train a healthy, happy therapy dog is with positive reinforcement.

Despite all the attention therapy dogs receive when they are on the job, it's not always easy for either the dog or the owner. Since dogs must be bathed within 24 hours of the visit, William wakes up at 4 A.M. to bathe Hank so that he's clean and completely dry by the time they arrive at the hospital. At the end of a therapy dog's long shift of nonstop attention and the stress of meeting so many people while also encountering noisy equipment, busy hallways, and unusual smells, William finds that Hank needs to sleep for the rest of the day.

But that seems like a small price to pay to William, who views his therapy-dog experience as an extraordinary opportunity to serve. "The quality of people I meet under the most difficult circumstances is remarkable. No one wants to stay in the hospital; everyone wants to get home," he says. The therapy dog "gives them an opportunity to take the focus off the difficulties they're facing." I agree completely.

If you believe that you and your dog might be right as a therapy-dog team, I encourage you to look into volunteering with a local therapy-dog organization. Training and certification programs are provided by the Delta Society and by Therapy Dogs International.

Obedience Training

RALLY OBEDIENCE

RALLY OBEDIENCE (also known as Rally or Rally-O) is a sport in which your dog proceeds through an obstacle course performing a series of specific obedience tasks. The course typically consists of 10 to 20 signs that instruct the team what to do. These events are a fun and fulfilling activity for many dogs and their owners, and a wonderful way for your dog to socialize with other well-trained canines.

The two most popular sanctioning bodies for Rally in the United States are the AKC and the APDT. Both have three levels of competition: The AKC labels theirs Novice, Advanced, and Excellent; the APDT's levels are One, Two, and Three. Both the AKC and the APDT have a series of awards and titles that dogs can earn in Rally contests, and both organizations encourage junior competitors.

To earn the distinction of AKC Rally's Novice class, your dog must be able to successfully perform everything covered in our Fundamentals Training Program, such as *sit-stay*, *down-stay*, *recall*, and focusing on you. She must also be able to walk at your heel around a designated course, make turns, change speeds, start and stop abruptly, back up, weave, and spiral in front of judges. You are allowed to give hand signals, encourage your dog verbally, pat your leg, and clap your hands throughout the course, but no food lures or treats are allowed. APDT's Level One Rally covers skills similar to AKC Novice; the main difference is that in APDT Level One, you can keep your dog on leash.

To earn the more advanced Rally certificates, your dog performs complex turning and heeling patterns, including abrupt pivots and diagonal turns, turning in the opposite direction from you, following cues while moving (and at a distance from you), and going over jumps without hesitation. To earn the Excellent Class, at each station you may give only a hand signal and encourage your dog verbally.

AKC OBEDIENCE TRIALS

IF YOU AND YOUR DOG ARE READY to enjoy even greater challenges in obedience training, I invite you to consider the extraordinary world of obedience trials. How far can you go in AKC obedience trials? All the way to the National Obedience Invitational, where dogs vie for the National Obedience Championship (NOC). But to be invited to compete, your dog must first earn all three levels of Competitive Obedience Trials: Novice, Open, and Utility. The Novice trial is similar to the CGC test: The only additional tasks are perfect *recalls* at any moment and off-leash *heeling*. The Open Class includes off-leash *heeling* with many turns and changes of speed, jumps and hurdles, and drops to a *down* in the middle of a *recall*. The Utility Class has been jokingly dubbed "Futility" by many dog owners because the tasks that dogs are asked to perform are extremely challenging, and this certificate is very difficult to earn. For example, utility dogs are able to go into a pile of objects and find a specific object that has the handler's scent on it, follow directional cues to retrieve a specific glove, be cued to go away from the handler and then jump specific hurdles on the *recall*. If a dog can successfully perform these tasks, it's likely he will have accumulated enough points to earn an invitation to compete for the NOC.

CANINE FREESTYLE DANCING

ANOTHER WAY TO PRACTICE OBEDIENCE training is canine freestyle dancing, in which you choreograph a dance routine with your dog. That's right; in canine freestyle you're the choreographer and your dog is your dance partner. For this training, your dog will, in essence, be performing a series of tricks that, when put together, look like a graceful dance routine. (You may find that it's easiest to teach some dance moves by using clicker training along with targeting devices, and then replacing the training aids with hand signals and verbal cues.)

Similar to human dancing competitions, canine freestyle routines are set to music. Beginners often start with a 30-second routine and build up to a 90-second routine. More advanced performers perform entire songs. Lately, some performers have taken to wearing costumes, including something for the dog. In addition to "couples dancing," some canine freestyle clubs and training programs have choreographed group dances that become that group's signature exhibition performance.

Any cue or behavior that a dog does reliably can be adapted into a canine freestyle routine, including all the skills you learned in the Fundamentals Training Program. Canine freestyle is a fun way to practice skills, teach new skills, invent moves, and chain together a routine. It helps dogs and their owners develop superior communication, response, cues, and skills.

There are a number of associations, websites, and local groups that have performance events. There are also some helpful books, DVDs, and Web videos that will help you get started. If you're looking for some special inspiration on canine freestyle, I highly recommend you learn about Carolyn Scott and her Golden Retriever, Rookie, who are considered the Ginger Rogers and Fred Astaire of canine freestyle. Rookie and Carolyn had an extraordinary bond; when you see a video of them you'll notice immediately how completely focused they are on each other. Together, they introduced canine freestyle to countless people around the world. In addition to performing on television and at contests, they danced at nursing homes, schools, and churches. Rookie danced well into his teenage years, which I hope inspires us all to remember that old dogs can indeed learn new tricks. Sadly, Rookie crossed to the other side of the "Rainbow Bridge" in 2008. I like to imagine that heaven is even more joyful with Rookie performing with the angels.

High-Energy Canine Sports

MANY DOGS REQUIRE ACTIVITIES that burn off a lot of energy. For these dogs, high-energy canine sports are a great option.

AGILITY COURSE

THE DOG AGILITY OBSTACLE COURSE is an exciting competition to watch. Each team—which consists of your dog and you, or a handler—races through an obstacle course that includes a variety of jumps, weave poles, bridges, and tunnels. The teams race against the clock and lose points for mistakes, such as missing an obstacle and having to go back to try again, knocking over a hurdle crossbar, hesitating while sprinting through a tunnel or while racing up and over a tall A-frame, or jumping off too early after running across a suspended bridge or teeter-totter. Sometimes the mistakes can be human error, such as not being able to keep up with your dog, or using imprecise body position, which can cue your dog to go the wrong way. Agility training takes a lot of practice and is great exercise for you and your high-energy dog.

Agility has become so popular that there are now commercial sponsors and cash prizes for some of the higher-profile competitions, which include a featured invitational competition at the annual AKC Nationals. There are agility athletic organizations, such as the United States Dog Agility Association, that

Just like their human counterparts, canine athletes need to train hard to do well.

present regional, national, and international meets. In recent years, the AKC has taken a squad of 12 duos to the FCI Agility World Championships in Europe. The FCI, or Fédération Cynologique Internationale, is essentially the International Kennel Club or World Canine Organization.

FLYBALL RELAY RACES

ANOTHER GREAT OPTION for high-energy dogs are flyball relay races. In these events, a team of four dogs races in relay fashion. The first dog runs down a 51-foot course over four hurdles; pounces on a mechanical box that releases a tennis ball, which the dog catches in his mouth; then returns over the jumps. When the dog crosses the start/finish line after a successful run, the next dog is released. Two teams of four dogs face off in a side-by-side race, and the first team to finish is the winner. Dogs and handlers train and compete with the same high-caliber precision that elite human sprinters use in their relay races.

In the past year, more than 250 teams belonging to the North American Flyball Association (NAFA) have run the whole race in under 20 seconds (yes, that's four dogs in under 20 seconds total!), as measured by electronic timing systems. NAFA's website (flyball.org) displays a dizzying array of statistics, including a breed analysis of which dogs are fastest. Not surprisingly, Border Collies and Jack/Parson Russell Terriers dominate the list. Since flyball has become such a fast and precise canine sport, NAFA's rulebook takes longer to read than it would take most teams to complete a race. Visit NAFA's website for the most up-to-date listings of competitions and clubs, which bear names like Spring Loaded, Instant Replay, and Rocket Relay. At NAFA events you will likely find out about flyball training in your area, or you can learn how NAFA can help you start a club if there isn't one nearby.

Even small dogs can get lots of air!

DISC DOG

NOT LONG AFTER the Wham-O toy company first introduced the Frisbee flying disc across America in 1958, people realized that many dogs loved catching them, too. As people became more skillful and creative at playing with flying discs, they included their dogs in their innovative play. Today, the disc dog world embraces a variety of competitions, including long-distance throws that champion dogs race more than 50 yards to catch in midair. Disc dog fanciers also have competitive canine freestyle choreographed routines that feature the dog's athletic jumps and fast-paced throws of several discs. There are disc dog clubs, competitions, and classes across America, as well as exhibitions and special shows. Dogs with a lot of energy and jumping ability excel at catching the flying disc.

Specialized Skill Training

MANY BREEDS WERE ORIGINALLY BRED to take on jobs: tracking, hunting, retrieving, water work, and herding. Today, those dogs' instincts and abilities are very much alive, and often need a high-energy outlet that doesn't involve ripping up your sofa or digging up your garden. I have participated in most of the training programs in this section with various dogs of mine. Together, we have traipsed the woods and fields, spent hours in the water, and worked while surrounded by a herd of sheep.

TRACKING

DOGS' ABILITY TO SMELL is far beyond our human sense. That's why they are able to find people trapped in rubble, sniff out contraband and dangers, provide forensic details at crime scenes, detect cancer, predict epileptic seizures, and tear open your child's backpack to eat that week-old jelly donut.

To earn the AKC's title of Champion Tracker (CT), a dog must be able to pass two very difficult tests. He must first earn a Tracking Dog Excellent (TDX) by following a scent over 1,000 yards that has been "aged" at least three hours before the dog starts, and includes at least five changes in direction and human cross tracks. He must also earn the Variable Surface Tracking (VST) distinction by tracking in a real-world situation, which may include rainy or snowy weather and an "aged" track over various surfaces rich with naturally fragrant vegetation, streams, sand, and smooth concrete. When a dog earns the TDX, VST, or CT, everyone celebrates; it's like being on a golf course when someone aces a hole-in-one.

The best way to learn about tracking is by going to a tracking event; they usually need volunteers to help prepare the courses on a Saturday, and tests are typically held on Sunday. The AKC website is a good place to start your own tracking of tracking events and training in your locale.

HUNTING SKILLS:
LURE COURSING, GUNDOG, EARTHDOG

HUNTING SKILL EVENTS INCLUDE lure coursing, gundog hunting tests and field retrieving, and earthdog. *Lure coursing* involves chasing a lure over a field course that includes abrupt turns to simulate an animal's escape. Lure coursing has traditionally been limited to purebred sighthounds (dogs that hunt by sight rather than by scent), but it has recently been expanded to include all kinds of dogs. Typically, a field of two or more acres is set up with a lure course rig: A lure like a plastic shopping bag is tied to a very long and strong motorized fishing/trolling line that is looped around a maze of pulleys. A few dogs race at the same time to catch the lure. The sport is not recommended for dogs younger than one year old because of joint stress. The AKC and the American Sighthound Field Association (asfa.org) sanction many lure coursing events. Other groups have developed their own versions of this sport, including steeplechase lure courses that combine some of the types of jumps that are also found on agility courses.

Gundog hunting tests were developed to help hunters evaluate their dogs' abilities. The AKC sanctions hunting and retrieving events, with separate competitions for pointing breeds, retrievers, spaniels, and hounds—all of which have different special jobs on the hunt. Other popular organizations that sanction hunt dog events and tests include the United Kennel Club and North American Hunting Retriever Association. Hunting tests include quartering (racing ahead to locate the game and then going back and forth between game and hunter on cue), trailing prey, and sit-to-flush (sitting silently for a cue to chase birds into the air). In retrieving trials, a dog must find and retrieve a shot bird, often aided only by the general sound of a gunshot and a vague sense of where the bird has landed. Retrievers are judged on the ability to find the bird quickly, pick it up cleanly so that it is balanced in the dog's mouth, run back to the handler directly, and give the bird to the handler and judge for inspection to see that it has not been mauled by a "hard mouth." Skilled hunt dogs earn designations, starting with Junior Hunter (JH) and advancing to Senior Hunter (SH), and ultimately Master Hunter (MH); many are then invited to compete at the National Amateur Field Championships (NAFC).

Earthdog tests provide a structure for terriers, Dachshunds, and Miniature Schnauzers to show off their hunting instincts and develop the skills they were bred for long ago: rooting out ground animals that would otherwise vex farmers and hunters. Earthdogs courageously "go to ground" inside a tunnel and follow a scent to a den. Earthdog course builders design and dig a network of tunnels for canines to find their quarry. Some trainers like to use a section of wide PVC pipe to lure-train their dogs into the tunnel, and then add on more sections of pipe, including 3-way and 4-way fittings. Some tunnel mazes are permanent structures that are used by clubs for training and hosted tournaments. I think the tunnel builders have as much fun creating vast earthdog mazes as the dogs have navigating them. The AKC and American Working Terrier Association (AWTA) have established noncompetitive tests for introducing earthdogs to quarrying and for evaluating higher skills up to the Master Earthdog designation.

WATER WORK AND DOCK DIVING

AS WE'VE DISCUSSED, all dogs need to be taught to swim, even if they are bred for the water. Some dogs, once they get in the water, would be content to play there all day. For them, there are water work and dock diving. In well-managed canine water programs, safety is always covered before a dog sets one paw in the water. Many programs require (and often provide) dog life jackets. Not surprisingly, the Portuguese Water Dog Club of America has an active water-dog program.

Water work includes rescue exercises, such as towing a person on a life ring, boat work, a variety of retrieving and delivery skills that include underwater retrieving, and even water scent work. Swimming competitions require the dogs to navigate around a set of buoy markers. Training programs include summer camps for you and your dog to vacation at together.

In *dock diving*, dogs take a running or standing broad jump off the end of the dock and into the water. Winners are the dogs that jump the farthest. If you have a water dog, you can probably guess that the main training technique is to lure the dog by throwing a toy in a nice arc so that your dog pops up off the end of the dock for greater distance, rather than leaping out flat. Toy lures are allowed during competition. Dogs compete in categories based on size, experience, and age. For safety, cover the dock with a nonslip carpet and make sure that the water is at least four feet deep and cleared of all branches and debris.

Isn't it funny, though, that many of those same dogs consider bath time a form of torture? (Note to self: Ask the AKC to sanction a bathing event.)

SHEEPHERDING

WHEN I SAW COMPETITIONS in which one Border Collie would herd some 20 sheep around a course, I decided to try sheepherding. Although I had fun working at it twice a week for about three months, I was an utter failure, not because of my Border Collie, Jock, but because I didn't have any of what sheepherding handlers call "stock sense." Standing smack in the middle of a herd of livestock was overwhelming for me, especially when I couldn't see Jock. If you're thinking of trying out sheepherding, the first question you should consider is how much stock sense *you* have. Before you introduce your dog to the sheep, try herding livestock yourself, without your dog. See what it's like to work the sheep, "reading" and anticipating their movements, so you'll know how to teach your dog—assuming *he* has stock sense. The most complete and current listing of upcoming sheepherding trials can be found at the United States Border Collie Handler's Association (USBCHA) website (usbcha.com); the AKC is also developing a sanctioned sheepherding program. At these trials, you will witness extraordinary dogs and meet owners and prospective trainers.

AKC Conformation Show Dog Basics

THE FACT IS THAT few dogs *conform* to the AKC's "breed standard" physical structure and appearance that is necessary to become successful in the show ring. The original focus of these AKC conformation dog shows was to give awards to the best dogs in order to improve the breeding stock. In addition to having superior genetics, a champion show dog is trained to *gait* properly (move a certain way that's deemed correct for the breed) and *stack* correctly (stand still and pose in that breed's correct posture while being inspected all over).

Just because a dog was born to champion show dog parents doesn't mean that she can be a show dog, too. Champions have a certain body structure, as well as a temperament that comes alive and sparkles in the ring with that *je ne sais quoi* "look at me" charisma. Show dogs trained with positive reinforcement can have a competitive edge because they often exude an easy confidence and distinctive personality that can make all the difference between the rare champions among the many competitors. Show dogs must love the traveling, and so must you enjoy devoting your weekends to these shows and the weekdays preparing for—and recovering from—them. To do well at dog shows, it must become a total way of life that is enjoyable for the human as well as for the dog.

If you're thinking about becoming a show dog "parent," start by visiting a few shows as a spectator. Talk to the fanciers—fans, breeders, owners, exhibitors, handlers, groomers, and vendors—at appropriate times, when it seems that they aren't busy preparing. Most shows have time set aside for this kind of interaction; after all, they're also social events. A few shows are *benched shows*, which means that there are structured hours when attendees are invited to look at the dogs up close and speak with their owners and handlers. At a benched show, dogs and people must be able to keep their poise and be sociable for many hours. When you're at a show, if you're anything like me, you'll be tempted to pet these beautiful animals, but don't touch them without getting permission. Buy a copy of the show program to orient yourself to the schedule and to help you take notes on dogs and people that you have met so that you can follow them at future shows. That will be your first step toward becoming a fancier yourself. Wear comfortable shoes; there is a lot of walking and standing around at dog shows. If you take the big leap into showing your dog, start at *match shows*, which are for practice and experience, and are usually more informal.

Nowadays, most champions are shown by professional, paid handlers who often specialize in presenting a certain breed. Less common is the show dog handler like Norm Randall, who is called an "all-rounder" because he can show a variety of breeds successfully. Before retiring, Norm showed 67 different breeds, including my Boston Terrier, Jasmine. Showing a small Boston Terrier is much different from showing a Giant Schnauzer, which is different from showing a Flat-Coated Retriever, and different still from showing an Ibizan Hound. Since pro handlers often earn bonus prize money if "their" dog wins, they tend to be very selective about the dogs (and the humans) they take on as clients. Although they generally own their own dogs, most of the best pros make their living showing the dogs of their clients. The reality is that most handlers also have day jobs, and must fit in their preparations and travel for dog shows around their work schedules. They devote their weekends to dog shows because they love dogs and being around the show ring, and are happy to help each other out.

Some AKC-recognized dog shows are restricted to specific breeds. Called *specialty shows*, they often feature separate competitions for amateur and professional handlers, and classify the dogs by sex, age, and previous competitive track record. There are more than 170 AKC-recognized breeds, each with its own AKC-sanctioned club, alphabetically from Affenpinscher to Yorkshire Terrier.

Each breed club helps maintain a consistent breed standard via dog shows and events, promotes responsible and healthy breeding practices, provides educational programs and materials—as well as opportunities to meet others who enjoy that breed.

Other shows, called *group shows*, focus on one of the seven dog groups: Sporting, Hound, Working, Terrier, Toy, Non-Sporting, and Herding. The Sporting Group includes America's most popular dog, the Labrador Retriever. The Hound Group includes the Beagle, which was America's most popular dog during most of the 1950s and has become known across the world via the *Peanuts* comic strip's dog, Snoopy. The Working Group includes the Portuguese Water Dog, which has become more recognized since the Obama family brought Bo home. The Terrier Group includes the Cairn Terrier, which has been immortalized as the character Toto in the *Wizard of Oz* movie. The Toy Group includes the small Chihuahua, which sadly has recently become one of the most common dogs in America's animal shelters. The Non-Sporting Group is a diverse group that includes Dalmatians, which also, sadly, increases the rescue shelter population every time a *101 Dalmatians* movie comes out. Also in the Non-Sporting Group is my beloved Boston Terrier, which was originally a cross between the Bulldog and the now extinct White English Terrier, and is considered the first genuinely American breed, having been recognized by the AKC in 1891. The Herding Group includes Scotland's

Rough Collie, which became popular in America when I was growing up watching *Lassie* on TV.

AMERICA'S MOST FAMOUS DOG SHOW: "THE WESTMINSTER"

IF YOU HAVE WATCHED a dog show on television, you probably saw an "all-breed" competition such as New York's Westminster Kennel Club Dog Show. First held in 1877, seven years before the American Kennel Club was established, "The Westminster" is America's longest-running canine contest. From among the 2,500 invited dogs that have won prizes at other significant dog shows, Westminster judges select one grand prize–winning dog that is anointed Best in Show. Winners earn a place in history, but there is no prize money. Westminster dogs do increase in value as breeding stock and a few rare champions receive short-term commercial endorsement opportunities. Most competitors are involved in pursuit of honor and for their love of the breed.

The path to Westminster's Best in Show finals features two preliminary contests during the two-day competition: Best of Breed and Best of Group. In Best of Breed, one judge selects one dog from among a highly elite field of the same breed. The same judge also selects a Best of Opposite Sex for that breed and from one to five Awards of Merit, but only the one Best of Breed winner goes to the next round, Group Judging. My first show dog, Jasmine, a Boston Terrier bitch, once qualified to show at The Westminster with her handler, Norm Randall, whose own Boston Terrier male was once a Westminster Best of Breed winner.

At the Westminster show's Group Judging round, each of the more than 170 Best of Breed winners is judged within one of the seven dog groups to determine the seven Best of Group winners. In each group, the one all-rounder judge awards four dogs a prize, but only each first-place winner advances to the finals, where one dog is judged Best in Show.

Since 1934, the Westminster show has also featured a Junior Showmanship competition that judges young handlers' skills, not the dogs' conformation. More than one hundred handlers, age 10 to 18, who have won 10 or more Junior Showmanship first place awards over the past year, are invited to compete. Eight finalists compete for the title Best Junior Handler. The skill and poise of these young people are inspirational.

Acknowledgments

THE LOVE THAT DOG TRAINING PROGRAM has been shepherded and groomed by a loyal team. To all, Larry and I offer our gratitude. As in dog training, all imperfections in this book are a result of our own shortcomings, not those who have "gone to ground" with us like tenacious terriers.

To President Obama and the First Lady, Malia and Sasha: Thank you for entrusting me with Bo and for doing so much training follow-up with him. Bo Obama's development into such a wonderful dog is to the credit of our First Family. You are showing the world that positive reinforcement dog training makes a difference for families.

To Senator Kennedy and Vicki, thank you for your warm relationship and the more than dozen years working with you, your staff, Splash, Sunny, Cappy, and his littermate the world now knows as Bo.

Highly skilled staffers coordinate the lives of very public people. So that I could enjoy the privilege of working with these wonderful dogs, thanks especially to Dana Lewis, Catherine McCormick-Lelyveld, and the First Lady's staff, and to all who have worked with the Kennedys, especially Delmy Contreras.

Thank you to Art and Martha Stern of Amigo Kennels for your relationship as ethical and loving breeders extending back to those wonderful years with my own Portuguese Water Dog, Ebony.

To Dr. Ian Dunbar, we offer our profound gratitude; thank you for inspiring generations of dog trainers and encouraging this book. Thanks to Karen Pryor, Dr. Pamela Reid, and Best Friends Animal Society staffers Ann Allums, John Garcia, John Polis, and Barbara Williamson, who contributed their loving understanding of dog behavior and the human–animal bond. Whatever recognition this book receives, we share with many great dog trainers and humane educators; may this book advance the growing platform for positive reinforcement training.

Thanks to all my dog training students, clients (two- and four-legged), and interns for giving me the gift of a career that has been a fun and soulful adventure for more than 20 years. Thanks to my dog training website angel, Kelli Lee, and special thanks to my co-instructor, Ludwig Smith, who often filled in while I was writing this book.

The making of any book is a unique story. *The Love That Dog Training Program*'s journey began with my coauthor, Larry Kay, who (if he ever takes a sabbatical from his writing career) would be a superb dog trainer and advocate for pets transforming the lives of kids and families. Thank you, Larry, for going beyond the call of duty to make this book into one that makes a difference.

Special thanks to our agent, Kristine Dahl, and the ICM team, particularly Colin Graham and Laura Neely. Thank you, Ellis Levine, for introducing us to Kristine. Like a fleet-footed sighthound, Kristine saw how to shape the proposal and find the ideal publisher.

And to that ideal publisher, Peter Workman: Larry and I feel blessed to have been brought into the Workman "family." Everyone in this elite pack takes on roles beyond their pay grade. Special thanks to all who shaped this book, particularly editor-in-chief Susan Bolotin and art director Lisa Hollander. Photo maestro Anne Kerman and her team made the photo shoot in Workman's studio a howling (though always well behaved!) success. Special thanks to blue-ribbon editor Aimee Molloy, who trained our words to do tricks and guided two authors through the editorial agility course at full speed. While we feel remiss in not acknowledging everyone at Workman Publishing individually, please accept our thanks for consistently valuing our authors' input and making this project a true win-win partnership.

My personal gratitude goes to my extended family and friends for the power and trust in the way that you have loved me. Thank you to William Waybourn and Ripley, who added to my therapy dog experience by opening the doors to serving our wounded warriors with you at Walter Reed Army Medical Center. My dogs have taught me more than I taught them, including perseverance, unconditional love, and that we don't need to choke our best friends with a chain to get them to do what we want.

Most of all, to Courtlandt, Blaise, and Paige: My love and respect for you is at the essence of my life. Even though I became a dog trainer to have a career while being a mom, above all that the greatest gift I have been given remains that of being your mother.

Larry Kay's Personal Thanks

THE FIRST TIME I saw Dawn in her classroom I understood what a talented trainer she is and how much she loves guiding people and dogs into beautifully bonded relationships. She proves that effective dog training is really human training. Thank you, Dawn, for making our collaboration a great adventure. Testing your system on my "golden oldie," Higgins, proves that we can indeed teach old dogs new tricks when the love bond is spirited.

Special thanks to everyone at Animal Wow, especially the ever-talented Sharon Brown and Lauren Wygant, for helping kids discover themselves as they discover pets. Thank you to Andrew DePrisco, Katy French, and all my colleagues at BowTie and *Dog Fancy* magazine.

I am blessed with brilliant colleagues, true friends, and a family that is my bedrock. My scribe tribe has given great advice and support, especially animal philosopher Dr. Gary Steiner, and authors Jan Burke, Steven Goldman, and Dr. Darryl Tippens. To Jennifer Wexler, Jonn Howell, and the men of the Mankind Project's Valley Oaks iGroup: Thanks for your good humor and seeing the truth in me even when I am blinded by my own shadow. Thanks to my Hesby Oaks neighbors who allowed Higgins and me to practice Dawn's system with you and your dogs. To all my loving family in Los Angeles, Chicago, the Northwest, and Buenos Aires: You inspire the best in me, thanks for the lifelong belly rub.

Robert Benchley (grandfather of Dawn's client, the writer/performer Nat Benchley), is widely quoted as having said that "a dog teaches a boy fidelity, perseverance, and to turn around three times before lying down." Thanks, Higgins, for teaching this boy many essential life lessons; someday I'll master that lying down technique.

Index

Photo Credits

COVER AND PRINCIPAL PHOTOGRAPHY:

Evan Sklar.

ADDITIONAL PHOTOGRAPHY CREDITS:

AGE fotostock: Ton Koene 226 bottom; **Associated Press:** ix, 226 top; **Canine Companions for Independence:** 255; **Fotolia:** 28 bottom center; **Getty Images:** Gerard Brown 260, James Forte 233 bottom, GK Hart/Vikki Hart 19, 51, 261, Jonathan Kantor 37, Tracy Morgan 230, Steve Shott 41, LWA/Dann Tardif 233 top.

Special thanks to Dawn Animal Agency and their wonderful canine models: Pat, Golden Retriever; Sally, Portuguese Water Dog; Murphy, Chesapeake Bay Retriever; Luna, Mixed Breed; Sam, American Staffordshire Terrier; Wilma, Boston Terrier.

About the authors

Before becoming the dog trainer to President Obama's family, **Dawn Sylvia-Stasiewicz** trained each of Senator Ted Kennedy's Portuguese Water Dogs. Sylvia-Stasiewicz, who has been a professional dog trainer in the Washington, D.C./Northern Virginia area for more than 20 years, runs popular Merit Puppy dog training classes and trains and boards animals for the Washington elite. She brings a mom's approach to training, basing her work on theories of positive reinforcement.

Larry Kay, a Los Angeles–based writer, created the award-winning *Animal Wow* dog care DVD for kids and is a contributing editor to *Dog Fancy* magazine. His writing credits include PBS documentaries, educational films for the New York City Board of Education, and children's edutainment software for Disney, The Muppets, and Atari/Humongous Entertainment's *Freddi Fish.* Larry is inspired by his 13-year-old Golden Retriever, Higgins, who now excels at lying in the sun, pondering the days when he chased squirrels.